CERAMICS

CERAMICS

Mastering the Craft

RICHARD ZAKIN

Chilton Book Company / Radnor, Pennsylvania

On the cover: Walter Ostrom. Canada. ''Fish Vase with Greek Pot,'' 9 inches high. Wheel-thrown with hand-formed elements. Majolica with resist techniques and colored glazes. Photo: Elaine Dacey Ostrom.

On the back: Susanne Stephenson. USA. ''Red Rock Vase,'' 23 inches high. Thrown, combination slip and vitreous engobe applied to unfired, leather-hard clay. Fired at cone 04. Photo: Suzanne Coles.

Designed by Arlene Putterman
Manufactured in the United States of America

Library of Congress Cataloging in Publication Data
Zakin, Richard
        Ceramics : mastering the craft / Richard Zakin.
            p.   cm.
        Includes bibliographical references.
        ISBN 0-8019-7991-9
        1. Ceramics.   I. Title.
TP807.Z338   1990   89-45966
666'.3—dc20   CIP

2 3 4 5 6 7 8 9 0   9 8 7 6 5 4 3 2 1

DANIEL RHODES was one of my teachers at the New York State College of Ceramics at Alfred University in 1965 and 1966 and his canny advice was important to my growth as a ceramist. My classmates and I used his book *Clays and Glazes for the Potter* as our lodestar. I had a chance to see him in another light when I rented a studio from him for a time in 1966: he was a most unusual landlord for he somehow never remembered to collect the rent. This knowledgeable, composed, and self-reliant person never forgot the human side, and I celebrate his memory.

CONTENTS

ESSAYS BY THE ARTISTS

TECHNICAL PHOTO SERIES

FOREWORD

Back in 1964 when we accepted Richard Zakin into the MFA program of the New York State College of Ceramics at Alfred University, I remember having some questions. I wondered if this student, who was trained in painting and who was devoted to music and the intellectual life, would be able to embrace the significance of pushing his hands around in clay. Will he understand the importance of mastering the skills and techniques of the potter's craft? And, most important, will he be able to accept the relevance of these sorts of things in forming a personal ceramic art aesthetic? Although many painters do make the switch to clay, it must be hard to leave the world of ideas in two-dimensional space and instant color for three-dimensional space and the transformation process inherent in making ceramic forms. Everything changes in the fire! The final look and feel of the work is not determined by the artist. The conceptual basis for ceramic art involves seeing the crucial relationships between ideas, understanding a bewildering number of processes and methods, and having intimate knowledge of the earthy and sensual materials. Richard quickly put my doubts to rest. His ceramic expression was filled with insight and understanding. He was able to grasp the whole of the craft. He understood the importance of knowing materials and processes and of having the skills and technology for ceramic art. He has become one of the authorities in the field.

With the publication of this new book, Richard Zakin shows us just how comprehensive his knowledge is and how clearly he can structure and explain this sort of material to others.

Over the years of our friendship, I have watched him grow from an energetic young student, sitting in my lectures hearing about the technology of the ceramic medium for more or less the first time, to becoming a definitive voice in our field. His first book, *Electric Kiln Ceramics* (Chilton; A & C Black, 1981), opened up an important aspect of the craft to people everywhere at all levels of experience and interests. That book filled an important gap in the literature of standard reference books for ceramic art. It also became obvious then that a new author had come along who would help inform and educate ceramists who needed help and encouragement.

This book has a much wider scope. It encompasses all aspects of the potter's craft and will become another essential book in the standard reference list. It was written by a person who is an artist and educator, as well as an author.

Contemporary American ceramics has developed and matured to a position of world leadership since the mid-1940s. There are many reasons for this rise to the top, and for the development of an American style in ceramic art. I use the word "style" here after a definition of the word once given by George Bernard Shaw: "Style is force of assertion." This style was created by talented American ceramic artsts, writers, and teachers. Some of our best have been all of the above, including Richard Zakin. Something fresh and different and exciting has happened here in less than 50 years. Bernard Leach once said it would take America 100 years to learn to make good pottery and to have some sort of ceramic tradition. He was wrong about that, but his landmark *Potter's Book* (1946) was a major influence on the post–World War II surge of interest, information, and inspiration that got us all going.

The teachers and students at Alfred University were another reason. I was affected and very much inspired by the "Alfred tradition" and the remarkable teachers here. Richard Zakin also carries on some of that tradition. Charles Binns was the first director (1900) and founder of the New York State College of Ceramics, which is a college of Alfred University. From the very beginning he taught that art and science were crucial studies for the ceramist. That idea has continued to this day. Binns also believed that books were needed and that authorities in the field should write them. Binns was the first Alfred teacher to write books. He was followed by Dan Rhodes and Larry Lawrence, who have written books for artists,

and several others here who have written books for ceramic science and engineering as the field has become more specialized. Alumni authors of distinction have included Donald Frith, John Kenny, Susan Peterson, Hal Reiger, and, of course, Richard Zakin.

In this book Richard takes us on a very comprehensive journey through the information and ideas of the potter's craft. He includes photographs of pieces made by leading artists as well as comments by them concerning various aspects of their work. This book is unique in its scope and the depth of its information and photographic documentation. It will become a standard reference in the field and will help bring us into the twenty-first century, maintaining a world-class reputation in ceramic art. Writing this book was indeed a monumental task. There are many fine books that give us various pieces of the puzzle of ceramic technology. This book attempts to be the one book we need to cover most of the ground. Few people could do a book like this and even fewer would ever dream of trying. But America's leadership role in ceramic art has depended on people with the energy, talent, knowledge, and motivation to do the hard work that makes quality and produces leaders. Richard Zakin continues the tradition.

VAL M. CUSHING
Professor of Ceramic Art
New York State College of Ceramics
at Alfred University

PREFACE

Now that I have finished this book, I am struck by the sheer size of the subject I have had the nerve to tackle. No one person can know the whole field of ceramics, but I have tried to include as many aspects of our craft as possible. Of course, I had a lot of help from friends expert in one or another aspect of the craft, and for that I am most grateful.

I am glad that I took on this challenge because it has encouraged me to think a good deal more about the nature of ceramics. It has been especially rewarding to look at the work of a great variety of ceramic artists and to try and understand the principles underlying their approach to clay. Preparing this book has given me the opportunity to meet and talk with many wonderful people—people who have committed themselves to something they see as important and special. It is a pleasure to thank everyone who has helped me during this quest.

In particular I thank Jim and Nan McKinnell and John Glick for their canny and wide-ranging advice. Two potters in England, Colin Pearson and Angus Suttie, were particularly helpful. I also thank Anne French and Dr. Tony Ford of the Crafts Council of Britain for their help. They all greatly contributed to my understanding of ceramics in England.

The following people were helpful in my explorations of glaze materials and glaze analysis: Val Cushing of the New York State College of Ceramics at Alfred (he was my first teacher in this field); Professor Robert Schmitz of the School for American Craftsmen in Rochester, New York; Robin Hopper, potter and writer; Nigel Wood of the Central School of Art in London; and Peter Pinnell, who teaches at the Kansas City Art Institute. I feel that Peter, who spent a lot of time helping me, deserves special mention.

A number of those who helped me are or were at the State University of New York at Oswego, where I teach. These include: Professor Joseph Lipsig, who helped me with the questions I had about the physical makeup and behavior of ceramic materials; Jim Graves of the Penfield Library also helped me with these matters. Professor John Kane spent many hours helping me with computer-aided recipe analysis. Professor Sewall Oertling, an Orientalist in the Art Department of SUNY at Oswego, read my chapter on ceramic history and offered valuable advice.

I am especially grateful to Dr. Barbara Perry, curator of ceramics of the Everson Museum, for furnishing photos of work from the Everson's justly famed ceramic collection.

I would like to thank two of my advanced students, Robin Leventhal and Gary Grossenbeck, who helped me prepare and test my clay body and glaze recipes. I also am indebted to Tim McHenry and Dottie Baker, who read the manuscript and made helpful suggestions.

Finally, I thank my photographer, Professor Thomas C. Eckersley, for his valuable and always timely help.

CERAMICS

Introduction

Ceramics is an ancient occupation, at least seven thousand years old. During that time we humans have learned a great many ways to work with clay so that, centuries later, ceramics has become a complex field. This book has been written for those who want to know as much as possible about every aspect of ceramics, as well as for those who would rather not be encumbered with facts and details they do not specifically need to do their work. I have tried here to touch upon as many aspects of ceramics as possible and to deal with the mainstream of ceramic practice, as well as the aspects that are less well known but that offer promise of relevance for contemporary ceramists.

In Chapters 1 through 3 I discuss clays and clay bodies, the conventional and the unusual: their workability, firing temperature, and their interaction with glazes. It is common now for ceramists to purchase prepared clay bodies from ceramic supply houses. Since this practice has rarely been discussed, I have included a section on what to look for when buying and using prepared clay bodies.

Every ceramic object is a balance between form and surface. Chapters 4 through 10 describe the wide range of glazes and other surfaces we can choose from, among them salt glazes, raku, wood-ash glazes, low-, mid-, and high-fire glazes, slips, and engobes. Many contemporary ceramists purchase low-fire prepared glazes: these, too, have not been discussed before in a book of this type. The noted low-fire ceramist Martha Holt has prepared a marvelous photo series on her use of these prepared glazes which accompanies her essay in Chapter 6. Also discussed are the low- and mid-fire temperatures of cone 02 and cone 3 since these offer great opportunities for exploration to contemporary ceramists. Chapter 7 deals with testing, mixing, and applying glazes. Chapter 10 describes methods of glaze analysis, both molecular analysis and a materials-based assessment. Molecular analysis can tell us with great accuracy what oxides are in the fired recipe. A materials-based assessment, while less accurate, can help us arrive at an understanding of the complex interactions that influence the glaze and its character. Although either can be used alone, ideally these two approaches are complementary.

Contemporary ceramists use many methods to create their forms—from hand-forming to forming on the potter's wheel to mold forming. Chapters 11 and 12 describe and illustrate these methods as they are used to create vessels, sculpture, and wall pieces. The discussion of wall pieces is, I think, especially important since this format has not been covered in any detail elsewhere.

Kilns and firing are the subjects of Chapters 13 and 14. I pay special attention to oxidation and reduction-firing methods and their impact on the work. Other firing methods are discussed as well, as are the basics of kiln design.

Short essays by contemporary ceramists from around the world appear throughout the book and offer valuable insight into the creative process. In these essays various artists describe not only their methods but also their feelings about the craft. Of course, a book of this scope must encompass more than one point of view. In fact, it needs many voices, for no one ceramist can reflect the diversity of the field. For the same reason, the 300 photos placed throughout the book represent the work of many ceramists.

Finally, I have included several appendixes—on the history of ceramics, safe practice for the ceramist, and the use of computers in ceramics. I also offer suggestions for setting up your own studio and note the basic materials you will need. The final appendix lists recipes for clay bodies, slips, engobes, and glazes at a number of firing temperatures.

Finally to the intangibles that we deal with every day in our work. They are tough and elusive and hard to write about, but they are at the heart of our craft. The photographs of ceramic pieces in this book are tangible and persuasive reports on the way we grapple with these problems that are central to our work and to the nature of ceramics.

CHAPTER 1

Ceramic Materials

Understanding the structure of our material universe is especially important to ceramists because it affects the character of our materials in ways that directly influence our work. The materials we use to make our clay bodies and glazes—those rather anonymous-looking powders—are compounds made up of atoms and elements. These compounds are affected by the elements that compose them and the way in which these elements are structured. The elements in a glaze compound affect such things as its fluxing (melting) and glass-making character. Structure, too, is important; the structure of clay, for example, has a great deal to do with its character and helps make a material which is workable and which can be fired.

The structure of our material universe can be understood as a step-by-step progression of these basic building blocks of matter—from atoms, to elements, to molecules, to compounds.

THE BASIC BUILDING BLOCKS

All matter is composed of *atoms,* the fundamental units of all material things.

An *element* is a grouping of identical atoms.

Molecules are structural units composed of atoms. They may be composed of one kind of atom or several kinds.

Compounds are formed by two or more elements or molecules in defined proportions. All ceramic materials are compounds; some are fairly simple, whereas others are complex, containing many different elements.

Before firing, some ceramic materials are compounded with oxygen and others with carbon. *Oxides* are compounds of metallic elements and oxygen. (Since firing is an oxidizing process, oxides are little changed in the fire.) *Carbonates* used by ceramists are compounds of metallic atoms and carbon. In the fire they are converted to oxides; the carbon is released as the gases carbon monoxide and carbon dioxide.

Crystals are compounds whose structure is three-dimensional and composed of repeated identical units. Each crystal type has its own unique structure and properties that help define the structure and properties of the materials they make up. Crystal development occurs in all ceramic materials and strongly influences their appearance and character.

Particles are composed of crystals. They are significant to ceramists because a number of materials, including clay, are made up of particles. Particle size, as well as particle-size variations, strongly influence the char-

FIG. 1–1 Steve Heinemann. Canada. "Under the Rocks and Stones," width 99 cm. Press-mold formed. Earthenware; multiple firings.

acter of the clay. It is at the particle stage that our senses of perception come into play. Here we arrive at things we can see and feel. This is the world of materials and their physical characteristics—the characteristics that we interact with day by day as we work in our medium.

ELEMENTS FOUND IN CERAMIC MATERIALS

Elements are composed of identical atoms. While no pure elements are found among our ceramic materials (we work with complex compounds), at times it is useful for us to understand their makeup. If we know the element composition of a recipe, we will understand a great deal about its fired character. The following is a list of the elements commonly found in clays and glazes.

Silicon (when compounded with oxygen, it becomes silica)
Aluminum (when compounded with oxygen, it becomes alumina)
Antimony
Barium
Boron
Calcium
Carbon (found in carbonates such as calcium carbonate, or whiting)
Cobalt
Copper
Fluorine
Gold
Iron
Lead
Lithium
Magnesium
Manganese
Nickel
Oxygen
Phosphorus
Potassium
Sodium
Tin
Titanium
Vanadium
Zinc
Zirconium

If ceramists have one indispensable element, it would have to be silica, an element found in almost every ceramic recipe. Silica is a common ingredient in many of the compounds found in the earth's crust. Aluminum, along with silicon, is the main building

FIG. 1–2 Ken Fergusen. USA. "Bowl with Hares," 19 × 15½ inches. Wheel-formed with hand-built additions; reduction-fired black stoneware with green slip. Photo: E. G. Schempf.

block of clay. It is also found in slips, engobes, and glazes, where it controls glaze flow and durability and encourages mat surfaces.

The other elements on the list are found in compounds used by ceramists to "dope" or modify silicon and aluminum in order to make them more useful—often by encouraging melting—in clays, slips, engobes, and glazes.

COMPOUNDS USED IN CERAMICS

Compounds are combinations of two or more elements. Two important compounds used in ceramics are whiting and soda feldspar. Whiting is composed of calcium and carbon. Soda feldspar, somewhat more complex than whiting, is composed of silica, alumina, sodium, and potassium. Clays, too, are compounds. They are made up of silica, alumina, and varying percentages of other elements that encourage melting or color the clay.

We use various compounds in our work. They are used because they can survive the rigors of the ceramic fire and because they produce interesting results. The ceramist's list of useful chemicals is fairly small because most materials burn away in the high temperatures of the ceramic kiln. All organic materials burn away at these temperatures, as do many minerals. Among the compounds used in ceramics are:

Clays
Feldspars and frits
Silicates
Ground silica(also called flint or silica dioxide)
Fluxes (these encourage melting)

Clays

Ceramists use five main types of clays:

Ball clay	Kaolin
Dark-colored clay	Stoneware clay
Fire clay	

Feldspars and Frits

Feldspars are naturally occurring compounds composed of silica, alumina, and melting materials and are economical and extremely useful in ceramics. Because they contain a good deal of silica as well as some alumina and melters, they supply most of the elements that clays, slips, and glazes must contain to produce good results in the kiln. Therefore they can be used as the primary material in many ceramic recipes. Ceramists use several types of feldspar:

Lithium feldspars
Potassium feldspars
Sodium feldspars

TABLE 1–1   THE CERAMIST'S MATERIALS CUPBOARD

1. Feldspars and Feldspar-like Materials

soda feldspar
potash feldspar
nepheline syenite
spodumene—a lithium feldspar

Optional:

pumice
volcanic ash

2. Silica—ground silica (flint)

3. Clays

ball clay
kaolin
stoneware clay (buff-colored clays of mixed particle size)
fire clay
red burning clay
dark burning clay

4. Silicates

talc
wollastonite

5. Melting Materials

bone ash

dolomite
Gerstley borate (available only in the United States and Canada)
titanium dioxide
whiting

Optional:

magnesium carbonate
tin oxide

6. Frits

high-soda frit (over 10 percent soda)
boron-containing frit (between 8 and 20 percent boron)

Optional:

high boron frit (over 20% boron)
barium frit

TOXIC MATERIALS

The following materials, though useful, are toxic. More information about these is found in Appendix B.

barium carbonate	Compounds that
lithium carbonate	contain:
(substitute	cadmium
spodumene)	lead
finely ground	fluorine
manganese dioxide	vanadium

Frits, a kind of ground glass, are manufactured in a process that begins with a recipe, proceeds to the melting of the materials in a crucible, and finally to cooling and grinding. Although somewhat expensive, this process has its advantages. Most frits, like feldspars, contain silica, alumina, and melters. Frits, however, contain elements not found in natural feldspars and can be formulated to contain melters in greater amounts than those in natural feldspars. The result is a powerful melting compound precisely tailored for a specific job.

Silicates
Silicates are compounds of silica and melters. Ceramists use two silicates—talc and wollastonite.

Ground Silica (Flint)
Ground silica is derived from ground quartz. It is used in ceramic recipes when additions of pure silica are desired.

Fluxes
Fluxes contain no silica and are composed only of elements that modify the melting

High-, Medium-, and Low-Clay Percentages in Clay Bodies

Clay Bodies with High Clay Content—stoneware, terra-cotta

Clay Bodies with Medium Clay Content—porcelaneous bodies

Clay Bodies with Low Clay Content—porcelains, talc bodies

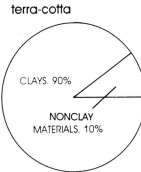

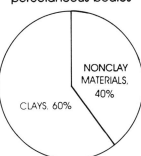

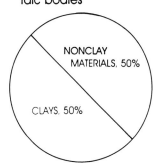

Slips, Engobes, and Glazes—clay-to-nonclay ratio

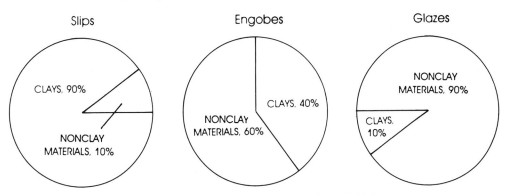

Slips

Engobes

Glazes

CHART 1–1 VISUAL COMPARISONS OF CERAMIC MATERIALS

properties of silica. Ceramists use a number of fluxes:

Barium carbonate
Bone ash
Dolomite
Gerstley borate (available only in the United States and Canada)

Lithium carbonate
Magnesium carbonate
Tin oxide
Titanium dioxide
Whiting
Zinc oxide
Zirconium opacifiers

Materials Used in Glazes

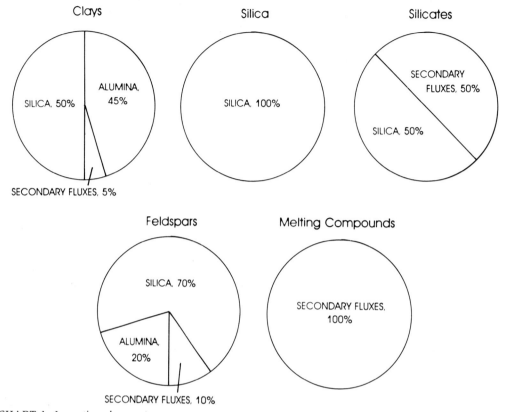

CHART 1–1, *continued*

Colorants
Colorants are used to alter the color of clay bodies, slips, engobes, and glazes.

Chrome
Copper
Cobalt
Iron
Manganese
Rutile (a compound of iron and titanium)
Vanadium

Glaze and Body Stains
Glaze and body stains are compounded from clay, colorants, and materials that modify the color response of the colorants. These compounds are more stable than the original colorant and far less toxic.

EUTECTICS
It would seem natural that a combination of two materials would have a melting point dictated in a straightforward way by the melting point of each material. If this were so, material A melting at 1000° C and material B melting at 1200° C would, if mixed half and half, create a compound whose melting point is 1100° C. This makes excellent sense, but it is not how nature works.

Because of the way compounds react to heat at the atomic level, the melting point of a compound is usually lower than that of its individual components. Furthermore, different oxide proportions will produce different melting temperatures. The classic example of this phenomenon is a combination of whiting (calcium) and feldspar fired to cone 8. By itself whiting is a dry powder after firing and feldspar a stiff mass. The 75 feldspar, 25 whiting combination will have the greatest melting power and will, in fact, be a glass. In these proportions calcium and feldspar form a eutectic and melt strongly.

What this means is that some combinations of oxides in a recipe will cause more fluxing than expected. This phenomenon is especially important for the ceramist who works in the low fire.

BUYING CERAMIC MATERIALS

The market for ceramic materials obviously is a specialized one. Most of our materials are specially prepared for ceramic use and must be purchased from a ceramic supply house. Ceramics dealers are not that plentiful and may be hard to find in your area. Look for advertisements from suppliers in craft magazines. A good supplier will be reliable, offer reasonable prices, have a good stock, and be familiar with that stock. Proximity is a big plus because it is expensive to ship heavy ceramic materials. These days suppliers will often know a fair amount about the craft (or have someone on staff who does) and be willing to help you with technical matters.

CERAMIC RECIPES

In ceramics more than in many other arts, technological matters strongly influence the look of the finished piece. One place where this is strongly in evidence is in the phenomenon of the ceramic recipe.

Ceramic recipes are composed of materials that are sources of silica, alumina, and various other elements that influence the character of the melt. Ceramic recipes have a certain stylized character that allows them to be compared one to another and to be

FIG. 1–3 Barbara Harmer Tipton. Canada. "Cup Drawing," 6 inches wide. Wall piece, wheel-thrown, altered, and assembled; fired to cone 6 in an electric kiln.

used easily by contemporary ceramists. For example, they are usually formulated for a total of 100 percent in order to allow easy comparison with other recipes. Colorants are often written as percentages over and above 100 percent because, at least in theory, other colorants can be used in their place with no substantive change in the character of the fired product. Furthermore, all ceramic recipes draw from a limited palette of materials—those that have been proven in use and are readily available from ceramic suppliers. While we have a limited choice of materials, their proportions vary a great deal. These different proportions are what give each recipe its unique flavor.

CHAPTER 2

Clay and Clay Bodies

Clays are earthy mixtures created by erosion. When moist, they can take on any shape, and when fired, they become extremely durable and permanent. These unique characteristics are shared by no other materials. At the same time, clays are common and are abundant throughout the world.

When it is moist, clay will readily take on practically any shape; this characteristic is called workability or plasticity. When clay dries, it will keep that shape, and when it is fired, it becomes permanently fixed in that form. Clay derives these features from the unusual nature of its physical structure. Every ceramist should understand the atomic and molecular makeup of clay.

Clays are composed of very common atoms: silica, oxygen, alumina, and lesser percentages of other elements. Both the silica and alumina atoms are grouped together with atoms of oxygen. Layers of silica/oxygen structures alternate with layers of alumina/oxygen structures and are the building blocks of clay crystals.

Clay crystals are unusual because they take the form of thin platelets (half a micron thick) rather than the pebble-shaped particles that make up most materials and objects. Owing in part to electrical attraction, these tiny sheetlike platelets cling to each other. When clay is moist, the platelets are separated by a layer of water, which allows them to skid along each other's surface. This process results in a material that, while dense and substantial, can be easily shaped and will keep that shape.

As a ceramic piece dries, the spaces between the particles shrink and each platelet becomes tightly layered upon its neighbors. This affects the character of the piece: it becomes smaller, more dense, and quite hard. When fully dry, the piece is ready for firing. During the firing the space between the platelets shrinks even further; the bond between each platelet becomes extremely tight and the material extremely dense.

The most common clays are made from eroded or decayed feldspathic rocks, usually through such natural weathering processes as freezing and thawing and the action of flowing water and precipitation. Clays that are formed by this process are often carried far from their original site and thus tend to contain many impurities. These clays are medium to dark in color, fine particled, and highly melting.

In a related but somewhat different process, clay may also form in one spot, sometimes by the action of precipitation and sometimes by geothermal action, as in geysers or geologic steam. These clays are light in color and contain fewer impurities; they usually have a large component of coarse particles and are refractory.

FIG. 2–1 Linda Nadas. USA. "Mountain." This piece is evidence of a strong wish to express the plasticity and "markability" of clay.

FLOCCULATION AND DEFLOCCULATION

Flocculation and deflocculation are both caused by changes in the watery medium surrounding the clay platelets. These changes influence the way in which the platelets attract or repel each other. An acidic watery medium encourages flocculation, which is the electrical attraction of the clay platelets, while an alkaline watery medium encourages deflocculation, which is the electrical repulsion of clay platelets.

When particles attract, their surfaces are parallel to each other. This configuration is tightly packed with particles, each one surrounded by a layer of water. Thus it requires a great deal of water. Therefore the effect of flocculation on a clay is to thicken it so that it requires more water to make it plastic (in the case of a body) or fluid (in the case of a slip).

When particles repel, their configuration is random. The particles are not so tightly packed and the random configuration requires far less water. The effect of deflocculation on a clay is to thin it so that it requires less water to make it a slip.

Clays are flocculated to make them more plastic and workable. This is especially useful for clay bodies that are marginally deflocculated as a result of the presence of alkaline fluxes in the recipe (often the case with mid-fire porcelain-like bodies).

Clays are deflocculated in order to create slips that are fluid and yet contain little water. This is crucial to the success of slipcast forming (see page 207).

CLAY BODIES

The term "clay body" denotes a composition made up of two or more clays or of a combination of clay and nonclay materials. While it is possible to extract clay from the earth, clean it, and use it to form ceramic pieces, ceramists rarely do this. They prefer to form their pieces from clay bodies. These mixtures offer the ceramist great advantages in terms of workability and durability. Even though clay bodies take time to make, their advantages are so obvious that the extra work is a trivial matter. Potters have been making clay bodies for millennia. Even the earliest potters tinkered with their clay, often by adding ashes, sand, and other clays and minerals to the mixture. Clay bodies can be customized for use at particular firing temperatures, or they can be used with particular forms or with particular forming or finishing techniques.

WORKABILITY

After firing temperature, but often even before color, the most important consideration

Paul Astbury

CLAY WITHOUT DISCIPLINE

Clay has no discipline and no order to say that it cannot be this or that. It is a three-dimensional brushstroke that has the power to transform, to metamorphoze, with the whim and quickness of mind. It can be made to look like any shape and to take on any appearance or quality. Clay does not force a particular discipline upon the artist—it is free.

A clay pot exists within its own domain. No other material can make a pot so well. Clay in sculpture is visible only because the artist has said that it should be.

Clay opposes discipline in other materials. It is an opposite—more like mind and matter combined. Something malleable is more vulnerable to the whims and wishes of the mind than something that is not. Clay imitates the malleability of the mind. It transforms dreams into actuality, relying on the mind to form it and give it structure. Because of this formlessness, there is no school of thought or movement with a common aim. Artists who use clay retain their individuality of approach. Their only common bond is the use of clay. Only each artist knows why he or she uses clay. If there is one common reason, it may be that we are attracted by the lack of discipline imposed and each one of us comes to understand this in our own way.

Paul Astbury. England. "Vanished World," wooden table frame and TV, 5 × 4 × 5 feet. Porcelain clay with oiled areas, silver foil, paper, and paint; the porcelain is fired to 1260°C (2300°F).

in choosing a clay body is workability. This concept is called "plasticity" or "bendability," and indeed our feelings about workability are strongly influenced by these characteristics. However, as Frank Hamer points out in *The Potters Dictionary of Materials and Techniques* (London: Pitman, 1975), plasticity is only one component of workability; the other is strength. Plasticity is the ability to bend. Strength is the ability to withstand the stress of forming without collapsing.

Strength is related to thixotropy; the ability of a material to become fluid when disturbed. Highly thixotropic bodies appear to be firm until they are agitated—the very action that occurs during the forming process. At this point these clay bodies seem to become limp, relaxed, and much wetter and, as such, are not easily formed.

Plasticity and strength are enhanced if the clays in the body contain particles of various sizes. A well-thought-out clay body, for example, will contain a fine-particled clay, such as ball clay; a clay with a good amount of midsize particles, such as stoneware; and a clay that is coarse in particle size, such as fire clay. Since alkaline materials deflocculate clay (which cause the platelets to repel each other and diminish workability) highly alkaline fluxes should be avoided. Materials that are not highly alkaline, such as talc or potash feldspar, should be used instead. Workability is also enhanced by adding fillers such as grog or chopped nylon, both of which have larger particle sizes than most clays and thus further diversify particle size.

MATERIALS USED IN CLAY BODIES

Clays

Ball Clay
A low-impurity clay, light cream in color, ball clay is neither highly refractory nor strongly melting and thus can be used at all firing temperatures. Because it is fine parti-

cled, ball clay shrinks a great deal. It is quite plastic and can be formed easily and naturally.

Stoneware Clay
A medium-impurity clay, tan-gray in color, stoneware clay has moderate melting powers and the particle size is mixed, which contributes to excellent workability. Mid- and high-fire buff and dark clay bodies are usually based on stoneware clays.

Kaolin
Kaolin is a white, low-impurity clay valued for its color. Porcelain bodies are based on kaolin clays. The particle size is uniform so workability is limited, and kaolin is quite refractory (nonmelting).

Dark-Colored Clays
High-impurity clays with a high iron content are an intense earth red. These clays have strong fluxing powers. Their particle size is varied, which contributes to good workability, but this is often offset by the alkaline character of the impurities. In the low fire, they may serve as the basis for the clay body. In the high fire, they are used to modify the color and the melt of the clay body.

Fire Clays
Fire clays are medium-impurity clays, tan-gray in color, added to clay bodies to improve workability and durability because of their coarse particle size. These clays vary in their melting powers from moderately melting to quite refractory.

Nonclay Materials

Ground Silica (Flint)
The only source of pure silica for clay bodies is ground silica. If silica is added to the clay body along with a flux, such as feldspar, the two partially fuse, binding the clay particles together. This significantly hardens the clay body.

Silicates

The two important silicates used in ceramics are talc (ingredients—silica, magnesium, and calcium) and wollastonite (ingredients—silica and calcium). The composition of talc and wollastonite is approximately one-half silica and one-half melter. This silica/melter combination causes a partial fusing during the firing, which strengthens the clay body.

Talc, a powerful and economical clay body flux, is used frequently in clay bodies, especially those intended for the low fire. In the low fire, talc bodies discourage glaze crazing; in the high fire, talc bodies encourage resistance to heat shock.

Wollastonite, a strong flux similar in action to talc, is highly valued in clay bodies, especially tile bodies, because its particles take on a fibrous form, which stabilizes the body and helps it to resist warping.

Feldspars

Nepheline syenite (ingredients—silica, alumina, soda, and potash). One of our most powerful clay body fluxes, it has a high soda content and is useful in both the low and mid fire.

Soda feldspar (ingredients—silica, alumina, soda, and potash). This powerful melting compound is high in soda and especially useful in the mid and low fire.

Potash feldspar (ingredients—silica, alumina, potash, and soda). This strong flux (though not as strong as the other feldspars, which contain more soda) does not volatilize in the high fire and therefore is especially suited to that range.

Spodumene (ingredients—silica, alumina, soda, potash, and lithium). This lithium feldspar is a strong melter and is mainly used in clay bodies because it encourages resistance to heat shock. (*Note:* Gases released by spodumene during the firing may be dangerous; always fire in a well-ventilated kiln room.)

Frits

Frits are useful for fluxing clay bodies, especially those meant for the low fire. The most useful frits are those which contain significant amounts of soda. Soda frits are powerful melters and are fairly neutral in their effect on the workability of the clay body. Frits must be used with great care in clay bodies, especially low-fire bodies. Highly fluxed low-fire bodies have a narrow maturation range and are easily overfired.

Fluxing Materials (No Silica Content)

Fluxes, which contain no silica or alumina, are used less often as additions to clay bodies than feldspars, frits, or silicates. Two fluxes, bone ash and dolomite, do, however, contribute in a unique way to clay bodies and find some use as body additions.

Bone ash (ingredients—calcium and phosphorus). This material encourages very strong melts and is used in mid-fire porcelain bodies, where it imparts translucency and a warm tone. Because it is highly alkaline and deflocculates the body, bone ash is used most often in slipcast bodies rather than bodies meant for hand-forming. (Deflocculated bodies do not lend themselves to hand-forming.)

Because bone ash is so highly alkaline, wearing gloves while working is essential. A good dust mask also should be worn when working with this dry powder.

Dolomite (ingredients—calcium and magnesium). Adding 5 to 10 percent dolomite to mid-fire porcelaneous bodies will encourage workability, a good melt, and translucency.

Fillers

Fillers are coarse materials that are added to the clay body to strengthen it and to help "open" it up so that it can dry evenly and thoroughly. They also reduce shrinkage and warping and promote safe firing. The most commonly used fillers are grog, sand, organic particles, and chopped nylon.

Grog

Grog is a coarse-particle filler made from ground fired clay. Although it can be made in a wide variety of colors, grog usually is made from a buff clay and looks rather like sand. Grog helps reduce clay shrinkage, warping, cracks, and heat shock. In addition, it strengthens the clay body and makes complex construction less risky. Adding grog opens up the clay body and allows it to retain moisture. Grogged bodies therefore are not as likely to crack or blow up in the fire.

Grog is usually added during the clay-mixing process, but it also can be added directly to wet clay that has already been mixed. As a starting point, add half a cup of grog for every ten pounds of clay. When adding to already-mixed clay, moisten the grog to prevent drying out the clay body.

Sand
Sand is similar to grog in its action, though its edges are not as sharp. Common sand contains a high percentage of impurities, including iron, and these may express themselves as spots and running areas marking the surface of the clay body. White sand has few impurities and in the fire will act more like grog.

Organic Materials
Organic materials such as sawdust and coffee grounds can be added to the clay body to strengthen it while it is wet. These materials will burn out during firing. If the clay body is fired to a mature and dense state, the resulting openings will shrink and the body will shrink a great deal as well. If the clay body is fired to a point short of maturity, the holes will remain and the body will be quite open. While a mature, dense body is desirable for its low absorption of water, an open body is desirable for a finished piece that will undergo a great deal of stress, as is often the case with sculpture bodies.

Chopped Nylon
Chopped nylon is composed of short lengths of fine nylon filaments. Mixing chopped nylon into the clay body produces particle-size and -shape variation, which reduces warping and cracking. It also opens up the body, thus encouraging workability and reducing

the possibility of explosions. Chopped nylon burns away during the fire, but those who fire in the electric kiln need not worry; the effect is negligible.

Chopped nylon is best added while the clay body is being mixed; it can be added after mixing, but with more difficulty. As a starting point, add a teaspoon of chopped nylon for each one hundred pounds of clay. When adding to already mixed clay, moisten the nylon so that it will be distributed more uniformly.

Foam Pellets
Tiny plastic foam pellets can be used as a filler in clay bodies. Like sawdust and coffee grounds, these pellets also contribute strength and workability to the unfired clay; and they too will burn out in the fire. Pellets, however, do not produce as much smoke in the firing and so are useful in bodies that will be fired in the electric kiln.

TYPES OF SILICA AND THEIR EFFECT ON CLAY BODIES
The physical characteristics of clay bodies affect their behavior. For example, silica exists in a number of forms, each of which influences the clay body in a different way. All silica in clay bodies is chemically the same, but the structure differs. Much of the silica in a clay body is bonded chemically with alumina and flux. Other silica resembles a very fine sand or silica flour. The type of silica that bonds chemically with alumina or flux is known as ''chemically bound''; the type that is not bound with alumina or flux is known as ''free silica.''

Free Silica
Free silica is useful because it forms a glassy binding that welds the clay particles together and strengthens the clay body. We are used to thinking of silica as refractory, but this form of silica is strongly melting because it is very fine grained (below 600 mesh).

Anna Calluori Holcombe

THE RELIQUARY BOX SERIES

Reliquary boxes are meant to house important religious and ceremonial itiems; mine have functional as well as suggestive elements.

The concept of the box has always held mystery and surprise for many cultures. Packaged Christmas presents and jewelry boxes come to mind. The boxes can be used to contain things, but that is not my primary emphasis. The space inside is small and shallow because I use the double-walled method of construction; therefore, their use becomes ambiguous. The boxes offer no hint to specify what might have been kept or should be kept in them; rather, they invite the viewer to consider the possibilities.

My "reliquary boxes" are made of earthenware clay and built by the slab method. Nylon fiber is added to the clay to make the slabs easier to handle and put together. I prepare preliminary sketches to work out ideas and then transfer them to graph paper and use them as a stencil to ensure that the parts of the box will fit properly together. Then I paint and spray commercial underglazes and glazes onto greenware to add surface pattern and color. The pieces are cone-fired to cone 04 in an electric kiln. I often add mixed-media elements—wire, wood, plastic—to the fired piece.

Anna Calluori Holcombe. USA. "Homage to Egypt," from the Reliquary Box Series, 17 × 19 × 3 inches. Earthenware clay body strengthened with chopped nylon fiber, finished with terra sigillata and mixed-media additions. Photo: Jim Dusen.

Chemically Bound Silica

Chemically bound silica may be of several types: two with a definite structure—quartz and cristobalite—and one that is amorphous (that is, it has no structure)—glass. In the structured arrangements silica atoms are grouped together with atoms of oxygen. These atoms form a "silica tetrahedron," or triangular pyramid. The tetrahedrons in turn are organized along orderly structural lines.

Quartz, for example, has one such arrangement, whereas cristobalite has another. These structural arrangements dictate the way the silica will react during the cooling cycle of the firing. At 573° C (1063° F), quartz suddenly undergoes a shrinkage of 1 percent (this is called "quartz inversion"). Most glazes are still quite fluid at this point and are little affected by quartz inversion. At 226° C (439° F), cristobalite rapidly contracts by 3 percent. At this point the glaze is solid. This puts the glaze in a squeeze—the body contracts, but the glaze is unable to. This compression of the glaze can help prevent crazing.

Cristobalite can be a powerful tool to help cure crazing problems in low-fire work, where crazing is an especially difficult problem. We can encourage the formation of cristobalite in clay bodies by using magnesium in the body (talc is a good source of magnesium), or we can add cristobalite and also prolong the firing, especially at or near its height.

When is cristobalite a problem? Cristobalite can render high-fire bodies brittle, and refired bodies containing cristobalite often crack. Therefore ovenware should not be too rich in cristobalite or it may crack in the oven.

The silica-alumina bond also has its own structure—mullite. Mullite ($3Al_2O_3 . 2SiO_2$) is an aluminosilicate created in the clay body during firing. These long, needlelike crystals interlace and help strengthen the body. Mullite is guaranteed at temperatures above cone 1 (1150° C/2102° F). Therefore if a durable clay body is a priority, it is a good idea to fire above cone 1.

CLAY BODY RECIPES

Clays
Most clay body recipes contain two or three clays of varying particle size and character. Usually a recipe contains a fairly large amount of one clay and smaller amounts of other clays whose purpose is to modify body color, workability, maturation temperature, and durability. Moderate amounts of either fine-particled or coarse clays added to the body encourage particle-size variation and improve workability; often a little of each is found in the recipe. White or light-colored clays are added to raise the firing temperature and lighten body color; darker clays are added to lower the maturation temperature of the body and darken its color.

Nonclay Materials
Most clay body recipes contain both clay and nonclay materials. The clay, of course, is the backbone of the recipe, but the nonclay materials are also significant and strongly influence the character of the body as well.

Nonclay materials are added to a clay body to modify its silica or melter content or to change its color or workability. Ground silica (flint) raises the silica content of the body (this encourages dense bodies). Feldspars, frits, and silicates contain silica and flux; not only do they raise the silica content of the body, but their melter content lowers its maturation temperature as well. Secondary melters (which contain no alumina or silica) may also be added to the body to lower its maturation temperature, although they are not as effective in this regard as materials that contain silica, such as feldspars and frits.

CLAY BODY TYPES
Individual clay body recipes are grouped in categories, such as stoneware bodies or porcelain bodies. While each clay body recipe has unique characteristics, it also shares many characteristics with other bodies in its category.

It is not unusual for ceramists to come to prefer to work with recipes that belong to a favorite category. The reasons for these preferences vary, but the most often mentioned are workability, durability, color, and visual texture, suitability of firing temperature and firing atmosphere, and the economy and availability of materials.

Clay body types move in and out of fashion. In the 1950s, an interest in functional ceramics for everyday use made durable stoneware bodies the norm. In recent years, many ceramists have turned to pieces that are low fired, highly colored, and nonfunctional. This has encouraged the popularity of high-talc bodies, which are useful with the brilliantly colored glazes of the low fire.

Today there is a good deal of interest in clay bodies whose category can be called unconventional. As ceramists seek to establish their own identity and create their own unique imagery, they develop recipes and strategies that enable them to explore the frontiers of the medium and produce many unusual types of clay bodies. Some of these are discussed on pages 34–37.

The following are clay body types in common use.

Low-Fire Bodies

Low-fire bodies are fired at temperatures between 920° and 1100° C (1700° to 2000° F). Their ingredients encourage as much durability as possible from the comparatively low temperatures at this part of the firing spectrum.

Low-fire bodies are divided into two types: white and buff firing bodies and darker-colored bodies. The white and buff bodies are composed of half clay and half melter (often talc). Talc bodies are fairly workable and can be used with transparent and translucent glazes as well as opaque glazes. Although the surface and color of talc bodies are not especially appealing, these bodies tend to be workable and reliable. Because of their light color, talc bodies take glazes well.

The dark-colored low-fire bodies have a high clay content and derive their color from the high iron-bearing clays that are a major ingredient in these recipes. These bodies have an appealing color and good workability but sometimes are marked with a white haze on the surface of the piece where it is unglazed.

FIG. 2–2 Richard T. Notkin. USA. "Cooling Tower Teapot" (variation #22), 6⅜ inches, Yixing Series. Cast-formed stoneware. Courtesy Garth Clark Gallery, New York and Los Angeles.

This haze is the result of the efflorescence of calcium. The classic antidote for this is to include 2 percent barium carbonate in the clay recipe. The barium unites with the calcium in the body in such a way as to create a nontoxic mixture. For those ceramists who would rather not keep barium in their studios, a useful alternative strategy is to apply a red terra sigillata to those areas of the piece that will remain unglazed.

While an earthenware body could, theoretically, be designed to be mature and water-tight, this is difficult in actual practice. Highly fluxed earthenware bodies do not have a tolerance for marginal overfiring, which is a normal occurrence in most kilns. Therefore low-fire bodies must be fired to a point somewhat short of maturity. Low-fire bodies also lack durability because of the absence

Denys James

CARVED AND OPENED FORMS

After years of rapid hollow-slab construction, I was drawn to the opposite method—starting with a solid mass of clay. Then I slowly bend, cut, open, and carve the form. I smooth much of the surface until I achieve a balance between roughly cut textured areas and the almost-shiny smooth areas.

I continue this interplay of contrasts by leaving the smooth surfaces unglazed and applying a lithium carbonate and stain solution to the textured recesses of the bone dry form.

Denys James. Canada. "Step Up, Step Through #5," 14 inches. Solid-formed low-fire clay, unglazed; oxidation fired to 1060°C (1940°F).

of mullite crystals, which grow in clay bodies fired above cone 1.

For all these reasons low-fire bodies are more open and less dense than those meant for the high fire. Such bodies can absorb liquids containing organic matter, which may then spoil. This makes them unsuitable for many food-handling purposes.

On the other hand, dense bodies shrink, warp, and sag. Low-fire bodies suffer from none of these problems. As a result, the cer-amist who works in the low fire does not need to worry as much about structural questions as other ceramists. You may notice that low-fire pieces feature flat tops, unsupported sections, and sharp changes of direction, all of which would be likely to deform if the clay bodies were fired to maturity.

Stoneware Bodies

Stoneware bodies, both mid- and high-fire, are workable, strong, dense, and reliable. They are fired at temperatures between 1150° and 1300° C (2100° and 2400° F) and are especially appropriate for functional ware because they stand up well to constant use and frequent cleaning. They usually contain about 90 percent clay, with the remainder evenly divided between ground silica and a potassium or sodium feldspar. Clays that are fairly refractory make up the bulk of the material in these bodies, with some coarse, some mixed, and some fine particles for good workability and durability.

Mid- and high-fire bodies range in color from a light ivory or buff to dark reds and browns. They tend to be somewhat rugged in character, which in good part accounts for their natural appeal. In reduction, their character is especially pleasing. The color is rich and warm and the visual texture is quite active; upon inspection, for example, a tan body will appear to contain particles ranging from a light tan to a medium brown, occasionally punctuated with black speckles—a result of the transformation of red iron oxide to black in the reduction fire.

In oxidation, many stoneware bodies, especially the light buff bodies, lack much of this appeal. Many ceramists add materials such as manganese or illmenite particles to oxidation-fired stoneware bodies to improve their appearance. Unfortunately these tend to look like poor copies of reduction-fired bodies. In general, the oxidation-firing ceramist has to be content with clay bodies that lack richness when compared to bodies fired in reduction. On the other hand, few body types offer as much usefulness and reliability as oxidation-fired stoneware bodies.

Sculpture Bodies

Sculpture bodies, a special variant of normal stoneware bodies, have a high content of coarse clays and aggregates. These coarse bodies can be rich and varied in color and texture. They are durable, resist shrinkage and warpage, and are useful for large sculpture and vessel forms.

FIG. 2–3   John Neely. USA. Wood-fired "bowl", with a natural ash glaze, 5 inches.

Porcelaneous Bodies

Porcelaneous is a term used to designate a clay body that contains a high proportion of nonclay materials (generally about 30 percent). The rest of the body is clay. The firing temperature for porcelaneous bodies ranges from 1160° to 1300° C (2130 and 2400° F). In character, they are about halfway between stoneware and porcelain. Most examples are white, but they can be medium or dark colored as well.

White porcelaneous bodies are made solely from ball clay and kaolin; buff-colored bodies are made from less pure clays such as stoneware, and dark-colored bodies are made from darker clays. Color is often influenced by the porcelaneous body's significant nonclay content, which moderates and "grays" the color. While not as workable as true stoneware bodies, procelaneous bodies still have good workability, and the ceramist who works with these clay bodies is far less constricted in choices of form than is the ceramist who works in porcelain. While not

Harris Deller

TECHNICAL NOTES

HARRIS DELLER'S PORCELAIN

Grolleg	*55*
Potash feldspar	*13*
Flint	*20*
Pyrophyllite	*12*
Bentonite	*2*
Molochite (fine)	*7*
Molochite (coarse)	*3*

CUSHING'S BLACK SLIP GLAZE

Albany slip	*65*
Nepheline syenite	*10*
Barium carbonate	*10*
Talc	*15*
Chromium oxide	*1*
Manganese dioxide	*2*
Cobalt carbonate	*2*

Harris Deller. USA. "Teapot with Cross Hatching and Aggressive Spout," 19 inches. Wheel-formed and altered porcelain fired to cone 10 in a reduction atmosphere. Photo: Gary Shermer.

Cylinder and cone shapes are thrown and, while wet, pushed and compressed to suppress the volume. As the porcelain dries, the volume is further compressed and altered. The contour of the volume is defined by pinching the clay and cutting away the edge with a knife. When the pieces are dry enough to hold their own weight, they are turned over. Pieces selected for the bottom part of the form then have a slab attached to them. The contour and volume of the shapes are continually refined as the pieces dry. The compressed volumes are assembled in pairs, one on top of the other, and allowed to dry further. Using a knife, straight-edge, and rasp, I articulate and refine the top, bottom, contour, and volume. An extruded spout and handle are added to the teapots and lids are made.

When the forms are dry, they are scraped with a metal rib to remove fingerprints and sureform marks. Pattern is incised into the forms with a stylus. The forms are then bisque-fired. After the bisque firing, the forms are covered with a black glaze. The glaze is sponged off, leaving a heavy concentration in the incised areas. The forms are sanded with coarse sandpaper to ensure the whiteness of the porcelain.

The works are loaded into the kiln, where each is carefully buttressed with fire brick to control the slumping. The porcelain is fired to cone 10 in a reduction atmosphere for hardness and brightness. The kiln is cooled and the works are removed. Some may be sandblasted and others are left as they are.

FIG. 2–4 Henry H. Lyman, Jr. USA. Porcelaneous whiteware teapot. Cone 6 oxidation in an electric kiln. Photo: Rick Singer.

translucent, their texture and surface tend to have much of the refined characteristics of porcelains. Porcelaneous bodies are especially compatible with the oxidation fire because of their reserved character.

Porcelain Bodies

Porcelain has such special associations that we must remind ourselves that essentially it is merely a clay body. True porcelain is pure white (sometimes ethereally white) and very hard and dense. Thin porcelain is almost translucent.

The composition of porcelain is narrowly defined: it must be evenly divided between clay and nonclay materials. The clays must be either all or almost all kaolin and the nonclay content must be composed only of silica and feldspars.

FIG. 2–5 Eileen Nisbet. England. "Thistle," 40 × 9 × 27 cm. This piece and the one in Figure 2–6 are made of porcelain clay hand-rolled into slabs. The shapes are cut, shaped, and joined. The surfaces are textured or pierced or inlaid and painted with colored slips. The work is fired to 1250° C in an electric kiln. Pieces may be painted with ceramic enamels and fired again to 790° C.

Karen Thuesen Massaro

HUMOR AND IRONY IN CLAY

Change, real and implied, is a key element in my work. Achieving movement within and surrounding the piece continues to engage me. Humor and irony have crept into many pieces as contradictions in the observer's expectations.

Subject matter for my sculptures includes familiar objects such as pencils, soap bars, irons, string, chairs, and fruit. Although identifying characteristics are maintained, form, surface, and position are changed. Words and thoughts stir in my mind as I work on the sculpture.

Various possibilities of interpretation add to the liveliness of the work.

The "Paired Fruit Servers" are faithful in form to their subjects. Clusters of fruit are draped by patterns that call the eye to move in and out of the surface plane. Any addition of real fruit to their ceramic counterpart heightens the visual drama. These are physical pieces juxtaposing the real with its abstraction.

In another piece, "Camay Corner," architectural elements build a precise triangular corner. Closer inspection reveals that bars of soap are the building material. A small inlaid manufacturer's label is sufficient to change one's reading of the wall. In another piece, a cast iron of stacked segments is tipped to exaggerate the

Karen Thuesen Massaro. USA. "Paired Fruit Servers I," 17 × 11 inches. Porcelain, assembled slip-cast sections; cone 10 oxidation. Photo: Lee Hocker.

way it sails over cloth. There is no doubt that it can flatten the small unruly waves. (Older irons are wonderful forms in themselves. I kept the characteristics I most admire.) A ball of twine sits on a table. Upon closer scrutiny, the rolled-up ball of porcelain string doesn't make sense; it is a visual nonsequitur.

Clay yields readily to a sense of animation.

I use this potential as a communicative tool. I don't center my work on humor. Rather there is a lightness of heart, a willingness to play with the medium. For me clay nurtures a sense of well-being. This is a personal response derived from both ceramic processes and the fired material. I want my work to share space in a living way with its observer.

True porcelain must be fired at high temperatures, from 1280° to 1300° C (2300° to 2400° F), in either an oxidation or reduction atmosphere. Porcelain bodies look rich when fired in any atmosphere; in oxidation they take on a creamy cast and in reduction a grayed cast.

Workability is limited in porcelains, in part because of their low clay content and in part because the clays they do contain have limited plasticity. Form choices also are limited because the material, being so close to a glassy state, will often warp or sag in the fire. Forms

that would be appropriate in a less dense body will be disastrously altered when made in porcelain. Ceramists who use porcelain bodies learn to work around the problems, making compromises in size and form that enable them to work well with the material.

According to Nigel Wood, author of *Oriental Glazes* (London: Pitman, 1978), Chinese potters during the Sung Dynasty used local clays whose significant mica content helped them create bodies that were quite plastic. Contemporary ceramists unfortunatley do not have access to such clays. In North

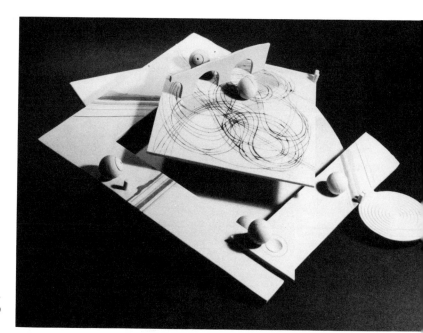

FIG. 2–6 Eileen Nisbet. England. "Game," 46 × 35 × 10 cm.

FIG. 2–7 Susie Symons. USA. Porcelain planter, 8 inches. A self-glazing porcelain with soda ash; cone 10 reduction firing.

FIG. 2–8 Paula Murray. Canada. "Beached Bowl," 10.5 cm. Paula Murray has developed "a firing process that utilizes the delicacy and strength of high-fired porcelain in conjunction with low-temperature salt-glaze surfaces." This piece was slipcast formed and a dry, crawling slip applied to the surface. The piece was fired to translucency, glazed and fired in a cone 04 reduction salt fire. The round-bottom bowl has been placed on a group of stones found in a riverbed.

FIG. 2–9 Sandra Byers. USA. "Pod," 2⅜ inches. Wheel-formed porcelain, pinched, cut, and incised; finished with a microcrystalline oxidation-fired mat glaze, fired to cone 9½. Photo: William Lenke.

Fig. 2–10 James F. Mc-Kinnell. USA. Porcelain plate, 14 inches diameter. Wheel-formed with a red copper slip applied over a wax-resist design; reduction fired at cone 9–10.

FIG. 2–11 James F. Mc-
Kinnell. USA. Porcelain plate,
14 inches diameter. Wheel-
formed with sgraffito decoration; reduction fired at cone
9–10.

FIG. 2–12 Nan B. Mc-
Kinnell. USA. Miniature vase,
$2\frac{1}{4}$ inches. Hand-formed; reduction fired at cone 9–10.

Clay and Clay Bodies
28

FIG. 2–13 Geoffrey Swindell. England. Wheel thrown and altered porcelain, 4½ inches. A copper oxide is applied under a mat white dolomite-containing glaze, then oversprayed with a shiny glaze. Note the precise control of the glaze surfaces.

America, however, we do have a low-impurity micaceous feldspar called Plastic Vitrox, whose platelet-like particles encourage good workability (but cause some extra shrinkage as well).

Porcelain is known for its richness. The unadorned white body is called porcelain bisque: its character is at once sparse, pristine, and yet rich in its smooth, pure white surface. Porcelains covered with a clear glaze are celebrated for their simplicity and elegance. Using colored glazes on porcelain can transform a run-of-the-mill glaze into a subtle, lively surface (see Figs. 2-5 through 2-13.)

COLORED CLAY BODIES

All clay bodies have color, and some colors, such as the brick of a red earthenware body or the striking white of some porcelains, are beautiful. In fact, if the ceramist wishes, the body color itself can serve as the final finish for the piece. The idea of using clay bodies whose color or surface is so rich that the ceramist needs no glaze is very appealing. While the ceramist will encounter many problems when working with colored clays, the results often can be worth the trouble.

Colored clay techniques may be as simple as using a rich red or white body that derives its colors from the natural color of its clay

Virginia Cartwright

Making my pots is the fun part. Glazing them is what I don't like to do, so over the years I've devised ways to avoid it. At first I began to look for clays that were fine-textured and terra cotta or dark brown in color. Later I found a black clay called "Cassius Clay" (humorous as well as smooth!) from Aardvark Clay Company in Santa Ana, California. All of these clays gave me the look I wanted—the look of leather-hard pots. To me, a pot is never more beautiful than when it is at this stage of drying.

I later discovered the appeal of colored porcelains. Potters all over the country are excited about the possibilities provided by colored clays, and most are using the neriage and nerikomi techniques. There is no name that I know of to describe the technique I use, so I call it "inlaid colored clay."

I color the clay by using dry porcelain scraps from my studio, about four to six cups at a time. I premeasure them (to avoid mess later when they are wet) and dissolve them in warm water.

I let this mixture sit for a few hours, and then pour the excess water from the top. I use about one tablespoon of Mason stains for every cup (I go by the premeasured amount of dry scraps) of newly dissolved porcelain and dissolve *that* mixture and beat it into slurry. I pour the slurry onto a plaster bat and spread it to a thickness of about $\frac{1}{4}$ inch, like a thick cake frosting. It dries quickly this way.

Next, I layer about five to seven sheets of these colored clays (about 3 by 6 by $\frac{1}{4}$ inch each) to form a slab. Some of these layers can be white or stoneware clay. I roll the clay after adding each layer. I then cut the layered slab in half, put one half on top of the other, and roll it again. This last step is repeated until the lines are fine and the loaf is about $1\frac{1}{2}$ to 2 inches thick. I place the loaf on end and cut extremely thin slices. I use a cutting device that I make with fishing line and mat-board guides. Some people use a cheese cutter, but I find this to be more awkward and to offer less control.

I apply the thin slices to a medium-thick slab. It's possible to use patterns from various layers and patch them together, creating an

Virginia Cartwright. USA. Colored clay teapot, 6 inches. Wheel-thrown with hand-built elements.

Clay and Clay Bodies

endless variety of patterns. Before I roll out the clay, I place service-station-type commercial paper towels over the design (otherwise it will smear and stick to the rolling pin). The more the clay is rolled, the more fluid and wonderful the pattern becomes. This gets to be so exciting that it's hard to stop.

I've been doing this inlaid technique for five or six years now, and only now am I starting to feel a little overdosed with it. Sometimes I look at all my work and I see pattern everywhere. Sometimes I long for just one plain and simple pot!

My latest works, in fact, are plain, very thin translucent porcelain pieces with no design. I continue to enjoy giving workshops about inlaid colored clay, though, because students love it so much. It's like being in a candy store!

---

constituents. Often, however, these techniques require additions of oxides or stains. Stains are much safer to use than oxides for coloring bodies. Because the ceramist must touch and manipulate the clay, the opportunity for exposure to dangerous materials is far more threatening than that posed by working with a slip or glaze colored with the same substances. Therefore most of the colorants, including cobalt, chrome, and manganese, are not recommended for use in colored clays. Stains are much less toxic and with care can be used safely for colored clay techniques.

The ceramist may use a monochrome (one color) or polychrome (multicolored) clay technique. Monochrome colored clay techniques require using a clay body whose color is unusually rich, such as blues, greens, reds, blacks, and whites. Polychrome techniques are simply an extension of monochrome techniques. Clays of various colors are used together to create rich surfaces and vivid imagery. The ceramist may run into problems

FIG. 2–14 Claudi Casanovas. Spain. Plate made of colored clays, hand-formed, sandblasted, and fired to 1280° C (2336° F), 14 × 68 cm. Casanovas's pieces look as if they had been formed by a complex geological process.

FIG. 2–15 Gail Carney. Canada. "Paper Doll Series," 23 inches. Black basalt clay, hand-formed.

FIG. 2–16 Jennifer Lee. England. Dark asymmetric pot with ridge, amber ellipse, 19 × 15 cm. Hand-formed using colored clay bodies. Jennifer Lee uses both mineral colorants and commercial stains, which she grinds in a mortar and pestle with water and sieves before adding them to an off-white stoneware body. The pieces are fired to a temperature between 1230° and 1260° C in oxidation or reduction. Oxidation favors cooler colors, whereas reduction favors warmer ones. The latter part of the firing is prolonged to ensure rich, saturated color. The surface is polished after firing.

FIG. 2–17 Ewen Henderson. England. Sculpture constructed from slabs created from a white and a dark clay. The dark clay, the center core, is surrounded by white clay on either side. During the firing the dark clay "boils" through the light-colored clay to create complex imagery.

FIG. 2–18 Dorothy Feibleman. England. "Pink Yellow Spiral Coil." Dorothy Feibleman works with laminated sheets of colored porcelain clays. Color is derived from commercially prepared stains. These pieces need no glaze. Photo: Richard Ball.

with the boundaries between inlaid areas. The inlays tend to shrink away from each other, leaving a fine crack between each inlaid section, thereby creating an obvious fault. One of the best ways to deal with this problem is to use low-clay bodies, which shrink very little.

UNCONVENTIONAL CLAY BODIES

Self-Glazing Clay Bodies
The concept of a clay body that also contains a glaze is extremely appealing: How much better it would be to use a clay that would

---

Neil Forrest

TRADITION, FORMAT, AND MATERIAL

My chosen medium is a thixotropic self-glazing clay body, otherwise known as Egyptian paste. Egyptian paste has many properties that lend itself to my biomorphic forms. During drying, the soluble salts in the clay (sodium carbonate and borax) migrate to the surface as the water evaporates. The salts remain on the surface as a deposit or scum, then melt into an alkaline glaze during the first and only firing.

Color and pattern are achieved by adding glaze stain to the Egyptian paste body, using the colored clays to construct patterned tiles. I use these tiles in two ways: either as leather-hard tiles that are shaped and laminated onto hand-built Egyptian paste forms, or as prefired flat tiles mortared onto large fiberglass armatures as veneers.

Egyptian paste clay can be temperamental. To encourage proper glazing, I force the salts to migrate upward by drying the tiles and forms on Formica panels. Once the salts failed to appear and I discovered that the large-grain borax was not dissolving in the wet clay. By substituting smaller-grain borax, I was able to increase the solubility to produce the scum and hence a glassy self-glaze.

These processes and materials yield new challenges that are ultimately manifested in the subject matter.

Neil Forrest. Canada. "Horseye and Leaves," 20 inches. Egyptian paste, low fire.

be naturally glazed during the firing! Such clay bodies do exist. In fact, the earliest glazed pieces, made of Egyptian paste, fall into this category and these ceramic recipes continue to attract attention (see the work of Neil Forrest in his essay).

Self-glazing bodies contain water-soluble fluxes that migrate to the surface of the piece as it dries. These fluxes are deposited as film over the surface of the piece. When fired, the fluxes combine with the silica and alumina in the body to create a thin layer of glaze on the surface. Unfortunately, these melters are alkaline and greatly diminish the workability of the body. Therefore ceramists who use self-glazing bodies often employ press mold forming or slip casting techniques: neither process calls for workable bodies.

Experimental Low-Clay Bodies

Low-clay bodies can be seen as a type of porcelain, perhaps as a kind of porcelain carried to the extreme. Porcelain is traditionally composed half of clay and half of nonclay materials. However, many of the charcteristics that we associate with porcelain are enhanced by lowering its clay content even further.

Working with clay bodies that contain little clay is quite an experience for the ceramist who is used to normal clay bodies. For one reason, they are usually difficult to manipulate. Some ceramists become accustomed to their difficult character and may even come to enjoy their unique qualities. While they vary from recipe to recipe, these characteristics are translucency, striking color,

Susan and Curtis Benzle

Our vessels are made up of multiple layers of porcelain, all laminated and compressed while the clay is still wet. Any one piece will have up to six layers of clay. The viewer is confronted with a constantly changing imagery that is dependent on the quality of the available light. We have come to have a strong concern for light as a source of aesthetic inspiration.

Curtis and Susan Benzle. USA. "Summer Breeze," 7 inches.

and rich surfaces, as well as low shrinkage and durability.

Many low-clay bodies are translucent since clay naturally discourages translucency. Stains can be added to low-clay bodies, and their color tends to be saturated and quite striking. The low clay content prevents undue shrinkage and also helps them to resist warping and cracking. After firing, they can be extremely dense and rock hard. Those that are highly fluxed become completely smooth and glassy, thus blurring the line between a clay and a glaze. In fact, they will often look quite finished and need no glaze.

Low-Clay Colored Clay Bodies
When colorants or stains are added to normal clay body recipes, the ceramist runs into many problems. Most clay bodies are much harder to color than glazes and require larger additions of colorant or stain if their color is to be effective. Clay bodies highly charged with colorant tend to be unworkable and, when fired, very brittle.

An elegant solution to this problem is to use a dense and glassy body as the base for a colored clay technique. These bodies contain little clay (50 percent or less) and accept color more readily than a body with a normal clay content. This is because clay bleaches colorant additons. While workability is limited, their surfaces can be striking, often reminiscent of a polished rock (see the work of Sally Urban Silberberg).

Low-clay bodies may be colored with colorants or stains or even with high-impurity clays. This latter strategy can be interesting, producing color that is warm but not at all heavy. Recipes are similar to those used in the eighteenth century by Böttger and von Tschirnhausen, the developers of porcelain in Europe, for their red porcelain.

Low-clay bodies also can be used to produce colored clay inlay and marbled imagery. They lend themselves to these techniques because of their low shrinkage. The inlays are less likely to shrink away from each other and the ceramist can move from one color area to another smoothly and seamlessly.

The best way to add color to a clay body is to add the colorant to a clay slurry. Slurry can be blended with a high-speed mixer and then dried on an absorbent surface. This is the only way to guarantee that the color will mix completely with the other ingredients of the body.

Clay Bodies with Highly Active Fluxes
One interesting type of clay body contains highly active fluxes such as boron and lithium. These bodies are light and frothy and marked by a pattern of fine bubbles. Many ceramists first encounter these bodies as kiln accidents. Their effects can be quite spectacular, for they have a tendency to boil and bubble, with neighboring pieces becoming welded together during the firing.

Colored Grog Clay Bodies
Grog is a granular substance added to a clay body to improve its workability. Adding colored grog to a clay body not only improves its workability but also can enhance its visual appeal. Adding multicolored grogs in large amounts can create a richly textured surface. These grogs can be made in the normal manner by crushing sheets of colored clay to a desired particle size and firing to bisque temperature.

Theoretically, it is also possible to make an unfired grog, so long as a binding material is added to hold it together. An appropriate binder would be glue, wax, or resin. When unfired grog is added to a clay body, the surface, if cut or sanded, would reveal upon firing a smooth, visually textured surface similar to terrazzo.

Sally Urban Silberberg

As in Nerikomi, a block of clay is constructed by layering thin slabs of clay and thick slips. Eventually the rough size is achieved and the piece is molded and compressed into shape with a wooden mallet and thin plywood forms. Over the next few days, additional cuts are made (horizontally, vertically, and diagonally) and separate layers of clay added. These fulfill both a visual and a structural role. The block is now composed of thousands of separate pieces of clay, bound together by slip. In Nerikomi, the block itself is now sliced to create thin sections of the structure to build with, but my rough form of clay now becomes the outside dimensions of the sculpture. All future work on the piece will be reductive rather than additive.

The form is allowed to harden to the consistency of hard cheese and then covered with plastic to allow the moisture to equalize. As I carve into the block, exposing the structure, the graphic information, and the vulnerabilities of a material that refuses to allow perfection, the sculpture begins to respond to the surrounding space. All the tedious labor of construction is poised on the "edge."

For weeks afterward, the work is gradually refined and surfaces smoothed and eventually sanded if they were cut, with some left in their raw, torn state. While the piece is still leather-hard, I use a small drill bit to form air vents for the firing. The work is dried thoroughly and very slowly bisque-fired. After the bisque, the smooth surfaces are sanded for the last time with a fine emery paper and the piece is fired in a gas, reduction atmosphere to cone 8.

Porcelain fulfills all my criteria. Here is a material that can be easily colored with oxides and stains, is pliable enough to work with but retains its original structure, will harden to a consistency that is easily carved, and with firing achieves the permanency of rock!

Sally Urban Silberberg. USA. "Miter." 9 × 11¼ × 13½ inches. Porcelain; Cone 8.

CHAPTER 3

Clay Making and Buying

Clay bodies are important to us because they influence the character of our work and can make a real difference in the way we feel about ourselves as ceramists. Suppliers who prepare mixed and bagged clay; bodies for ceramists have become common; many ceramists buy their clay from them. Other ceramists, however, insist on buying dry materials and mixing them in their own studios. Both approaches require judgment and knowledge, and both will be covered in this section.

USING PREPARED CLAY BODIES

Clay bodies are much more convenient to purchase than to make since the mixing machinery is bulky, dangerous, and expensive, so most ceramists purchase their clay bodies from commercial suppliers.

Commercial suppliers usually mix a wide range of clay bodies from very low-fire to high-fire stoneware and porcelain. In recent years, the best suppliers have become quite sophisticated when dealing with the problems of mixing clay bodies. The winners in the marketplace have been those who have been willing to take the trouble to do it right. On the other hand, ceramists have become

sophisticated as well and are more discriminating in their selection of a supplier.

What to Look for in Commercial Clay Bodies

Unauthorized substitutions can be a real problem when buying commercial clay bodies. The supplier may make a substitution because another material is more economical or because an older material may be getting scarce. Ask your supplier to notify you if any substitutions are being made.

Attention to detail is another problem. The mixing machinery must be cleaned between different kinds of loads. Even though this is a tedious task, good suppliers make sure that they do it well. Weighing materials for the clay bodies must be done accurately, too; here again, the supplier must make sure not to cut any corners.

The ceramist must tell the supplier how the clay body will be used and fired. A good supplier may be able to suggest alternative recipes. Always make and fire a few test tiles from any new clay as soon as possible and then perform an absorption test (described later in this chapter).

Finally, while price is a factor, the ceramist's investment of time and effort always outweighs the cost of the clay body itself.

The most important consideration in choosing a clay body supplier is quality.

CLAY MAKING

Even if you buy most of your clay bodies from a ceramic supply house, a time may come when you will want to make small lots of a special clay body, such as a low-clay porcelain or a colored body. Some ceramists make their own clay just so that they can control this part of the process to ensure uniformly high quality.

Mixing Clay in Small Amounts

For small test lots, clay can be made up in a plastic bucket in the same way as a glaze. If the clay becomes too wet, allow it to dry on a plaster bat or a pile of newspapers. Then wedge the clay after completing the dewatering process.

The same methods can be used to mix clay on a slightly larger scale (up to 10,000 grams or 20 pounds). To mix larger amounts of clay, fill a large bucket with wet clay slurry and mix with a propeller mixer affixed to a small electric drill. Dry the clay on drying bats made from bisque-fired clay, plaster of paris, or piles of newspaper. This is a slow process but not terribly demanding, and it produces highly workable clay bodies.

Mixing Clay in Large Amounts

Moist clay bodies are extremely difficult to mix because clay is heavy and unyielding when moist. Therefore, to make clay in large lots, you must purchase mixing machinery that has been specially designed for this purpose. The most common types are moving blade mixers and pug mills.

Moving blade mixers rely on a large motor and blade to cut through the moist clay. This is a kind of "brute force" method, but it is effective and popular. Pug mills work only on a small portion of the body at a time.

They can mix more effectively than blade mixers, but they often need a premixing device to ensure that the overall mixture will be uniform. Pug mills can be built with a de-airing chamber to produce a smooth mixture that requires little wedging.

Each type of mixer has its advantages. Large blade mixers may be superior for mixing clay bodies from dry, bagged materials, while pug mills are best for reworking scrap and discarded work.

Mixing Clay Safely

Clay mixers generate a great deal of clay dust, which is dangerous and can lead to silicosis. Having an effective method of ventilation is extremely important, and always wear a good dust mask. Ideally, wear protective overalls and a hat as well. Clay mixers are dangerous; their powerful mixing blades can injure, break, or sever limbs and should always be treated with extreme care. Above all, never put your hand or arm into the mixer while it is in operation. To the person who has never mixed clay, this may sound like an obvious precaution, but anyone who has ever used a clay-mixing machine knows how tempting it is to assist the mixing process when it seems to need help. At all costs, resist this impulse.

MATERIALS SUBSTITUTIONS IN CLAY BODIES

Ceramists who make their clay bodies from dry materials must always be ready to substitute materials if necessary. Sometimes a particular material may be in short supply or is no longer available. Or just as likely, a new material may have been introduced to the market and is now readily available. Substitutions are also necessary when using a recipe that was developed in another area and calls for materials not available in yours. Clays in particular are subject to variations in availability, but appropriate substitutes can be made for most clays. Keep in mind that the new recipe may have somewhat different characteristics, so be sure to test before using it.

Clays

Clays fall naturally into one of four or five categories, groupings that are distinguished by impurity content, particle size, and shrinkage. Because the differences between any clay in a given category are less significant than the similarities, it is not uncommon for the ceramist to substitute one clay for another in the same category.

Clays that are high in impurities are usually red or brown in color because of their iron content. Clays in this category will differ from one another as a result of the type and amount of impurities they contain, but it is usually possible to substitute one high-impurity clay for another in a clay body recipe. Other clay types, such as stoneware clay, ball clay, kaolin, or fire clay, are perhaps even more uniform, and it is usually easy to substitute one for another in the same category.

Nonclay Materials

Nonclay materials used in clay bodies fall into the following categories: soda feldspars, potash feldspars, lithium feldspars, frits, and silicates. If you need to substitute, use another material from the same category. Be sure to test the results, though, because the new recipe may have a somewhat different character than the original.

CLAY BODY SHRINKAGE

All clay bodies shrink. A piece that is 20 centimeters high when formed will be 18 centimeters high after the final firing. Shrinkage depends on the amount and type of clay in the recipe. Nonclay materials do not shrink and so will not contribute to clay body shrinkage. High-clay recipes will shrink more than bodies that are low in clay.

The type of clay is also important. A fine-particled clay, such as ball clay, will shrink more than one that is coarse particled, such as a fire clay. It is understood that a plastic and workable clay body will shrink more than a clay body that is made up mostly of coarse clays, such as a sculpture body. While there is no ideal shrinkage rate, a total shrinkage of 10 percent is considered acceptable in a clay body suitable for hand-building or throwing.

Testing for Clay Body Shrinkage

To test for shrinkage in the clay body, start with a sample of the clay recipe that has a water content typical of the clay bodies you usually use. Then, do the following:

- Make up a test tile 13 by 4 by .7 centimeters.
- Carefully draw a 10-centimeter mark on the tile.
- Let the tile dry and fire it to the desired temperature.
- Measure the new length of the drawn line.
- Subtract the length of the line from 10 centimeters, the length of the original line.
- Divide this figure by .10. The result will be the percentage of shrinkage.

CLAY BODY ABSORPTION

One of the most important characteristics of a clay body is its moisture absorption rate. A body that can absorb a great deal of moisture (perhaps equal to 18 percent of its fired weight) is said to be open, while a clay body that can absorb very little moisture (perhaps 2 percent of its fired weight) is said to be tight or dense.

The absorption rate is controlled by a number of factors: the firing temperature, the amount of clays and fluxes in the recipe, and the fluxing power of those clays and fluxes. When the firing temperature is raised, the body will become progressively more dense. To lower the absorption rate, use larger amounts of strongly fluxing clays and fluxes. To raise the absorption rate, use larger amounts of refractory clays and lower the flux content.

Testing for Water Absorption

Testing a clay body for water absorption can be done accurately by following a simple procedure. The test is not difficult, but it will take some time and patience.

The Procedure
- Make up a test tile.
- Fire the test tile to the desired temperature.
- Remove the tile from the kiln and let it cool until it is just at room temperature.
- Weigh the tile carefully on a gram scale.
- Soak the tile in a container of water for at least twelve hours.
- Remove the tile from the water container and wipe dry with a paper towel. Use a light touch so as not to absorb water from the body of the tile.
- Weigh the tile. It should weigh only slightly more than it did before it was immersed in water.

Determining the Percentage of Absorption

To determine the percentage of absorption, use the following equation:

1. Subtract the weight of the tile after immersing in water from its original weight. The resulting figure is the weight of the absorbed water.
2. Divide this figure by the weight of the tile *before* immersion.
3. Move the decimal point two places to the right to obtain the percentage of absorption.

An Example

$$\text{Weight of the fired test tile} = 22.3 \text{ grams}$$
$$\text{Weight of the test tile after immersion} = 26.7 \text{ grams}$$
$$26.7 - 22.3 = 4.4 \text{ grams}$$

The weight of the absorbed water is 4.4 grams.

Divide the weight of the absorbed water by the original weight of the fired tile:

$$4.4 \div 22.3 = .1973$$

To find the correct absorption figure, move the decimal point two places to the right: 19.73 is the percentage of absorption.

Normal Absorption Figures

low fire	8 to 12 percent
stoneware food containers	4 to 5 percent
decorative stoneware	5 to 8 percent
porcelain	1 to 3 percent
sculpture bodies	10 to 20 percent

If the clay body you are testing strays too far from these limits, do not use it. If you have mixed the test from a recipe, find another recipe. If the clay body was purchased from a supplier, ask for a different one that is better suited to your needs.

CONTROLLING CRACKING AND WARPING

Cracking

The stress that the clay body endures during drying is a major cause of cracking. Those places where sections are joined are particularly prone to cracking: hand-built pieces, which have many more joins than wheel- or mold-formed pieces, are particularly prone to problems. The areas of the piece that are under stress, especially where clay forms are joined together, should be reinforced with clay during the forming process. For example, fill the sharp corner where two slabs come together with a coil of clay. This coil is called a "fillet" and it will look highly finished and be quite strong.

Wheel-thrown pieces are subject to stress cracks where water has been allowed to settle (as in the bottom of a vase form). To avoid cracking, use as little water as possible during throwing. Carefully sponge away any water that has settled in the base of the piece during throwing.

Cracking during Firing

Cracks can be caused by an overly rapid firing cycle, especially during the early stages of the fire, or by rapid cooling. To prevent cracks that might occur during heating, always heat the kiln slowly. To prevent cracks that might occur during cooling, extend the cooling cycle. This procedure is called "soaking" and is accomplished quite simply. Rather than shutting off all power or fuel, fire the kiln for two or three hours with partial power or fuel.

Warping

Uneven shrinkage is the primary cause of warping. All clays and clay bodies shrink. The problem, however, is that shrinkage never occurs in a perfectly linear manner: it is always uneven. Warping, unfortunately, is a fact of ceramic life.

To minimize warping as much as possible, choose a clay body with fairly low shrinkage. Avoid clay bodies with a high percentage of ball clay. You may want to choose a body that contains a good percentage of coarse particles and fillers such as grog or chopped nylon, which strongly discourage shrinkage and warping.

Body fluxes also can encourage warping, especially those that melt in an abrupt manner. Some fluxes move quickly from the inert state to a highly melting state. These fluxes (among them boron) can cause warping in reaction to normal kiln temperature variations.

Another cause of warping is overfiring. Unfortunately, the term "overfiring" is open to interpretation because there is no one point at which a piece can be said to be overfired. Furthermore, bodies that have been fired at or even just beyond their optimal maturation point will be dense and rich in surface. Unfortunately they will be prone to warping and cracking as well. Sometimes the ceramist must be willing to forego some surface richness for good structural integrity. To prevent warping, fire the body at a somewhat lower temperature, alter the clay recipe (if possible), or change to a new clay body.

CHAPTER 4

Surface Finishes

From clay we derive form. Once that form is created, the ceramist will usually manipulate it in order to enrich the surface. We may add clay to the surface, engrave or press the surface of the clay, cover the surface with a special finish, or fire the piece in a special way. To a degree unmatched by any other artistic medium, ceramists manipulate both form and surface, and it is our job to balance the two as best we can. This is a difficult task because form and surface are almost always created at two separate times using different methods for creation.

The intertwining of form and surface is the engine that drives our medium and gives the best ceramic pieces a tension, a restless energy, and a sense of resolution. In our time, with its emphasis on the experimental and the personal, the ceramist has a wide range of surfaces to choose from.

CLAY ORNAMENT

One of the best ways to create imagery on the surface of ceramic pieces is to use clay. In fact, a good deal of our imagery is created in this way. Just as clay lends itself easily to the creation of form, it also lends itself easily to the creation of surface imagery. Some of the earliest potters excelled in the creation of clay imagery. The Jomon potters of an-

cient Japan took this approach in their large modeled and carved coil vessels.

Strategies for creating clay imagery are usually simple and straightforward. Imagery can be created in a number of ways.

Sprigged Imagery

To create sprigged imagery, the ceramist presses clay elements on the surface of the piece. These elements are usually slipped so that they will bond effectively. First, the ceramist cuts and forms the clay elements. Then the surface of the form is slipped and the elements are pressed into the form.

Carved and Engraved Imagery

Imagery can be carved or engraved into the surface of the clay. Scalpels are excellent tools for precise carving because they are sharp and slim and so do not get in the way of carving. Scraping and smoothing tools can be used to clean and refine the image.

Stamped or Pressed Imagery

Imagery can be created by pressing into the clay with stamping tools made from bone, wood, metal, rubber, or cork. First, make slabs for the ceramic piece and stamp them with various stamping tools. Then assemble the slabs, being careful not to damage the imagery.

Molded Imagery
Molded imagery is related to stamped imagery. Small press molds can be used to create the elements that will be applied to the form. Decorative handles and emblems have long been treated in this way.

To make press-mold elements, start with

FIG. 4–1 Marc Barr. USA. Untitled, 36 inches. Hand-formed white earthenware with colored slips and glazes, fired to cone 06.

a block of plaster that has set. Carve an image into the plaster and blow out any plaster dust. Then press clay into the plaster and clean the clay element. Finally, apply the press-molded element to the surface of the piece.

Sandblasting
To sandblast a piece, the ceramist directs a stream of sand, under pressure, upon the surface. The areas of the surface touched by the sand become abraded and engraved. To leave parts of the surface smooth, mask them with tape before sandblasting the piece.

Slip Trailing
In slip trailing, the ceramist creates a raised-line imagery with a thick slip. This is done with a device called a "slip trailer," a flexible plastic or rubber bulb with a narrow nozzle at one end.

Slip-trailed imagery is usually applied to a piece when the body is leather-hard. The procedure requires a steady hand and some experience, so always practice on test slabs first.

In the past, low-fire domestic wares were decorated with slip trailing and then covered with a clear glaze. Now this method is used at all points of the firing spectrum. As in the past, the ceramist applies transparent or translucent glazes over the imagery.

To create slip-trailed imagery, first prepare a thick slip. Immerse the nozzle of the slip trailer in the slip and squeeze the bulb to fill it. Squeeze the slip over the piece to create a raised, linear design. Finally, cover the piece with a transparent glaze and fire it.

CARBON REDUCTION: FIRE-MARKED SURFACES
Carbon reduction is a firing process that modifies the color and visual texture of the clay body. To fire in this way, the ceramist

Fiona Salazar. England. Vase. Earthenware clay body. Coil formed, then painted with terra sigillatas and burnished. Fiona Salazar admires ancient pots and draws inspiration from those that were finished in terra sigillatas.

Karen Koblitz. USA. "Still Life with Plums and Blue Leaves," wall relief, 18 × 20 inches. Slipcast elements, low-fire clay and glaze.

Roberta Kaserman. USA. "Star Ship," 15 inches high, 26 inches long. Mixed media, wood and clay. The clay elements are made from a porcelain body finished with terra sigillatas and gouache (the gouache is unfired).

Patti Warashina. USA. "A Step Out of the Dark," 27 × 25 inches. Mold-formed and altered with hand-formed and mixed media additions. Low-fire talc body finished with commercially prepared underglaze stains and glazes.

Angus Suttie. England. "Jug,"
36 × 52 cm. Hand-built, low
fire. "I want my work to attract
people's attention, not by being
beautiful or obviously super-
skillful, but by being intrigu-
ing, awkward, unusual, and
suggestive. I want to commu-
nicate."

Deborah Horrell. USA. "Hand
to Heart," 12 × 33 × 9 inches.
Mixed media. The ceramic elements are slip-formed, sandblasted, translucent porcelain
enhanced with colored pencil.

Elyse Saperstein. USA. "Roller Teapot," 11 inches high. Terracotta clay body, slab built, finished with terra sigillata and slips, fired to cone 02. Photo: John Carlano.

Sylvia Netzer. USA. "Gateway to Second Avenue," 6 × 3 feet. Tile and neon. The ceramic elements are low fire, finished with commercially prepared glazes. This piece was designed in collaboration with Marjorie Hoog. Photo: © David Lubarsky 1988.

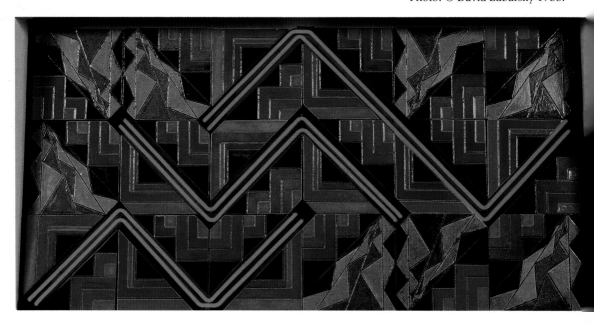

Martha A. Holt. USA. "Woman Tree #2," 35 inches high. Hand-formed, finished with low-fire commercially prepared glazes. Photo: Mark Perrott.

Nancy Jurs. USA. "Amaterasu," 5 feet high. Sculpture, hand-built stoneware, glaze and acrylics.

Kinpei Nakamura. Japan. "88-21," 58 cm high. Created from mold-formed elements, oxidation fired in an electric kiln. Nakamura is conscious of tradition and of the ways he differs from it. He buys his clay already made up and fires in an electric kiln.

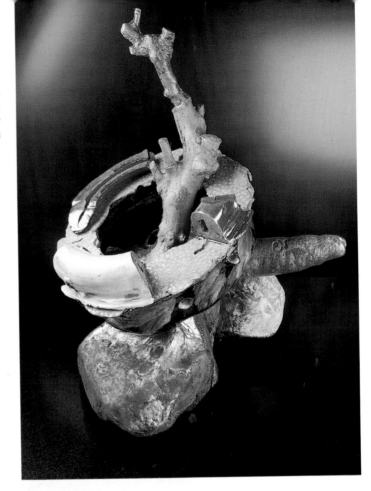

Robert Shay. USA. "Chaco," 4 inches high, 8 inches long. This work is made of stoneware multifired over a wide variety of temperatures and atmospheres. Some pieces contain parts made of fused glass, and many have cast bronze appendages held under tension with greenhide (gut).

Andrea Gill. USA. Vase, 27 inches high. Low fire, terra-cotta. Constructed with slabs and press molds. The work is fired to cone 06, finished with a majolica glaze.

Frank Boyden. USA. "Fish Vase," 11 inches high. Wheel thrown and altered. Wood fired (with no applied glazes) in an anagama kiln. Fired to cone 13–14. "When I started to make pots, I naturally drew on them. At present, I am putting one completely conceived drawing around a piece: I am always curious about the distortions that drawing must take on in order to fit contours; also, in how the drawing concludes itself from a large number of static points as one moves around the piece and how the drawing and the piece imply what is hidden." Photo: Jim Piper.

John Chalke. Canada. "His Master's Plate," 16¾ inches high. Hand formed, cone 6, multifired in an oxidation kiln. This piece is evidence of John Chalke's "long love for Oribe ware" from Japan. It has kept his interest and has been a source of many of his platter forms.

Judith Salomon. USA. Black bowl, 20 × 13 inches. Hand-built from cast slabs, low fire, whiteware. Bisque fired to cone 04, then glaze fired to cone 05 or 04.

FIG. 4–2 Claudi Casanovas. Spain. Bowl, 120 cm. Fired at 1280° C (2336° F). Courtesy Gallerie Besson, London.

FIG. 4–3 Mary Law. USA. "Peas in a Pod," 6 × 12 inches. Oval serving dish, wheel-formed and altered porcelain; slip trailing, covered with a clear glaze, fired to cone 11 in reduction. "I use my porcelain body (the throwing slops, actually) watered down, and I add Mason stains for color; then I trail the slips on leather-hard porcelain." Photo: Richard Sargent.

Ann Tubbs

Although I certainly recognize the usefulness of glaze and use it on my functional ware, I tend not to glaze my nonfunctional pieces. Most of all, I love to play with slips and engobes on the soft and leather-hard clay—my favorite part. Possibly this reflects my interest in two-dimensional work. I like the fluidity, the immediateness, the thick, luxurious slips, colored and contrasting with the darker body, and the possibilities of change and alteration and messing about with my fingers. I keep thinking that someday I'll build a salt kiln, but instead have gotten very comfortable with cone 06 to 6 electric and all the possibilities for colors and smoke firing.

Ann Tubbs. USA. "Boy and Dog #4," 18 inches. Wheel-formed, hand-formed, and extruded elements brushed with a sieved slip; fired in an electric kiln to cone 04–03 and finished in a sawdust fire. Photo: Stephen Johnston.

surrounds the piece with materials that will burn, leaving a residue of carbon that stains all or part of the surface black. The village potters of Africa and the Pueblo potters of the Southwestern United States use this method to create their black pottery. Some contemporary potters fire their pieces surrounded by sawdust, an effective carbon-reduction technique.

Sawdust Firing
In sawdust firing the piece is packed in a kiln structure surrounded by sawdust. The saw-

FIG. 4–4 Jennifer Elion. Canada. "Reliquary," 22 × 30 inches. Hand-built raku clay body with about 30% grog. Glazed and fired at cone 04 in the raku kiln; the base of the piece was left unglazed so that it would be carbon darkened.

dust is set alight and allowed to burn until combustion ceases from lack of fuel. As the sawdust burns, rich patterns of carbon smudging are left on the surface of the piece. Pieces fired in sawdust have a natural and direct quality that can be very appealing.

Sawdust firing has a number of advantages. First, it is economical—the sawdust is usually free for the taking. Second, the firing is done in a simple firing container rather than in a true kiln. The container requires only a top and walls with small openings to allow air to reach all parts of the densely packed sawdust and smoke to leave during combustion. A sawdust "kiln" can be made from bricks (common red brick will do) or a metal garbage can with holes pierced in the sides with a sharp tool to allow air to enter.

Sawdust firing has disadvantages as well. The surface of the piece cannot be as varied as a normal glaze surface and the piece will not be durable (though the sawdust firing can be preceded by a bisque fire to harden the piece) and will allow water to seep through its walls. Sawdust-fired pieces, especially large pieces, may develop cracks in the firing. Some cracks are to be expected in the sawdust fire and small ones are not considered to be defects.

Pieces intended for the sawdust fire can be painted first with terra sigillata, which takes the sawdust fire well and emphasizes the fire markings.

To fire a piece in the sawdust fire, select a strong piece that is compact in shape. (You may wish to fire it first in a bisque kiln.)

The Procedure
1. Add a layer of sawdust in the base of the firing structure.
2. Place the pieces to be fired in the structure and surround them with sawdust.
3. To make sure the fire burns slowly (the

FIG. 4–5 Robert Schmitz. USA. Thrown form with hand-built additions; pit fired at 871° C (1600° F).

safest option), pack the sawdust tightly around the pieces.

4. Cover the pieces with a layer of sawdust.
5. Place the metal lid over the structure but leave a gap of a few inches to create a draft.
6. Start the fire with pieces of paper and let the sawdust burn for a few minutes.
7. Close the lid of the structure.
8. For the first hour or so, make sure that the fire continues to burn; restart it if necessary. After half an hour, the fire should be well established and will not go out until all the sawdust has burned.
9. Unload the pieces the next day and brush off any burned sawdust.
10. Wet the piece lightly, then wax and buff it. If the piece is too delicate to wax and buff, spray it with a transparent acrylic medium or a liquid wax.

The African village potters create a utilitarian ware with a rich, lustrous, dark black carbon-reduced surface. The work is fired in the open in impromptu firing structures composed of the pots plus shards and fuel.

Firing takes place over a short period—perhaps an hour or two. At the end of the firing, the potters pull the still-hot work from the fire and pour oil over it. The oil quickly burns and stains the surface of the piece carbon black. Finally, the piece is polished. Although simple, this method produces an elegant surface. A similar method, using heavy smoke reduction, is used by the Pueblo Indians in the Southwest.

APPLIED SURFACES: SLIPS, ENGOBES, AND GLAZES

Most ceramic pieces are finished by covering them with a mixture that modifies the surface of the piece when fired. These mixtures create durable surfaces that are tightly bonded to the clay body.

No one surface finish can be said to be universally useful or "good" because every ceramist's needs are unique. For one ceramist, the most desirable characteristic is the ability of the piece to withstand the stress of

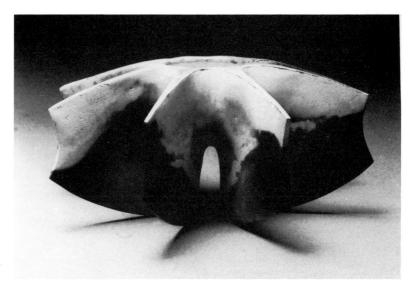

FIG. 4–6 Robert Schmitz. USA. Thrown form with hand-built additions; pit fired at 871° C (1600° F).

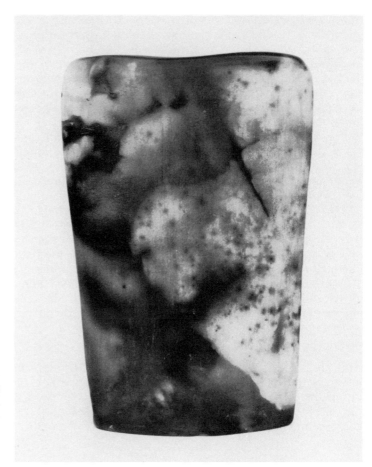

FIG. 4–7 Joan Mathieu. USA. Slab Pot. Burnished white stoneware body bisqued-fired in an electric kiln (cone 08–06), then sawdust-fired.

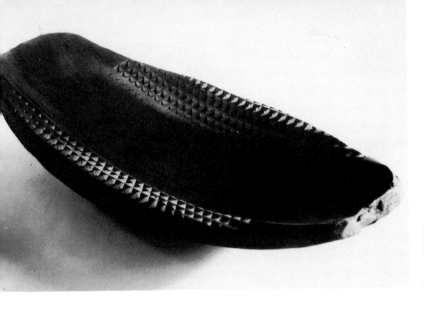

FIG. 4–8 Mikhail Zakin. USA. Slab-formed bowl, 12 × 7 inches. Cone 3 fired, then smoke reduced in hardwood sawdust while still red hot.

cooking and cleaning, whereas another may want a rich texture or color or want to explore more exciting application possibilities. The potter who wishes to create durable, useful vessels that can be easily cleaned will have a different idea of what constitutes a good surface than the ceramist who wants to apply a complex, highly textured surface upon a sculptural nonfunctional form. The ceramist has to consider the character of the form, the purpose of the piece, and the nature of the materials and tools at hand. The ceramist may choose a surface finish that will convey intangibles, such as a particular artistic creed.

Surface treatments go in and out of fashion; the surface treatment of a piece may follow the current fashion or perhaps be considered avant-garde. Or it may harken back to a traditional practice or even be completely independent of both fashion and tradition. There is no one standard that we can all accept as ''best.''

Just as there is no one set of criteria for choosing a good surface, no one method of application will be best for every ceramist. Some will want the application to result in a smooth, mechanically perfect surface, others may want to emphasize the accidental and the earthy, and still others will choose a highly painted, imagistic surface.

Surface finishes are perhaps the most complex and interesting part of our technology, rooted in our medium's past and at the same time constantly evolving and shifting direction. Most of our surface finishes are fired and are unique to our medium.

Ceramic surfaces are divided into two main types—those that are vitreous or glassy and those that are nonvitreous and essentially claylike. The vitreous surfaces are further divided into glazes and vitreous slips and engobes; the nonvitreous surfaces are divided into slips, engobes, and terra sigillatas.

CHAPTER 5

Glazes

Glazes are favored because they offer the ceramist a wide variety of choice in surface quality, color, visual texture, and richness of effect. Glazes resemble glass and indeed are chemically similar to glass. Glass, however, does not have a crystalline structure, whereas glazes almost always do. This structure is what gives glazes their visual textures and inviting satiny, surfaces.

The earliest glazed pieces seem to have come from Egypt. These pieces derived their glazed surfaces from alkaline salts in the clay body. Lead glazes were developed in Babylon. Then, during the Han Dynasty in China, high-fire glazes were developed that were derived from the wood-ash by-product of the kiln fuel. By the eighteenth century, when an understanding of chemistry began to emerge, ceramists were able to experiment with and employ a much larger selection of glaze materials. While we may not be any better than ceramists of the past, we have many more ways to affect the durability, behavior in the fire, visual texture, and color effects of glaze recipes than our forebears.

GLAZE MATERIALS PROFILE

Glaze materials fall into three broad categories: clays, glass makers (primary fluxes),

and secondary fluxes. In turn, these are divided as follows:

Clays
Light
Dark

Glass makers
Feldspars and frits
Silicates
Silica

Secondary fluxes
Fluxes
Opacifiers (materials that encourage opacity)

Glaze Clays

Glaze clays help keep the glaze in suspension and are sources of alumina and silica. They also may be sources of impurities that encourage melting and modify color. The darker-colored clays can be used to enrich glaze color.

The Glaze Materials

Kaolins (ingredients—kaolin and alumina). These low-impurity clays contribute no color to the glaze (often a desirable trait) and are refractory.

Ball clays (ingredients—silica, alumina, and a small amount of impurities). These clays contribute little color to glazes and are somewhat refractory.

Stoneware clay (ingredients—silica, alumina, and a moderate amount of impurities). These clays contribute some color to glazes, often warming them a bit, and are moderately fluxing.

High-impurity clays (ingredients—silica, alumina, and large amounts of impurities). Iron is the main coloring element in most of these clays. They contribute a great deal of color to the glaze and encourage warm tones, as well as being strongly fluxing.

The Glass Makers

Feldspars

Because they contain silica, alumina, and melters, the three ingredients necessary in a glaze, feldspars are practically glazes in themselves. Many useful recipes are composed almost entirely of feldspar, with only a small amount of clay added for suspension.

Nepheline syenite (ingredients—silica, alumina, sodium, and potassium). This soda feldspar is one of our most powerful glaze-melting materials.

Potash feldspar (ingredients—silica, alumina, potassium, and sodium). A favorite high-fire feldspar.

Soda feldspar (ingredients—silica, alumina, sodium, and potassium). A powerful flux, especially useful in the mid and low fire.

Spodumene (ingredients—silica, alumina, lithium, iron, potassium, and sodium). A strong melter that encourages rich visual textures and strong, saturated glaze color.

Frits

Frits resemble feldspars in many ways, but they may contain melting mixtures not found in nature. Most frits are powerful melters, and the most useful for the ceramist are those based on sodium or boron.

Soda Frits. These powerful melters contain significant percentages of sodium plus silica

and alumina. (*Note:* Soda frits have a high coefficient of expansion and contraction and may cause crazing if too much is used in the glaze.)

Boron Frits. Useful for low-temperature work, these frits contain significant percentages of boron plus silica and alumina. Boron frits do not encourage crazing.

Lead Frits. While not as dangerous as non-fritted lead sources, these strong melters can be toxic.

Silicates

The two silicates used in ceramics are talc and wollastonite. Their composition is divided between silica and flux.

Talc (ingredients—silica, magnesium, and calcium). A powerful flux. Because talc contains magnesium, it tends to keep glazes in suspension and encourages violet blues when used with cobalt.

Wollastonite (ingredients—silica and calcium). A powerful flux that encourages royal blue colors when used with cobalt.

Ground Silica (Flint)

Ground silica is a glass maker. By itself it is refractory, but, when used with other materials, it encourages glaze formation.

Secondary Melters (Fluxes)

Secondary melters contain no silica or alumina. They influence the character of the glaze melt.

Barium carbonate (ingredient—barium). Encourages lovely mat surfaces and rich colors, but it is toxic and its use should be discouraged.

Bone ash (ingredients—calcium and phosphorus). Encourages strongly broken visual textures. Bone ash has a strong affinity for red iron oxide and encourages rich, earthy brick reds, browns, and oranges. It is refractory up to cone 8, at which point it becomes strongly fluxing.

Dolomite (ingredients—calcium and magnesium). Below cone 8, dolomite is a weak melter; it encourages smooth glaze surfaces and muted glaze color. Above cone 8, it is a strong melter and encourages highly broken visual textures and fairly strong, saturated glaze color.

Gerstley borate (ingredients—boron, calcium, and sodium). A powerful and reliable flux at all firing temperatures but especially useful in the low and mid fire. (Not available in England or Europe.)

Lithium carbonate (ingredient—lithium). Since very similar visual effects can be derived from spodumene (a lithium feldspar), there is no reason to continue to use this dangerous material.

Magnesium carbonate (ingredient—magnesium). Below cone 8, magnesium carbonate is a weak melter, but it encourages smooth, dry glaze surfaces and muted glaze color. Above cone 8, it is a strong melter, encouraging highly broken visual textures and fairly strong, saturated glaze color.

Tin oxide (ingredient—tin). Encourages opacity in glazes and smooth, enamel-like surfaces.

Titanium dioxide (ingredient—titanium). Encourages rich visual textures and good glaze color. In small amounts (up to 4 percent), it is a strong flux; when used in larger amounts, it progressively mats the glaze. It may also cause pinholes in glazes and should be used with low-viscosity materials such as soda feldspars and Gerstley borate.

Whiting (ingredient—calcium). Below cone 8, whiting is a weak melter but encourages smooth glaze surfaces and muted glaze color. Above cone 8, it is a strong melter and encourages highly broken visual textures and fairly strong, saturated glaze color.

Zinc oxide (ingredient—zinc). In small amounts (up to 4 percent), zinc oxide is a strong flux; when used in larger amounts, it progressively mats the glaze.

Zirconium opacifiers (ingredients—zirconium and silicon impurities). Highly refractory, these encourage opacity in glazes, mute color, and encourage some visual texture.

GLAZE RECIPES

Glaze recipes are complex combinations of materials. Most recipes contain three to six ingredients. The ceramist can choose from about thirty or forty ceramic materials to create a recipe. As a result, a great number of combinations are possible, many with a unique character. While the experimenter may have a fairly good idea of how a recipe will look, the complete character of a recipe can be revealed only during the fire. Most successful glaze recipes are the result of knowledge, intuition, experimentation, and luck.

Ceramists encounter so many glaze recipes that it is difficult to keep track of them. In order to deal with this variety more effectively, we organize them by class or category. These classes or categories define glaze recipe types that have at least one attribute in common. Ceramists use impromptu systems of glaze classification all the time, and we deal with a long list of significant attributes, including appearance, important ingredients, and the way the ingredients are used and fired.

Glazes Classified by Their Silica, Alumina, or Flux Ratio

Balanced Glaze Recipes

For a glaze recipe to be balanced, it must have silica, alumina, and fluxes in proper proportion. The best way to ensure this is to look for a glaze that contains 55 to 65 percent feldspar and 6 to 10 percent clay. The rest (25 to 35 percent) can be secondary melters. Balanced glaze recipes are stable, useful, and reliable.

High-Silica Recipes

High silica recipes are glassy, durable, stable, and smooth. These glazes derive their silica from ground silica (flint), feldspars, frits, and silicates. For example, a high-silica glaze would contain 60 to 70 percent feldspar, 5 to 8 percent clay, perhaps 8 to 12 percent flint or a silicate, and 10 to 27 percent secondary melters.

High-Alumina Recipes

High-alumina recipes are durable, stable, and nonflowing. Their surfaces may be dry and mat or, if strongly fluxed, smooth and enamel-like; their color is somewhat bleached. Alumina is derived from clays, feldspars, and many frits. In a high-alumina glaze, the clays should comprise 10 to 20 percent of the recipe and feldspars (or frits with an alumina content over 8 percent) 60 to 70 percent of the recipe.

Recipes High in Secondary Fluxes (Melters that Contain No Silica)

These recipes are often florid with a great deal of visual texture. Unfortunately, they are plagued by poor durability, instability, excessive and erratic glaze flow, and crazing. Ceramists continue to use them, however, because they produce glazes that are rich and exciting. A content of 38 to 45 percent melting materials is appropriate for these recipes. Such a glaze recipe might look like this: 40 to 50 percent feldspar/frit, 5 to 10 percent clay, and 40 to 50 percent secondary melters.

GLAZES CLASSIFIED BY APPEARANCE

Transparent Glazes

Transparent glazes come closer to true glass than other glazes. Like glass, they have no crystalline character; rather, their character is that of a frozen liquid. Transparent glazes should contain between 55 and 70 percent feldspar and perhaps some ground silica or silicates—all sources of silica, which is our main glass-forming material. They should contain just enough clay to ensure that they do not flow readily (3 to 6 percent), and they should not contain high percentages of secondary melters. Overreliance on secondary melters is a "brute force" method for creating transparent glazes—a method that re-

sults in weak, unstable recipes. The percentage of flux should be kept in the 25 to 35 percent range.

Majolica

Classical majolica is both a blaze type and a glazing strategy. The glaze is low fire and derives its white color, characteristic opacity, smooth surface, and reactions to applied color from its significant tin content. In the majolica strategy, coloring oxides and stains are painted directly onto the glaze surface to create color imagery.

"Majolica" comes from the medieval name for Majorca, an island off the coast of Spain and at one time a source of Moorish pottery for Italy and the rest of Europe. The Islamic/Spanish pottery was characterized by rich flat patterning and highly stylized imagery. Majolica was later imitated, especially in Italy and Holland. The Italian work, known as *Faïence*, was often complex and features strongly spatial imagery, in imitation of Renaissance and Baroque painting.

Traditionally, majolica glazes were fluxed with lead, which encourages rich glaze surfaces and good color reactions. Now, because we are aware of the problems associated with lead and know that it is toxic, we often use other fluxes instead.

A number of contemporary ceramists have begun to experiment with majolica. Some use traditional techniques that are as authentic as possible, whereas others have begun to create a modern version.

Some ceramists are interested in leadless and in mid- and high-fire majolica glaze strategies. These, however, cannot duplicate exactly the character of the low-fire majolica glazes that contain lead. Even so, they can be quite rich and are more suitable than the lead-containing glazes for utilitarian pieces.

Lusters

Lusters are thin metallic films applied over glazes as the result of the conversion of normal glaze oxides into metallic oxides. The conversion occurs in a reduction atmosphere in the low fire, which produces carbon monoxide. Carbon monoxide lacks an oxygen molecule and will take the molecule from wherever it can, in this case from the coloring oxides. When they lose their oxygen molecules, these oxides are transformed into pure metals. In other words, the surface of glaze is converted from its normal state (and color) to a film of pure metal. The metallic oxides used in ceramics to create luster glazes are gold, platinum, bismuth, copper, and tin.

Luster reduction can be accomplished in two ways: by firing in a reducing atmosphere or by adding a reducing agent to the glaze recipe. Lusters fired in a reduction atmosphere can be made by the studio ceramist using low-fire recipes rich in secondary melters and containing an appropriate colorant. Once the maturation point has been reached, the kiln is heavily reduced. Reduction is continued until the kiln atmosphere loses its color (approximately 500° C or 1000° F). In the great lustered pieces from Iran and Islamic Spain, the ceramists employed this method to produce work of great intensity and beauty.

Commercially prepared lusters contain a reducing agent, usually an organic binder such as oil of lavender, that burns out during the firing and in doing so creates a localized reduction. There lusters can be applied directly from the container to an already glazed and fired piece and then fired to a point just above red heat: 600° to 700° C (1200° to 1300° F).

Crystal Glazes

Crystal glazes are characterized by metallic crystals that float on the surface of the glaze; they are created from low-alumina glaze recipes containing titanium or zinc. The first part of a crystal fire is normal, but in the latter part of the fire, once the desired firing temperature is reached, the temperature is allowed to drop for a few minutes and then is held steady in a long soaking period. The zinc or titanium crystals form and develop during this period. Appropriate amounts are 6 to 10 percent titanium and 2 to 8 percent zinc.

Visually Textured Glazes

Some glazes derive their visual texture from a reduction atmosphere in the kiln. A few glaze ingredients encourage visual texture in any kiln atmosphere; these are bone ash (mottled effects), lithium feldspars and titanium (light-colored spots and patterns of running glaze), wood ash (light-colored spots,

FIG. 5–1 Alan Caiger-Smith. England. ''Bowl with Broad Rim,'' width 26 cm. Red earthenware and tin glaze with dark vaporing from silver luster pigment; fired in a third firing with reduction.

FIG. 5–2 Cheri Sydor. Bowl, 17 cm. Wheel-formed, raku-fired, and fumed with applied silk thread. Photo: Bradley Strubble.

blooms of color, and patterns of running glaze), zirconium opacifier (a tight pattern of light-colored spots), and, above cone 8, whiting (patterns of running glaze).

Desiccated Surfaces

In recent years ceramists have become fascinated with glazes marked by "decaying wall" imagery, which many find evocative of the fire. Desiccated surfaces are dry textured, deeply fissured, parched, curdled, and partially vitrified. Often the body is revealed where the glaze has pulled or flaked away. These effects are often achieved by using recipes that are abnormally high in secondary melters (perhaps as much as 60 percent) and contain a high precentage of calcium, magnesium carbonate, or a zirconium opacifier. For best effect, they must be fired below cone 8, since underfiring is an important part of the process.

FIG. 5–3 Barbara Harmer Tipton. Canada. Gray cup and saucer, 8 × 10 inches. Wall piece, wheel-thrown, altered, and assembled; fired to cone 6 in an electric kiln.

Alan S. Bennett

My work is like fishing. Wedging the clay is like cleaning and waxing my line, sharpening the hooks, and tying new flies. Creating the form is like casting and moving the lures. When I reach the point where I realize the form is just right, it's like a bass striking! Glazing is like playing the fish and fighting and reeling it in. I don't use a line that is so strong that the fish has no chance, and I don't use predictable glazes; I like challenges.

FISH GLAZE

Magnesium carbonate	*45*
Borax	*18*
Feldspar	*23*
China clay	*14*

This dry surfaced glaze is marked by a pronounced crawling texture; where it has pulled away from the body the body is shiny and fluxed.

Alan S. Bennett. USA. "Catch," a group of pieces intended for the wall. Slab-formed from a body that contains 20% pyrophyllite for workability, warp resistance, and strength in the firing. The pieces are finished with a "desiccated" glaze and fired to cone 8 in a gas kiln fired in oxidation.

Smooth-Surface Glazes

Smooth-surface glazes are just the opposite of the highly textured recipes. These enamel-like glazes are often associated with the oxidation fire and the low and mid fire because smooth glaze surfaces are easy to create under these conditions. Smooth glazes are generally well balanced in their ratio of silica, alumina, and flux. Their significant flux, often sodium or potassium derived from feldspar or frit (55 to 65 percent), encourages good melts while not bleaching any of the colorants or stains.

Smooth-surface glazes are best applied with a sprayer that can be used to blend two or three colors. They lend themselves to novel color combinations created with the more unusual stain colorants. The results at their

FIG. 5–4 John Chalke. Canada. "Shift-Shape," $9\frac{1}{2} \times 6\frac{1}{2}$ inches. Hand-formed plate, multifired in an oxidation kiln to cone 6 and lower. This work is strongly influenced by Oribe ware, a style that originated in seventeenth-century Japan. John Chalke says of this: "When I first met Japanese Oribe ware (it was 1964), like so many new loves, part of the encounter seemed already to hold a disturbing familiarity. Much later I wondered how this possibly could have been so, then decided that one of those strange old/new crevasses had just been straddled by a bridge I had made from Haiku romance, desire, and fitting odd pieces of those seventeenth-century designs into missing knowledge gaps of the present day."

FIG. 5–5 Lana Wilson. USA. Teapot, 16 inches. Hand-formed, fired to cone 6. Lana Wilson is interested in alternatives to our classical glazes, complex, highly textured finishes that she calls "Lichen Surfaces." Many of these surfaces rely on the crawling and cracking characteristics of recipes that are rich in magnesium carbonate. Photo: Martin Trailer. © 1989. All rights reserved.

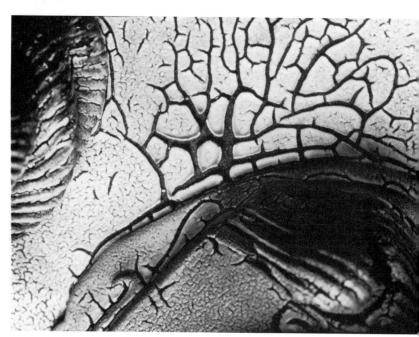

FIG. 5–6 Surface detail of the teapot in Figure 5–5 by Lana Wilson. Photo: Martin Trailer. © 1989. All rights reserved.

FIG. 5–7 Colin Gorry. England. Untitled vessel. Thrown and altered stoneware fired in oxidation. Courtesy Michaelson & Orient. Photo: Brian E. Rybolt.

best are serene and elegant examples of the potter's art.

GLAZES CATEGORIZED BY USE

Utilitarian Glazes
Ideally, glazes meant for utilitarian work should look no different than other glazes: they should merely be durable and easily cleaned. This means they should contain ample silica (50 to 70 percent feldspars/frits) and little flux (22 to 30 percent). Such stable and reliable glazes may not always have the strong visual textures that characterize less stable glazes, but sensitive glaze application can compensate for this.

Glazes for Outdoor Use
Glazes intended for pieces that will be placed outdoors should be durable and able to withstand the rigors of the weather. The two most successful surfaces are those with high amounts of silica and those with a high alumina content. Both contribute to good durability. Vitreous engobes with their high alumina content and great durability are particularly appropriate. (For more on vitreous engobes, see pages 106–108.) These surfaces are likely to contain 25 to 35 percent clay and 45 to 65 percent feldspar or frit, and should contain 10 to 30 percent secondary fluxes.

VOLATILE GLAZES
These glazes derive their character from the introduction of volatile materials into the kiln chamber during the firing. Two glaze types that fall into this category are salt glaze and wood-fired glaze; both are fired in the fuel-burning kiln.

FIG. 5–8 Michael Simon. USA. "Faceted Jar," 9 inches. Thrown, altered, and salt fired. "I think of this as a pot with three sides and three facets per side; the proportioning is done as I throw. All these pots are attractive to me because, at bottom, their proportions work." Photo: W. Montgomery.

Salt Glazes
Salt glazes are created in fuel-burning kilns designed specifically for the salt-firing process (Figs. 5–8 through 5–12). At the point when the kiln is nearing the highest part of the fire (near cone 9 or 10), the ceramist opens ports in the kiln wall and forces salt into the kiln. The silica and alumina in the clay unite with sodium (from the salt) to create a surface glaze. The violent chemical reaction produced as the salt is exposed to the heat of the kiln results in a surface marked by a strong visual texture and an active pattern. This surface distinguishes salt firing from

all other glaze treatments. Colored slips may be applied to the body before firing; the salt will cover the slips without obscuring them but will enrich their color and create a unique effect.

Wood-Fired Glazes

One of the most beautiful surfaces open to ceramists is that from high-fire wood firings (see Fig. 5–13). High-temperature wood firing produces surfaces marked by the deposit of rich wood-ash surfaces. These effects were first attained by the Han Dynasty potters in China between 200 B.C. and A.D. 200. During the firing the ashes of the wood fuel fall naturally upon the ware, are volatilized, and become a glaze. These glazes have a soft dappled imagery that covers the top surfaces of the piece and falls away gently toward the base. (For a discussion of the wood kiln, see page 224.) (*Text continues on page 68.*)

FIG. 5–9 Michael Simon. USA. "Triangular Vases." Thrown and altered using paddling techniques; salt fired.

FIG. 5–10 Walter Keeler. England. Teapot, 16 cm. Wheel-formed and altered; salt fired at cone 9.

Robert M. Winokur

The clay I use is a run-of-the-mill stoneware clay body—basically fire clay and Jordan with some ball clay, spar, flint, and grog. Glass sand is wedged in. (How much, I don't know.) I lay out the clay on the wedging board about $\frac{3}{4}$" thick, sprinkle sand over the surface until it "looks" right, wet the sand, roll it up, and wedge it. To confuse things a little more, I rework scrap clay in with each new batch so the clay already has some sand in it before I wedge in more. The sand is what gives the fired surface its classic salt-glaze orange-peel-pitted surface.

I use only one glaze right now. It's a blue wood-ash glaze that is an adequate blue mat stoneware glaze to which I add about 30% washed and mixed wood ash. Mixed wood ash is anything I burn in my wood stoves: broken

Robert M. Winokur. USA. "5 Westlakes Wall," 180 tiles mounted on four plywood panels, 5 feet 11 inches × 7 feet 4 inches. Stoneware clay body with blue wood-ash glaze over slips and engobes; cone 9 salt glaze.

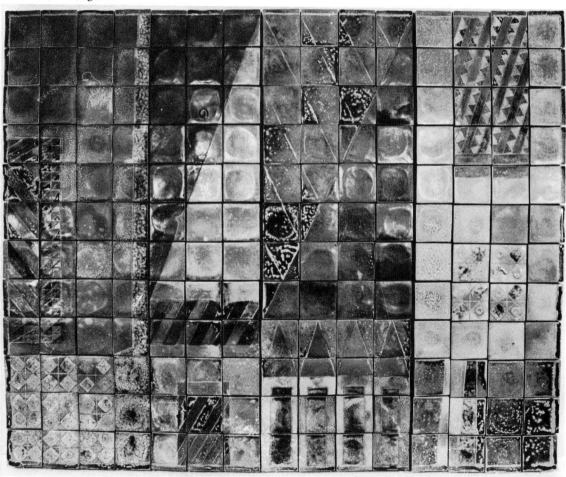

Robert Winokur placing the salt compound into an angle-iron "spoon."

Loading the salt in the kiln: the angle-iron "spoon" is inserted into the salt port and turned over to allow the salt to spill into the firebox.

pallets, shipping crates, old painted house trim. The glaze in a salt firing takes on a somewhat transparent blue runny, rivulet surface. Because it tends to run, I keep the glaze up high and give it space so it won't run off the wall onto the kiln shelves. This is the only concession I make, with regard to surface and form, to the fact that I am salt glazing.

I glean glaze, slips, and engobes from a range of sources, such as old Alfred [University] notes and technical books. Some made great tests and so became batches, but I rarely use them. I seem to favor six or seven of the twenty-five I have made up.

By history and tradition, salt glazing is essentially a once-fired procedure: I tip my hat to this and walk on by. I bisque-fire all my work and apply glaze slips and engobes afterward. I occasionally put salt in thick bisque cups and place them among the ware as I stack the kiln for firing, but I'm not sure this is necessary. It might be ideal for marginal kilns or when the ware is stacked very tight.

I use a pyrometer/thermocouple, cone packs, draw rings, and thirty-six to forty pounds of a mixture of pretzel-grade salt and sodium bicarbonate; $\frac{2}{3}$ to $\frac{1}{3}$. I do "normal" stoneware in terms of reduction, firing to cone 9–10 and then proceed to salt as the temperature drops. I shut off the burners and close up the kiln when I'm done and let any remaining salt in the fire boxes percolate. Since I throw salt in the kiln, I've lost all inhibitions about throwing anything else into the kiln during a firing—sandwich wrapping, fruit pits and skin. I used to throw in little packets of stannous chloride crystals at low red heat on the way down, but I gave that up. It ruined most of the lower third of the kiln, did nothing for the top, and the middle was iffy.

I like salt glazing because it provides me with the elements of chance, unpredictability, fortuitous accident, risk, and all the anxiety and excitement attendant with those elements. Raku would do the same for me, and I toy with the idea of doing a body of work in it, but it seems too fragile and impermanent compared to a high-temperature salt firing.

FIG. 5–11 Jane Hamlyn. England. "Oval Dish with Romanesque Handles," 20 × 30 × 16 cm. Thrown and altered ring on a textured base, with thrown and cut handles; salt glazed with colored slips at cone 9–10. Photo: Bill Thomas.

Rob Barnard

WOOD-FIRED POTTERY

The pitfalls facing potters involved in unglazed wood-fired work are essentially the same as those facing all ceramic artists today. That is, how does one create intelligent visual statements that make use of the language of ceramic art without perverting it or becoming trapped by it. This can be achieved by the ceramic artist only after he or she has grasped the vastness and diversity of the language and comprehended its structures.

Philip Rawson has suggested that the ceramic language has a set of structures—similar to the grammar and syntax of spoken language—that help us decipher each other's statements and that ceramic language, like every language, is based on common usage and signs. The pitcher, for example, is a generalized idea that we all share. The same is true of a mug or a bowl. We all recognized these forms probably long before we ever dreamed of making them. One reason for this is that we understand these objects from their cultural function.

When we begin to look at the ways these forms have been articulated in the history of ceramic art, we begin to see that some of these forms are merely clichés in the language—repeated over and over, using the same obvious signs—while others are compositions on the level of poetry that exploit, and not pervert, the language to appeal to our deepest feelings about life. This is when pottery ceases to be merely a functional tool for survival and becomes Art. Rawson believes that pottery, like other art, "operates very much at the level of feelings rather than the simple naming of facts" and that the meaning of each pot resides in feelings. It is, I believe, the expression of feeling inside the language of pottery and not the mere act of creating pitchers, mugs, and bowls that is the role of the modern potter.

So how does the potter go about transforming mundane objects into objects full of feeling and emotion? (Some in the field would tell you that it is impossible for this to occur while the object retains its usefulness, but this opinion is contradicted by tens of thousands of years of ceramic history.) To achieve this feat the modern potter has to make an exhaustive, ongoing cross-cultural study of the language of pottery and all its utterances. Great writers learn by devouring the written word. So potters must learn by devouring the visual and philosophical elements of the great works that make up the history of ceramic art. Unless we pursue this course we will remain, as Rawson says, "ceramically illiterate," condemned to repeating and mimicking the simple statements of others.

Rob Barnard. USA. Teapot, 8 inches. Wood ash with natural ash glaze; cone 9–10 wood-fired. Courtesy Anton Gallery. Photo: Jarvis Grant. © 1986.

Frank Boyden

In the past decade the firing of ceramics with wood has reemerged in the Unitd States as a viable and certainly energetic form of exploring clay. Not only has it produced some exceptional results and some powerful statements, but it has brought to the American ceramic scene an aesthetic that stands diametrically opposed to the flashy low-fired slipped, stained work of the 1980s. As an aesthetic, it creates a symbiotic understanding between the potter and his work and the process of firing. Wood firing can produce wondrous and magical results—results that border on the geologic, on thoughts of metamorphosis, on reflections of gifts from somewhere, and upon irrational and often romantic energy.

Such things are possible. It is all possible somehow. However, the finest work coming from our wood kilns is the result of a great deal of knowledge being pitted against the romantic and irrational aspects of the fire and the all-consuming process of setting up and firing a big wood kiln for two to ten days.

The rewards of wood firing can be rich and deep, and the best of the new work uses the anagama as a tool that can speak directly to contemporary concerns. The wood-firing process, however, is so powerful as a social happening that it can easily reduce itself to the Raku phenomena of the 1960s and 1970s, with results judged by the social ambience of the happening.

Today, a good number of anagama kilns are available. Most are located in institutions and are fired periodically and more or less unsystematically by different people or groups. There is little continuity in approaches to firing or in the use of clays or glazes. This is not bad in itself, but the results of such an approach do not produce seasoned, mature, powerful work, nor do they lead to a Zen-like acceptance of fleeting qualities, surface effects, and phenomena that are looked upon as gifts from the kiln.

Wood firing requires a long-term commitment. The process is tremendously time- and energy-consuming. To create strong work, the potter must attain over time a set of languages relating to a number of processes that are often unclear: the language of the clays used, of a particular kiln, of a specific wood, and, most important, of his or her own work. Through this the artist comes slowly to the language of

Frank Boyden. USA. "Raven Sentinel," 54 inches. Thrown and altered; Gas fired at cone 13–14. Photo: Jim Piper.

selectivity regarding the fired work. The richness of this process is deeply rewarding in every respect.

AN ANAGAMA FIRING

I will present one approach to firing porcelains and extremely vitreous white stonewares. My work in this area is directed at achieving brilliant color with a minimum or no use of glazes, and I work at extremely high temperatures (1400° C, cone 13–14).

I use EPK-based domestic porcelains, grolleg, and Limoges porcelains. The kaolins and ball clays used to formulate such bodies must contain iron. The irons will produce brilliant oranges, bright reds, purples, and blues. Even with small amounts from .07 to .2 percent, one can achieve brilliant white translucent clays that will color intensely given the right firing approach. If the clays lack sufficient iron, surface development can be enhanced by using iron-bearing Shino glazes that have been watered down and a light mist sprayed over the surface. (I use yellow ochre as an additive because of its fine particle size.)

Firing schedule: 55–65 hours, not including loading. I fire my kiln starting with bisque ware. It is easy to handle, does not blow up, and requires a shorter firing. I fire four or five different clays at one time because they produce varying results in different areas of the kiln. When loading, I use approximately one-half the loading space. The stack is extremely important since it directs the firing and flame movement and the final outcome of the work.

Pieces are placed so that they will deflect and move direct flame and ash where I want them to be. Since much of my work is drawn on, I place the work to give maximum effect to the drawings. It is the back side of pieces and hidden areas that most often develop the richest color, while ash often will obliterate areas on the front. I place a piece so that a drawing will emerge from an ash-covered surface into a colored ground on the back side.

Loading will consume an entire day. The kiln is closed and firing starts after dinner. I will have assistants fire the kiln for the first 12 hours, keeping a small fire and raising the kiln temperatures to about 600° over that time.

Since the kiln is 25 feet long, there will be a major difference in heat from front to back. Also, the kiln must be reduced three times for body reduction. This is absolutely essential for good color. About 18 hours into the firing, I reduce the front one-third at approximately cone 07. Reduction takes place for one and a half hours with the damper almost totally closed. Then I pour on the wood for very heavy reduction.

After reduction, I clean the kiln and repeat the process for the middle and back sections as they reach temperature. At this point cone 8 will be down in the front of the kiln and, depending on firing conditions, reduction will be completed at about 28 to 30 hours into the firing. From the start of the firing, I have used alder wood; now I will begin to switch slowly to fir, which provides much greater energy and allows greater control of the kiln.

Over the next 10 hours, I will slowly raise temperature; after this, I will have cone 14 in the front, cone 8–9 in the middle, and cone 5 in back. During this time, the kiln has been fired in a light to medium state of reduction.

At this point I begin to introduce wood into the ports, in the middle and back of the kiln. Slowly over the next 10 hours I will raise the middle and back to cone 11–12. I keep the front of the kiln between cone 10 and 11 so as to not lose heat in the front one-third. This is important since the work soaks and new ash deposited is drawn into the ash melt and the work is not crusty. The kiln is allowed to soak at this period for 6 to 10 hours with a mean temperature of cone 12.

Finally, over a period of 4 to 5 hours, the back is raised to cone 13 by introducing wood through the side ports. The kiln is then filled with large charges of kindling through the side ports only, since the front is now at cone 5 or 6. Now I introduce about 200 pounds of charcoal into the ports, seal the kiln as tightly as possible, and allow it to cool for 6 or 7 days. The introduction of kindling and charcoal produces fuming and will burn slowly for up to 20 hours, often producing beautiful lusters on the porcelains. This will work only when the kiln is essentially airtight. Such a firing will consume approximately $3\frac{1}{2}$ to 4 cords of alder and fir.

FIG. 5–12 Chris Staley. USA. "Faceted Auger Vase," 28 inches. Thrown and altered porcelain body; salt fired at cone 9. Staley has said of his work that "the firing process is critical—it leaves its own mark, which has a special life of its own. I feel that I've taken two methods and pushed them and as a result made them my own: my use of faceting and the application of a very thick slip."

RAKU

Some types of ceramics embody not one or even several strategies, but rather a whole group of specialized strategies and recipes. When these strategies and recipes are combined, they take on a life of their own. This is especially true of raku (see Figs. 5–14 through 5–16).

Raku is unique among glazed ceramic work in that it is a quick-firing technique. The bodies, forms, and glazes must be designed to withstand the shock of abrupt heating and cooling. Raku glazes are often crackled or otherwise unstable because they are cooled quickly. Their character can be complex and exuberant, featuring metallic flashing and richly crazed surfaces. Those ceramists who fire in raku exploit these effects and apply their brilliantly colored glazes with great energy.

These brilliant, low-fire glaze surfaces contrast with the clay body, which in the fire turns a soft, velvety black, the result of smoke reduction. Smoke reduction also affects the glazed surfaces of the piece. Coloring minerals such as copper take on a strong metallic appearance and craze lines become blackened and strongly emphasized.

Raku has encouraged the development of specialized recipes and work strategies, dictated by its quick firing and its rich, unstable glaze surfaces. The clay bodies tend to be coarse, and forms to be quite burly and compact. Glaze recipes are usually simple (visual

FIG. 5–13 Chuck Hindes. USA. "Saggar Shield," 30 × 24 inches. Hand-formed; wood fired at cone 9–10.

James Lawton

My kiln is a converted refrigerator, stripped of compressor and all plastic components, laid on its back and the bottom lined with common red brick. This gives me a super insulated, relatively airtight chamber that produces a reduction atmosphere without an immense dosage of combustibles. It also prolongs the cooling, thus cutting the mortality rate on the work.

I use dry hay or straw mixed with sawdust as my combustible and usually reoxidize the piece when its interior is still red. This seems to encourage the oranges I look for in the copper/lithium glaze.

My images are rendered with an underglaze slip sprayed on the bisque, beginning with a ground color (usually white or yellow gold) that is then airbrushed with other underglaze colors (the same white base with various Mason stains, 5 to 20%). Details are rendered with a small 000 brush with concentrations of the ceramic stains; highlights are put in by scratching through the colors to the base. A clear glaze is then applied over the entire image.

James Lawton. USA. "Bowl with Fins," 9½ × 18 inches. Thrown and altered with some molded and slab elements; raku firing. Courtesy Garth Clark Gallery, New York and Los Angeles.

"G" RAKU SLIP (FOR BISQUE)

Tennessee #9 ball clay*	250 parts by weight
Nepheline syenite	150
Talc	200
G-24 frit	150
Flint	50
Soda ash	100

*Any *white* occurring ball clay will do.

BASIC CRACKLE CLEAR GLAZE

Gerstley borate	70 parts by weight
Nepheline syenite	20
Kaolin	10

This glaze crackles (or crazes) minimally. I also use it as a base for bright liner glaze colors tinited with 5–20% Mason stains.

After each image is rendered and glazed, a liquid emulsion wax is applied and set to dry. The edges are cleaned up, leaving a raised outline of the image. The exterior glaze that surrounds, or "floats," these images is a lithium-based formula that is very sensitive to the raku process.

SANDY SCOTT RAKU BASE

Gerstley borate	28 parts by weight
Lepidolite	14
Spodumene	14
Lithium carbonate	14
Zirconium opacifier	14

Add 4% copper carbonate for turquoise breaking pink-orange.

I bisque-fire in an electric to (Orton) cone 08. I have used and built various types of firing chambers but have settled upon a fiber envelope design that lifts off the firebox shelves to give easy access to pulling the ware. I fire with propane (LP) gas or natural gas with a natural draft (Venturi) burner.

Richard Hirsch

RAKU RECIPES

Richard Hirsch has been working with raku for many years. The recipes he lists below are the ones he has used in creating his own work in raku.

WHITE RAKU CLAY BODY
Cone   06 Bisque

Hawthorn fire clay	35
Foundry Hill Cream	25
OM #4 ball clay	15
Spodumene	5
Talc	10
Mullite (100 Mesh)	5–10

RED TERRA SIGILATTA

Ball clay	50
Red iron oxide	50

Calgon	5
Water	400 milliliters

WHITE TERRA SIGILATTA

OM #4 ball clay	200 grams
Water	800 milliliters

To this white sigilatta base, I add ceramic stains to attain colored sigilattas, usually 1–10%. Also, I add a 5% frit 3110 to the stained sigilatta to ensure melting.

WHITE VITREOUS ENGOBE

Tennessee #5 ball clay	20
Flint	30
Frit 3110	25
Talc	10
Borax	5
Opax	10

Richard Hirsch. USA. "Ceremonial Cup #28," 16½ inches. Wheel- and hand-formed elements, fired to cone 04 in a raku kiln and sandblasted after firing.

RED LUSTRE ENGOBE

Add 5% red iron oxide and 5% red copper oxide to the White Vitreous Engobe recipe above.

RAKU WHITE CRACKLE

Gerstley borate	60
Custer feldspar	50
Barium carbonate	22
Flint	16

Tin oxide $\frac{1}{2}$%

RAKU CONE 04 SLIP (WHITE)

Calcined kaolin	20
Frit 3124	15
OM #4 ball clay	15
EPK kaolin	5
Flint	20
Zircopax	5
CMC	1

---

complexity comes from the fire, not from the recipe itself) and glaze application is often direct. Kiln designs emphasize easy access to the fired ware.

Raku was originally developed by the Japanese. The word "raku" means enjoyment; its connotations are that of quiet, reflective pleasure. In Japan, raku was most often associated with the aristocratic amateur or the tea master, rather than with the professional potter. Before the 1930s and 1940s, raku was unknown outside Japan. Since its introduction in the West, it has evolved to the point where it has become one of the most contemporary of our ceramic techniques. Raku as we know it did not exist until sometime after World War II.

We in the West were first introduced to the concept of raku by Bernard Leach in *A Potter's Book* (London: Faber & Faber, 1949). In a wonderful section of the book, Leach talked about his introduction to raku; it was also his introduction to ceramics:

> One day in 1911, two years after I had returned to the Far East, I was invited to a sort of garden-party at an artist friend's house in Tokyo. Twenty or thirty painters, actors, writers, etc., were gathered together on the floor of a large tea-room; brushes and saucers of color were lying about, and presently a number of unglazed pots were brought in and we were invited to write or paint upon them. Almost all educated Japanese are sufficient masters of the brush to be able to write a decorative running script of, to Western eyes, great beauty, and many of them can paint. I was told that within an hour's time these pots would be

FIG. 5–14 Steven and Susan Kemenyffy. USA. "Autumn Louise," c. 4 feet. Hand-formed raku sculpture.

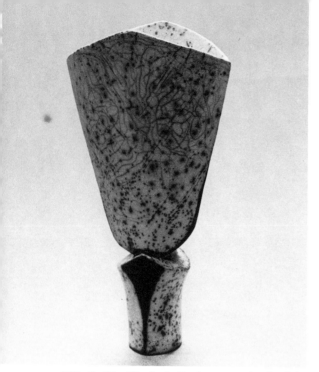

FIG. 5–15 Elizabeth Raeburn. England. Slab-built vessel, 22.5 cm. Fired in raku with a borax glaze, then postfired in reduction in wood shavings. Photo: Alan Winn.

glazed and afterwards fired in a little portable kiln, which a man was stoking with charcoal a few feet beyond the verandah in the garden. I struggled with the unfamiliar paints and queer long brushes, and then my two pots were taken from me and dipped in a tub of creamy white lead glaze and set around the top of the kiln and warmed and dried for a few minutes before being carefully placed with long handled tongs in the inner box or muffle. Although this chamber was already at dull red heat the pots did not break. Fireclay covers were placed on top of the kiln, and the potter fanned the fuel till the sparks flew. In about half an hour the muffle gradually became bright red, and the glaze could be seen through the spy hole melted and glossy. The covers were removed and the glowing pieces taken out one by one and placed on tiles, while the glow slowly faded and the true colors came out accompanied by curious sharp ticks and tings as the crackle began to form in the cooling, shrinking glaze. Another five minutes passed and we could gingerly handle our pots painted only one short hour before. (*A Potter's Book*, pp. 29–30)

In the process Leach describes, the decorator paints an image with monochrome slips, then covers it with a clear lead glaze. The look of

FIG. 5–16 Jeff Mincham. Australia. Coil-built form with carved elements and copper mat surface, 40 cm. Raku fired to 1000° C (1832° F).

raku, as well as the process, was strongly modified when Western ceramists adopted the technique. They were excited by the speed of the entire process and by the direct quality of the result. Impressed with this, they expanded raku's palette and its imagistic possibilities to include bravura color and imagery that reflected the vibrancy of their new interpretation of the raku method.

In some ways the contemporary method remains the same as the traditional Japanese method. We still place the glazed piece in an already heated kiln, watch the glazes melt, draw the piece from the fire with tongs, and still have an opportunity to examine the completed piece about an hour after it has gone into the fire. The sense of excitement that Leach conveys is still with us and the devotees of raku remain obsessed by it.

A Raku Firing

Special long-handled tongs, as well as a face shield and fireproof apron and gloves worn over snug, protective clothing, are necessary when working with raku.

Raku requires a special kind of low-fire kiln in which pieces can be loaded and unloaded during the height of the fire and withstand the rapid heat change. Several kiln types have been adapted for raku, including front loading, top hat (the whole body of the kiln can be raised and lowered), and car kilns.

Raku is a fuel-burning process. While Leach's potter used charcoal, we use propane or natural gas.

Because the raku firing demands constant loading and unloading of work, raku kilns tend to be fairly small. Instead of one big firing that may last for three days, three or four smaller firings will be done in a day. Most raku firings are group activities: one person at the kiln door, one using tongs to pull the ware from the kiln, one to help with the smoke reduction, and perhaps one or two others to help out. The first firing takes about two hours to get to the point where the glazes begin to melt. The fuel supply is then turned off and the pieces are removed with tongs. Additional firings usually follow: the kiln is loaded, the fuel supply is turned on again, and the process repeated.

Dangers Associated with Raku

During the firing raku is potentially dangerous. The ceramist may be exposed to fumes during the firing and cooling process. This exposure, however, is moderated because most raku firings take place out in the open. (Raku firings should never take place indoors.)

Many materials ceramists used in the past should be avoided, particularly lead glazes and dangerous colorants such as chrome, tin chloride, manganese, and vanadium. Spraying solutions such as tin chloride on a piece as it is taken out of the kiln is a potentially dangerous practice.

Physical safety is also important. During the raku process the ceramist works close to the fire, so burns are a risk. Raku firings pose environmental problems as well. The smoke produced during the reduction process makes firing raku in a city or built-up area unwise. The raku process is much more suitable to open country.

The ceramist who works in raku must also anticipate how the consumer will use the piece. Raku pieces should never be used for preparing or containing food. Raku clay bodies are porous, and even glazes that do not contain lead are likely to be soft and may break down in the presence of highly alkaline or acidic foodstuffs (for example, fruit juices).

Raku glazes can be dipped or sprayed on. Glaze imagery, often applied with a brush, is strong and direct, reflecting the character of the medium.

Post-Firing Treatments

Pieces taken from a normal firing are fairly cool and nothing other than refiring will affect their appearance. Raku taken from the fire is red hot, and the piece will change a good deal before it cools. At this point the raku potter can modify the surface of the glaze. The piece can be sprayed with water, which will encourage a complex, densely crackled pattern. The hot piece is then placed in a fireproof container filled with combustible materials such as sawdust or leaves, and covered with a lid. This creates smoke reduction, which modifies many glaze colors and causes any unglazed areas to turn a soft smoky black. The crackle pattern also darkens and becomes quite dramatic at this point. After 15 minutes to half an hour, the glaze has cooled and its appearance is "set." The finished piece is withdrawn from the container and washed.

Though not without dangers and drawbacks, raku has been a valuable addition to ceramics. It is unique and encourages a vibrant personal imagery and a direct approach to our materials and processes.

GLAZE TYPES CLASSIFIED BY INGREDIENT

Glazes are often categorized by identifying a significant material in the recipe. While other materials in the recipe also play an important role in determining the look of the glaze, this is a useful strategy in that recipes we identify in this way have a family resemblance.

Sodium and Potassium Glazes

Glazes containing sodium and potassium derive these elements from feldspars and frits. Their feldspar/frit content should be between 60 and 70 percent. These recipes tend to be durable, stable, and reliable with strong, unbleached color. Soda and potash feldspars are similar in that both contain sodium and potassium; the soda spars merely contain more soda than potash, while the potash spars contain more potash than soda.

Frits generally contain sodium. Sodium, a somewhat stronger flux than potassium, is especially useful in low- and mid-fire glazes; in high-fire glazes, potassium is preferred. Sodium has a drawback in that it encourages

crazing. If the amount of melting materials (those without any silica content) is kept below 30 percent, however, crazing can be minimized.

Boron Glazes

The useful sources for boron in glazes are Gerstley borate (available only in the United States and Canada) and boron frits. Gerstley borate is a secondary flux, while boron frits contain silica (and usually alumina) as well. Recipes that contain Gerstley borate in amounts from 20 to 40 percent or boron frits from 30 to 80 percent tend to produce strong, durable glaze surfaces, stable melts, and good color. Boron is a strong flux that melts at a rather low temperature, so it is useful in low-fire recipes and, in amounts up to 20 percent, in high-fire glazes as well. High-fire glazes that contain too much boron may be overmelted; these glazes lose most of their character and take on a hard, glassy look.

Boron is the only material in common use, besides silica, that is a glass former. Thus it is possible to create true glazes with Gerstley borate and a little clay. Recipes will be composed mostly of boron without much silica. While definitely glassy, they are not as durable as glazes that contain silica.

Titanium Glazes

Small amounts of titanium (.5 to 2 percent) cause strong melts and encourage extremely durable glazes and fine color. (See the section on eutectics in Chapter 1.) Larger amounts (6 to 12 percent) are usually refractory and encourage mat surfaces and rich visual textures. Unfortunately titanium also encourages pinholing, especially in the low and mid fire. If titanium is used with materials that contain sodium (soda feldspars and frits) and other low-viscosity materials, this can be minimized. The sources for titanium in glazes are titanium dioxide and rutile, both secondary fluxes, as well as some high-impurity clays.

Taxile Doat's Titanium Glaze Recipes

In 1905 *Grand Feu Ceramics* by the French ceramist Taxile Doat was published in English (trans. Samuel Robineau, Keramic Studio Publishing, Syracuse, N.Y.). The title, a blend of French and English, means "High Fire Ceramics." In this book Doat included many recipes for crystalline and "flowing mat" glazes; most of these derive their crystalline imagery or flowing mat surface from significant amounts of titanium or rutile (a blend of titanium and iron). Here are two of these recipes:

MAT IVORY YELLOW
(a flowing mat glaze, cone 9 oxidation)

*Feldspar**	*35.7*
Dry, pure clayey kaolin	*13.7*
Nemours quartzy sand	*43.6*
(a flintlike material)	
Chalk (whiting)	*15.9*
Ground natural rutile	*9.6*

*I have used a soda feldspar to good effect—R.Z.

MAT CRYSTALLINE YELLOW BROWN
(a crystal glaze, cone 9 oxidation)

Feldspar	*33.60*
Pure clayey kaolin	*12.89*
Quartzy sand	*47.00*
Chalk	*15.00*
Rutile	*9.60*
Red oxide of iron	*9.60*

Opacified Glazes

The ceramist adds opacifiers to a glaze to make it opaque. While a number of materials can be used to opacify glazes, tin oxide and zirconium dioxide are the most reliable opacifiers. Both of these materials can be considered secondary melters (although zirconium opacifiers contain a small amount of silica as an impurity).

Zirconium is highly refractory and its use is somewhat limited in the low fire; in the higher fire, its effects are varied. In mat glazes, zirconium encourages surfaces marked by a finely divided visual texture; in shiny and transparent glazes, it encourages surfaces that are shiny but lack depth. Zirconium opacifiers work well in the reduction fire.

Tin is useful at all parts of the firing spectrum, but is especially useful in the low fire because it does not hold back the melt; it also discourages crazing. It is less useful in the high fire, particularly in reduction, which may affect it adversely. Tin is more expensive than zirconium, and this also limits its use.

Tin and zirconium can be used together quite effectively. Opacity is improved and the surface quality can be as good or better than when tin is used alone.

One category of opacified glazes contains no colorant. Such glazes would be clear if they were not opacified, but with this addition they take on a white color.

High-Clay Recipes

High-clay glazes contain from 14 to 20 percent clay and tend to be mat, nonflowing, durable, and highly stable. Moderating the recipe by including soda feldspar will help minimize pinholing problems. The low viscosity of the soda feldspar compensates for the high viscosity of the clay.

Glazes Containing High-Impurity Clays

Glazes usually are made from white and light-colored clays, but dark clays can be used as well, particularly to enrich glaze surfaces and color. This is especially true of glazes fired in oxidation, which benefit from the rich character imparted by the dark clays.

The most important impurities in a dark clay are iron, titanium, and calcium. The iron will significantly darken the glaze, the titanium will encourage some visual texture and make the glaze more durable, and the calcium will encourage glaze flow and visual texture. Many glaze recipes in this book call for a dark, iron-bearing clay.

FIG. 5–17 Sandra Byers. USA. "Two-Lobed Pot," $3\frac{3}{4}$ inches. Wheel-formed porcelain, pinched cut and incised; finished with a microcrystalline oxidation-fired mat glaze and fired to cone $9\frac{1}{2}$. Photo: William Lenke.

Ash Glazes

Ash glazes derive their strong visual textures from ash's crude, granular particles and from its phosphorus content. All ash varies in its effects on quality and texture, depending on its source, the season, and the place in which it is gathered. The ingredients of ash are silica, alumina, calcium, phosphorus, and trace elements, but the proportions can vary a great deal.

Wood ash can never be counted on to work in any particular way, nor can this year's batch be counted on to act like last year's. Some ceramists insist upon using ash only from hardwoods, while others will happily use the more common soft woods; others use only the ash of reeds and straw. Consistency may be the most important factor. If the material accumulated for ash making is gathered at the same time of year from the same kind of plant or tree in areas that are similar to each other, the ash will likely give consistent results.

Ash should be tested before applying it to a piece. If it is to be used as an additive in a standard glaze recipe, it is best to add it to several different glazes (in test amounts) so that at least one of the mixtures will work well.

Wood ash for glazes should be burned in an open fire or fireplace and not in an airtight (Scandinavian-type) stove, which will impart very little texture to the glaze.

Testing Wood Ash

In a sense, this experiment is the ceramist's version of a materials assay. It is an effective way to find out which glaze types will work with a particular batch of wood ash.

Gather the wood ash (at least enough to fill a five-gallon bucket) and dry-mix it (a very dangerous proposition if carried out in a careless manner: please follow the safety directions in the section which follows. Add

FIG. 5–18 Eric James Mellon. England. "June Night," 10 inches diameter. Wheel-formed bowl with an ash glaze (from the Philadelphus bush) fired to 1300° C in an oxidizing atmosphere. "A mermaid with a fox is riding a horse. At the bottom of the composition is a moon goddess and at the top is a bird maiden."

10 grams and 40 grams of each sample to 100 grams of the following glazes:

1. high-silica recipe
2. high-alumina recipe
3. high-melter recipe
4. dark-clay recipe

Precautions

Lung irritations from wood ash (or any other caustic material) can be prevented by wearing a good dust mask, protective outerwear, and rubber gloves. Make sure that you use the appropriate filters in the dust mask and change the filters often. Protective clothing is a must when working with any caustic dust. Overalls are easy to find at industrial suppliers and are inexpensive.

Wood ash is also hazardous in the wet glaze as it is highly caustic. Ceramists who use wood ash glazes a great deal will find that their skin will crack and bleed from exposure to this material. Care should be taken; ideally rubber gloves should be worn.

Spodumene Glazes

Spodumene is a strongly fluxing lithium feldspar that is very useful in the low fire. Spodumene glazes produce rich visual textures and highly saturated alkaline color: for example, copper, which is normally green in the oxidation fire, becomes a strong blue in the presence of spodumene. Spodumene is low in viscosity and discourages pinholing. For these reasons, it is an admirable partner for titanium if used in the following percentages: spodumene, 12 to 24 percent : titanium, 6 to 12 percent.

FIG. 5–19 Neil Moss. USA. "Mashiko Jar," 36 × 20 cm. Cone 10 stoneware finished with slips glaze and oversprayed ash glaze. Photo: California Media Group.

Lithium is derived from lithium carbonate as well as from spodumene. Of the two materials, spodumene is preferable because the lithium in spodumene is locked into the compound in such a way as to minimize inhalation and ingestion problems. Lithium carbonate should be handled with care; it can cause organ damage and can have a strong effect on mental states. Gases created during firing should be vented effectively.

Zinc Glazes

Zinc, which contains no silica, is a secondary flux and a prime example of a material that is a strong flux in small amounts and a weak flux in large amounts (see Eutectics, page 8). Small amounts (1 to 2 percent) are often added to transparent glaze recipes to ensure a good melt. Larger amounts are usually quite refractory and encourage mat surfaces. Zinc is used in amounts of 8 to 20 percent to create mat, opaque glazes. If fired correctly, zinc encourages the growth of crystals in the glaze (see Crystal Glazes, page 55).

Lead Glazes

Lead produces beautiful results but unfortunately is toxic and the effects cumulative. Glazes may slowly and insidiously release lead into foods, especially acid foods. Lead's toxicity can be managed to some extent, but it will always be a problem for both the ceramist and the consumer. The use of lead frits reduces the danger but does not eliminate it. Even fritted glazes may leach lead under certain conditions. Therefore, studio potters should never use lead in glazes for pieces that conceivably could be used for serving food. Every ceramist should acknowledge that people will sometimes press a piece into service as a food container even if it never was intended for that purpose. In its unfritted form, lead is a secondary flux; when fritted, it falls in the glass-making category.

High-boron and high-sodium frits can be substituted for lead-containing materials. You may also wish to add .5 to 1 percent zinc oxide or titanium to enrich the glaze surface and enhance melting. In the low fire, you may find that these substitutions work best if the firing temperature is raised to cone 03.

Barium Glazes

Recipes containing barium are dangerous to both the potter and the consumer. While barium can be fritted, barium frits do not encourage the highly valued, soft mat surfaces of unfritted barium. Barium encourages the growth of small crystals in the glaze, which under high magnification reveals a corrugated surface. Barium glazes produce surfaces that look soft and mat rather than shiny. This is because their broken surface scatters light instead of reflecting it. Barium is strongly alkaline and has a strong effect on color, especially copper, which turns a strong, saturated royal blue. Barium is a secondary flux.

Unfritted barium is a dangerous material for the potter. Dr. Michael McCann, in his book *Artist Beware* (New York: Watson Guptil, 1979), has stated that the dangers from inhalation and ingestion are especially high; its effects can be cumulative and chronic symptoms can develop. For the consumer, barium glazes (especially the ones with the beautiful mat surfaces) can be the source of chronic symptoms that are hard to diagnose.

Tin oxide is a fine substitute for barium because it encourages the rich waxy surfaces that are a hallmark of barium. Used in amounts of 10 to 14 percent, tin oxide will produce soft, satiny surfaces. Unfortunately, it is one of our most expensive ceramic materials.

Both zinc and titanium, relatively inexpensive materials, may be used in amounts of 6 to 10 percent to achieve effects somewhat akin to barium.

Calcium/Magnesium Glazes

Calcium and magnesium are two oxides with a dual nature: they are quite refractory (nonmelting) until cone 8; at which point they become strong melters.

Material	Contents	Type
whiting	calcium	secondary melter
magnesium carbonate	magnesium	secondary melter
dolomite	calcium and magnesium	secondary melter
talc	magnesium, calcium, and silica	silicate
wollastonite	calcium and silica	silicate

High calcium/magnesium glazes are meant for the high fire, usually in amounts of 15 to 30 percent calcium/magnesium secondary melters or 25 to 50 percent silicates. These glazes are often marked by a rich pattern of rivulets playing over the surface of the glaze. In the lower fire, high calcium/magnesium glazes tend to be chalky and bleached in color.

Copper Red Glazes

Copper can be used to create red glazes in the reduction fire; the red color will develop in reduction with 1 to 3 percent copper carbonate. A wide range of glaze types will work; typically they are high in silica and low in alumina. The most desirable copper red glaze will have a ruby color, but this is somewhat hard to control. If too much copper is present, the glaze may take on a liverish tone. Glaze thickness, too, is an important factor in the production of good color. If the glaze is too thin, reds will not develop; if too thick, the colors will be muddy. Tin encourages bright colors. Copper reds are at their best when applied to light-colored and white bodies; the darker bodies tend to gray the color. Experimentation is necessary to obtain consistently good color.

PINHOLING, CRAZING, CRAWLING, AND UNDERFIRED GLAZE SURFACES

To some ceramists the title of this section will sound like the ceramic equivalent of the Four Horsemen of the Apocalypse. To others it will seem like a description of a group of exciting and exotic glaze surfaces. Many ceramists consider these phenomena to be defects and imperfections; others look upon them as a valuable testament to the violence of the fire. Most ceramists will want to know how to eliminate or minimize these phenomena, but others will want to know how to create and encourage them.

Pinholing

Pinholing is marked by small, widely dispersed breaks in the surface of the glaze, the result of glaze activity during the fire. Most glazes undergo an active phase at some point during the firing, but the evidence of this activity is smoothed over as the firing continues. Pinholed glazes, however, do not heal, usually because they are high in viscosity. High-viscosity glazes are stiff and nonflowing even in the heat of the fire; therefore, pinholes cannot smooth out.

To cure pinholing, add a low-viscosity material to the recipe, such as spodumene (a lithium feldspar), a soda feldspar, or a frit containing soda or boron. You may also subtract some of the high-viscosity material from the glaze, such as clay, titanium, or zirconium opacifiers.

To encourage pinholing, subtract low-viscosity materials and add high-viscosity materials such as clay, titanium, or zirconium opacifiers.

Crazing

Crazing is a phenomenon in which a highly ordered, geometric pattern of cracks marks the surface of the glaze. Although they weaken the glaze these patterns can be pleasing to the eye and some ceramists value crazed glazes. Oriental ceramists, particularly, prized these surfaces and often employed them in their work. On the other hand, ceramists who want durable, easily cleaned surfaces to cover utilitarian pieces see crazing as a defect.

Crazing is caused by glazes that shrink more than the body. As the glaze adjusts to this shrinkage, cracks are created in its surface. Crazing may show up immediately or it may be years before it becomes obvious. However, with the aid of a thirty-power magnifier it is possible to see any crazing in a glaze even if it is not yet visible to the naked eye.

Some of our materials, such as sodium, expand and contract a great deal and should be avoided if you do not want crazing. The ceramist's prime weapons against crazing are lithium and boron. To discourage crazing, substitute spodumene (a lithium feldspar) or a boron frit for some of the soda or potash feldspar in the recipe. Recipes that contain a high percentage of secondary melters (over 35 percent) are likely to craze.

To encourage crazing, avoid lithium and boron and use a great deal of sodium, which is found in soda feldspars and frits.

Crawling

Glazes that crawl will leave sections of the piece unglazed. Recipes that contain large percentages of high-shrinkage materials or high-viscosity materials will crawl; dirty or dusty glaze surfaces are also prone to crawling. Even underfired bisque can provide the kind of dry surface upon which glazes will crawl.

Crawling is common in recipes containing more than 15 to 20 percent clay. If you want to use such a recipe but do not want it to crawl, calcine most of the clay (see page 108). Zinc oxide that has not been calcined also shrinks a great deal. Use calcined zinc oxide to prevent crawling.

To encourage crawling, use recipes that contain a high-shrinkage clay, such as ball clay; use uncalcined zinc in the recipe and 20 percent or more of the clay.

Underfired Glaze Surfaces

An underfired glaze is fired at a temperature lower than that required for complete maturation of the glaze. Often maturation has started and patches of the glaze are mature and marked by glass formation; other areas, however, are dry, dull in color, and perhaps flaky. Most ceramists will not want these effects, but others will work very hard to get them! Their characteristic variations, from shiny to dull and from glassy wet color to dry chalky color, can be effective, especially when applied to work of a sculptural character.

CHAPTER 6

Low-, Mid-, and High-Fire Glazes

LOW-FIRE GLAZES

In recent years many studio potters have begun to work in the low fire for the pleasing effects they can achieve at this end of the firing spectrum, particularly the varied visual textures and vivid glaze colors. Ceramic stains play a big part here, for they work well in low fire.

Mixing Low-Fire Glazes in the Studio

Making low-fire glazes in the studio has the advantage of economy, since commercial glazes are fairly expensive. Many ceramists working in the low fire use both studio-produced glazes and commercial glazes. In this way they can combine the economy of studio glazes with the exciting colors and textures of commercial formulations.

Glaze Application

Glazes can be applied by spraying, dipping, and splashing. Most commercial low-fire glazes contain ingredients that also make them suitable for brush application. These ingredients, such as gums and colloids, can be added to glazes produced in the studio as well.

Cone 04

Cone 04 is one of the most popular firing temperatures among contemporary ceramists. Indeed there is a large support system for those who fire to cone 04. Because cone 04 is used a great deal in schools and is the favored firing temperature for those working in low-fire slipware (often called "hobby ceramics"), prepared clay bodies and glazes are widely available.

Cone 04 glazes should contain significant amounts of silica and strong melters. The major ingredient in the recipe should be a frit, with perhaps a litle soda feldspar, small amounts of powerful melters (which contain no silica), and 3 to 12 percent clay. High-impurity clays are appropriate for the low fire.

Unfortunately, many commercial glazes contain lead melters. If the lead compounds have been fritted, the only source of danger to the ceramist is from out-gassing during firing. Pieces glazed with these recipes, however, should never be used as containers for food because the glazes may leach lead. Lead-free cone 04 commercial glazes are available, but some colors and effects (such as brilliant reds and metallic lusters) cannot be prepared satisfactorily without lead.

Sandra Blain

For many years I was a stoneware potter making one-of-a-kind and utilitarian pieces and firing them in a gas kiln. An emphasis in all of my work was the use of textural material impressions, incising, and tool or finger markings. The relief areas were then emphasized with slip or oxides and a C/9 glaze sprayed or poured over. I never did anything with bright color. All of a sudden I realized there was a movement in this country and professionals were looking at avenues of low fire. I became very interested. A major breakthrough occurred when I was able to design a house with a large private studio. At about the same time, I found I had less time to work in the studio. Using my studio time to best advantage, I decided I did not want to spend time making clay, slips, and glazes and firing the kiln. I wanted to concentrate more on making the piece, emphasizing form and surface and firing in an electric kiln.

After my break from stoneware, I focused on ideas I had been accumulating through sketchbook drawings. These ideas related to my longstanding interest in the circus. I was still interested in the vessel with its sense of intimacy and its ability to contain space, but I now saw it more as a vehicle for expressing my personal aesthetics.

Sandra Blain. USA. "Circus Slide: Ringed Image-Tie," 21 inches. Low-fire earthenware painted with slips, covered with a clear glaze, and then lustered; multiple firings in an electric kiln.

Substitution Strategies for Lead

Some cone 04 glazes, such as transparent, noncrazing glazes, are difficult to create at low temperatures without lead. The best substitute for white lead often will be Gerstley borate; both contain no silica. The best substitute for lead silicates, which do contain silica, often will be a frit high in boron or sodium or a combination of the two; these, too, contain silica. Other materials, such as titanium and zinc, may be added in small amounts (1 to 2 percent) to harden and stabilize the glaze surface. High-soda and high-boron glazes are often soft and unstable and will benefit from these additions.

(*Text continues on page 87.*)

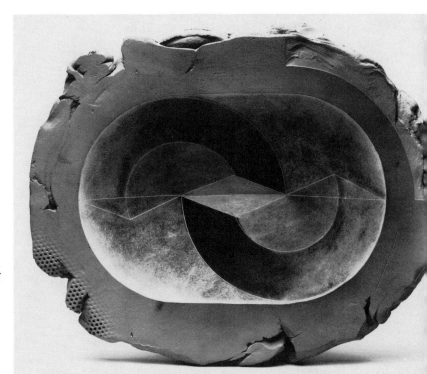

FIG. 6–1 Angelo di Petta.
Canada. Platter. Press-mold-
formed and painted with prepared glazes, some of which
were altered with additions of
such materials as lithium carbonate; fired to cone 04. Photo:
Gustav.

FIG. 6–2 Antonella Cimatti.
Italy. "Circo Dolce," 45 × 45
cm. Low-fire clay body with
polychrome glazes and ce-
ramic "pearls"; fired to 980° C
(1796° F).

FIG. 6–3 Jane Dillon. USA.
"Big Black Pot," 66 inches.
Multifired terra-cotta with slips
and low-fire glazes. Photo:
Bruce Cole.

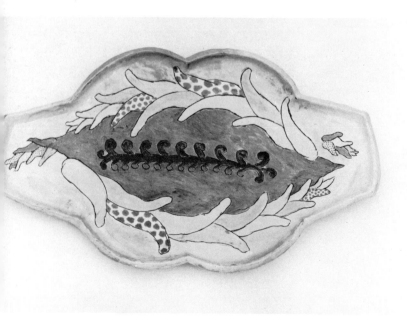

FIG. 6–4 Ian Symons. Can-
ada. Platter. Hand-formed; low
fire. Photo: C.I. Photography.

JoAnn Schnabel

A PERSONAL APPROACH TO GLAZING

I am striving to develop a personal palette of color, texture, and richness of surface in my glazing. I fire at 06–04 in an electric kiln; in low-fire glazes, what you see is what you get. Most of my glazes are stable and do not melt down enough to smooth over the surface once they are fired, so application is important. Because of the involved surfaces on my work, I use either a squeeze syringe to fill cracks with colored glazes or a brush to paint the glazes. Often I will rub the dry glaze with my finger to smooth the surface before it is fired.

I use a wide variety of glazes—commercial and my own. I pick each glaze for the particular qualities I am after for a piece, such as a lead mat glaze for a creamy soft finish. I use mainly commercial glazes for the convenience of having ten different purples to choose from. Many of my commercial glazes are "art" glazes that, once fired, reveal different colors where they are applied thin to thick. I often use these glazes in combination with each other, applying them in layers. This layering enables me to create surfaces that have a visual depth. For example, using two or three coats of a mat glaze with one or two coats of a semitransparent gloss glaze will give me a surface that has just a bit of a sheen where the gloss glaze is a little thicker. This surface also has a nice range of colors because the two glazes influence each other. Sometimes I will paint a glaze on top of another with a brush in a thick patterned application; after it is fired, the glaze becomes highly textured. In this way the glaze is integrated with the textured form and not just a layer of color on top of it.

I mix my glazes like a painter mixes paint, blending oxides and stains to obtain my own palette of colors. Usually I mix 2,000 grams of one color at a time. Because I don't measure the individual components of the colorant blend, once I've run out of a particular color of glaze, it really is gone. I feel this ever-changing palette keeps my glazes fresh and interesting. It also allows a continuous evolution and development in my glazes, as well as in the forms.

JoAnn Schnabel. USA. "2nd Basic," 25 inches. Hand-formed, finished with brush-applied commercial glazes; cone 04, fired in oxidation in an electric kiln.

Andrea Gill

These pieces are constructed out of low-fire terra-cotta clay using slabs and press molds. All surfaces are applied after the bisque; in many cases, the surface is not planned at the time of construction. The work is fired to cone 04 or 06.

I use two types of decorative techniques: majolica and colored slips. I started doing the majolica while I was in graduate school. As far as I knew, no one else was doing it at the time and I felt very much like a missionary for reviving low-fire pottery—although I am sure others were in fact doing the same thing! (This was in 1975.) At that time, I also began using a very dry, vitreous slip with a high percent (30%) of colorant with no glaze over it. I wanted a surface that looked like tempera paint on newsprint.

I have continued to use both techniques (majolica and colored slips), revising the formulas occasionally. I am also now using some glaze on top of the slip, applied very unevenly with a toothbrush. The majolica glaze continues to be plagued with pinholing and crawling, usually due to my somewhat sloppy technique.

For best results, I have found that bisquing and glaze firing to cone 06 and wetting the bisque before glazing seem to help. A smooth surface also helps: a layer of red slip (the clay body put through a 60-mesh screen) applied

"Interlocking Vase," 26 inches. Low-fire clay and slips, cone 06–04. Photo: Brian Oglesbee.

Andrea Gill. USA. "Clymantis Vase," 27 inches. Slip on terra-cotta clay. Photo: Brian Oglesbee.

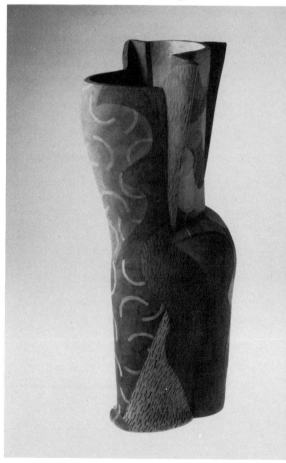

over any rough spots helps—in the case of my work, the whole pot; in thrown work, wherever it is trimmed. It is still a technique that is nerve-racking, since a great deal of time can be spent on a piece that for one reason or another can end up as landfill.

CLAY 06–04

Red art	*60*
Fire clay	*20*
Ball clay	*10*
Talc	*10*
Fine grog	*10*

Barium carbonate—about $\frac{1}{4}$ per 100 lbs.

SLIP FOR BISQUE

Nonplastic kaolin	*10*
EPK	*5*
Calcined kaolin	*15*

Talc	*10*
Frit 3124	*15*
Lead bisilicate	*10*
Flint	*20*
Zircopax	*10*

Add 30% colorant (Mason's stains or rutile). For dark colors (dark blues and greens), use 15% or less.

MAJOLICA
(Greg's revision)

Frit 3124	*76.1*
Barium carbonate	*3.0*
EPK	*15.2*
Calcined kaolin	*5.7*
Zircopax	*11.7*

(Add $\frac{1}{2}$% golden brown stain if glaze is too white.)

Low-Fire Commercial Glazes

Low-fire glazes can be purchased already mixed and ready for use. Studio potters who use them benefit from an elaborate infrastructure that has been established to distribute these glazes. These glazes are mainly intended for those ceramists working in low-fire cast-formed ware. They are sold in so many colors and textures that it takes considerable expertise to exploit their possibilities.

These glazes have had a strong influence on the way we think about ceramics, both how we think ceramics work should look and how it should be created. The use of these glazes is subject to some controversy. Some ceramists object to their flamboyant colors and textures, while others simply pre-

FIG. 6–5 Ian Symons. Canada. Casserole. Hand-formed; low fire. Photo: C.I. Photography.

Martha A. Holt. USA. Applying Commercial Glazes

1. Applying Velvet to greenware.

2. Applying black Velvet to bisque.

3. Sponging black Velvet off of bisque.

4. Applying glaze with a "silk sponge."

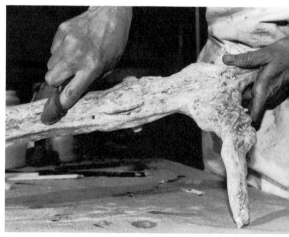

5. Rubbing glaze off with a nylon stocking.

6. Working on a nearly completed piece in the Lower Clay studio at Penland School in North Carolina.

Martha A. Holt

LOW-FIRE COMMERCIAL PRODUCTS

I want to talk about the surface materials I work with—low-fire commercial products, the positive and negative characteristics of these materials, and the reasons why you might consider working with them.

Many of us learned our craft in school. We acquired painting and drawing skills at the same time we were taking ceramic courses. Many of us were attracted to ceramics because clay was both three-dimensional and two-dimensional. We made the form and then applied the surface. But the tools and techniques we learned in painting and drawing classes were not applicable in ceramics. Glaze did not handle like paint. What we saw was not what we got. The color applied to the form was not the same color after the fire. And where were the pencils?

I began using low-fire commercial products in the early 1970s for four reasons that I consider pluses for commercial products. First is the wide range of colors available; second is the consistency of the results; third is the time and expense saved by not testing and mixing myself; and fourth, for concerns of safety—no

hazardous materials stored in half-opened bags, no dry-mixing materials together to create dust. I was using materials that someone else had spent a lot of time making standard and safe.

My working process was simple. The underglazes were applied with a brush to greenware and fired to cone 04. A clear mat glaze was airbrushed onto the bisqueware and fired to cone 06. This glaze cover is necessary to bring out the underglaze colors and to seal the surface. Without a glaze, the underglaze colors would be pale and dull and the surfaces too porous.

The results were unsatisfactory. The commercial surfaces did not compare to the richness that comes from studio-mixed glazes. On the minus side for commercial products, the surfaces were flat and boring. They lacked the subtle color shifts and mat/gloss surface changes characteristic of homemade glazes. But I had been seduced by the pluses of commercial products and was determined to find materials and methods that would compete with homemade glazes. In the early 1980s, with the help of friends, I was able to do this.

There are so many commercial products and manufacturers available. Obviously what you use depends on your need, what you want. But several products are so appropriate for the clay artist, and they are unique. The first, AMACO's Velvets is a product of the Reward Division of the American Art Clay Company (AMACO), Indianapolis, Indiana. Velvets are underglazes that were developed to be used without a glaze cover. Velvets are important for three reasons. First, they have a deep rich color and velvety texture. I think of them as having a surface like terra sigillatas. Second, they fire exactly to the color they are in the jar. This means that what you see is what you get. It is like applying paint: light blue is light blue, deep yellow is deep yellow. Third, the Velvets can be mixed. Value can be changed by adding black Velvet or white Velvet.

Ceramists also have access to a wonderful array of drawing materials that include underglaze pencils and underglaze chalk crayons. These materials handle like their names—pencils and crayons. The only drawback is that they contain no glassformer, so a glaze cover is required. But what a wonderful feeling to scribble on a piece of clay the way one scribbles in a notebook.

Once I found these products and others, I was ready to begin to confront the minuses of low-fire commercial products: flat surfaces, lack of subtle color shifts, absence of mat/gloss surface changes. My working process is as follows. I apply the Velvets to greenware with various sized brushes, mixing, and blending colors by eye, much like an oil painter. The initial bisque is to cone 04. To the bisqued piece I paint a wash of black Velvet (Velvet diluted with water) over the entire surface and sponge it off. This heightens the texture as the black Velvet remains in the undercuts and depressions. Next I scribble all over the surface with underglaze pencils and crayons. I will smudge the colors and rework them like pastels. If I don't like the color of Velvet, I can blend the pencils and crayons over the area and change the color. It is a very plastic way to work.

Because the pencils and crayons do not contain glassformer, their surface must be sealed or they will powder off. For this I use a clear cone 05–06 glaze, which I dab on lightly using a silk sponge. This is a simple way to apply a thin, even coat of glaze without having to use an airbrush. Once the glaze has dried, I rub off as much glaze as I can using a nylon stocking. The finished effect of this commercial surface is one of depth and interest. The colors change subtly when different types of underglazes are applied to greenware and bisqueware. The surfaces combine mat areas (where the glaze was rubbed off) and gloss areas (undercuts and depressions where the glaze did not rub off).

Commercial products offer variety, convenience, and safety, but the results are not always satisfactory. We must think in terms of building up surfaces in a more complex way than is required with homemade glazes. Some of the most exciting surfaces are by artists who incorporate commerical products into their already existing palette of glazes. Donna Nicholas's work is a good example of this. Experiment with them and try different firing methods. Commercial products used in raku and pit firing have tremendous depth and interest because the firing process creates accidental changes in the surfaces. Susan and Steve Kemenyffy use a variety of commercial products in their raku pieces. Don't limit yourself to the instructions on the bottle. A lot of these products hold up well at higher temperatures. The color and texture will change, sometimes for the better. I have used Velvets in a cone 9 wood kiln as well as on translucent porcelain in a cone 5 electric kiln. Wonderful vitreous engobes can be made by mixing 1 part Velvet, 1 part low-fire white casting slip (dry), and $\frac{1}{4}$ part clear glaze. These products have helped to increase my visual vocabulary.

From Martha Holt's Notebook

"An artist comes closer to nature by drawing. To understand a natural form is in a small way to understand the universe. The limbs and trees I draw are formed by the forces of nature—wind, water, gravity. To draw these forms is to escape being human for a small period of time and to return to nature."

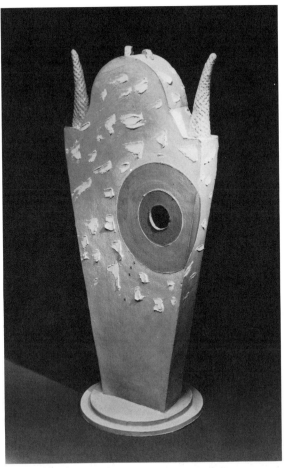

FIG. 6–6   Dave Gamble. USA. A hand-formed low-fire piece glazed with commercial glazes multifired to cone 05, 24 × 16 inches.

FIG. 6–7   American Art Clay Company. USA. Glaze-mixing equipment.

fer to make their own glazes. Other ceramists, however, delight in their wide color range, reliability, and interesting textural possibilities. (See Martha Holt's essay). Ceramists who use these commercial glazes often are more interested in new strategies for glaze application rather than in creating new glaze recipes. There is much to be said for this kind of approach with its emphasis on carefully made, one-of-a-kind artistic wares. Ceramists who work in this way are the direct heirs of the court potters of Asia and Europe.

Cone 02

Cone 02 is considered to be an unusual firing temperature and few ceramists work in it. However, it has much to recommend it. At cone 02 the ceramist still has access to all the advantages of the low fire without needing to use lead fluxes. Cone 02 glazes are brilliant in color and rich in surface, and they are surprisingly durable.

Cone 02 glazes should be high in silica and contain strong melters. Look for recipes in which frits and soda feldspar make up most of the glaze, with smaller amounts of

FIG. 6–8 Susie Symons. USA. Earthenware pitcher, 19 inches. Thrown and altered base with a hand-built top; fired at cone 03 in oxidation.

brilliant color effects, or on iron-bearing clays and natural colorants, which produce an earthy color balance. The result is a kind of split personality in that cone 3 can be used to give either a low-fire or a high-fire look.

Among the most useful glaze types for cone 3 are those which are smooth and enamel-like and rely on color for their impact; they are in fact strongly reminiscent of the low fire. Also useful at this firing temperature are earth-colored glazes and glazes with a great deal of visual texture. Earth-colored glazes derive their character from high-impurity clays; highly textured glazes derive theirs from lithium or titanium. Both are strongly reminiscent of the high fire. Glazes may be dipped, sprayed, poured, or applied with a brush.

Cone 3 glazes should be fairly high in

FIG. 6–9 Henry Serenco. USA. Wheel-thrown jar. Cone 3–4 fired in oxidation in an electric kiln.

powerful melters that contain no silica, and 3 to 14 percent clay. As in cone 04 recipes, high-impurity clays are appropriate at this temperature.

MID-FIRE GLAZES

Cone 3

Cone 3 is also an unusual firing temperature for the studio ceramist but is often used in the ceramics industry. Cone 3 is equivalent to 1168° Celsius or 2134° Fahrenheit. Glaze character is excellent and very versatile: it can be based on glaze stains, which exhibit

Low-, Mid-, and High-Fire Glazes

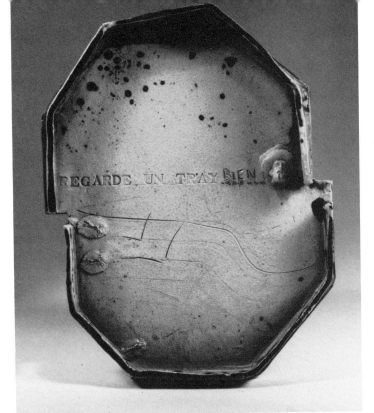

FIG. 6–10 John Chalke. Canada. "Regarde un Tray Bien." Hand-formed and multifired to cone 6.

FIG. 6–11 William P. Daley. USA. "Conical Chamber," 16 × 26 inches. Stoneware, unglazed, fired at cone 6. Photo: John Carlano.

silica and include at least 10 to 15 percent frit to ensure a good glaze melt and stabilize the glaze. For earth-colored glazes, the recipe should contain iron-bearing clays. Adding small amounts of zinc or titanium will harden and further stabilize these glazes.

Cone 6

Cone 6 is equivalent to 1222° Celsius or 2232° Fahrenheit. While cone 6 color is not as rich as that of the lower temperatures, its range is still wide. Both normal colorants and most glaze stains work well at this temperature. Most cone 6 glaze surfaces are not marked by the rich flow patterns and textures of the higher temperatures, but the glazes can be appealing and are highly durable and stable. These are practical virtues, and it seems that this is how we have come to think of this firing temperature. Glazes may be dipped, sprayed, poured, or applied with a brush.

Look for recipes that contain moderately strong fluxes, such as soda and potash feldspars, which are often more useful at cone 6 than the powerful frits. Keep calcium/magnesium melters below 15 percent; they are quite stiff at this firing temperature. Wood ash is particularly good in that it encourages rich glaze textures.

A number of glaze types are useful at cone 6, including glazes whose strong visual textures are derived from wood ash or lithium, earth-colored glazes whose color is derived from high-impurity clays, glazes whose mat surfaces and high viscosity create a stonelike look, and glazes whose low viscosity heightens the effect of carved or relief imagery.

In the past few years, a number of suppliers of low-fire glazes have introduced a line of glazes meant for cone 6. They seem to be trying to emulate the success of their low-fire prepared glazes with ones suited to higher temperatures. The potential market is significant, and there is no reason why these glazes should not also find favor with many ceramists.

HIGH-FIRE GLAZES

Cone 9

Cone 9 is equivalent to 1280° Celsius or 2336° Fahrenheit. Glaze color is muted and reserved but quite rich. Many cone 9 glazes are highly figured, with surfaces marked by complex patterns of glaze texture and flow. These glazes are durable and stable and the

FIG. 6–12 Robert Turner. USA. "Shore," 10½ inches. This piece and "Form I" (Fig. 6–13) were thrown and altered with additions of foreign materials placed in the wall of each piece; these additions bloat and melt during the firing. Fired at cone 9 reduction. Collection: Arizona State University Museum. Photo: Brian Oglesbee.

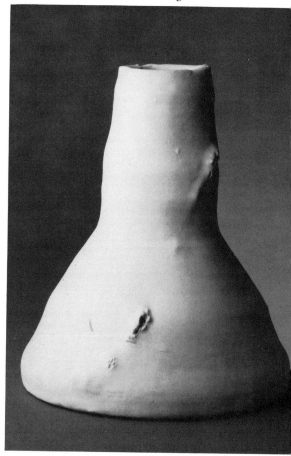

Eileen Lewenstein

In recent years I have worked almost entirely in porcelain, finding that the white body gives a lively enhancement to glazes I had previously used on stoneware. I have always been interested in the idea of forms that fit together with other forms: I expressed this earlier through boxes, where the lid was cut through the completely enclosed pot form, and in two-piece interlocking egg forms. I am now interested in related double and triple forms, the spaces between the pots being of vital importance to the concept of the whole.

THE BASIC GLAZE

Feldspar	*4*
Whiting	*31*
China clay	*40*
Flint	*18*
Dolomite	*7*

Color variations are created with small additions of metallic oxides.

Eileen Lewenstein. England. "Diptych," 7 inches. Thrown and altered porcelain; fired to 1250°C (2282°F) in an electric kiln.

bond between glaze and body is intimate and strong. Cone 9 is often associated with reduction firing. Reduction-fired cone 9 glazes are marked by robust, earthy color and dark mottled patterns coming from the reduced clay body. These add texture to the glaze surface.

Most ceramists who glaze at cone 9 apply their glazes by dipping the piece into the glaze or by splashing or pouring the glaze over it. These methods work well with cone 9's highly figured glazes.

Cone 9 recipes are rarely complex and they usually contain a few materials in good balance. Their activity comes from the character of the fire rather than from complex

Sandy Brown

For my oxidation-fired stoneware, I use a fuel-burning kiln made from ceramic fiberboard. The firing is cone 9, 1280° C (2336° F). The colors are oxides and commercial stains. A transparent glaze serves as a medium for the color, which I add in powder form to the recipe. I apply these colors freely in a painterly way, using wallpaper brushes, paint brushes, and glaze trailers.

TRANSPARENT GLAZE USED FOR GLAZE PAINTING

Nepheline syenite	*50*
Whiting	*20*
Ball clay	*15*
Flint	*25*
Boron frit	*10*
Bentonite	*10 (yes, 10%!)*

Sandy Brown. England. "Criss Cross." Softly thrown platter, bisque-fired, painted with oxides and underglaze stains, and covered with a transparent glaze; fired to 1270°C (2318°F) in an oxidation atmosphere. Photo: Russel Baader.

interactions of glaze materials. Look for high percentages of potash feldspar in these glazes; frits and the more powerful feldspars are rarely needed or used. Calcium/magnesium melters dominate the flux category. The glaze clays of choice are kaolin or ball clay, although the higher-impurity clays can be used as well.

Cone 9 lends itself well to tough, durable clay bodies and glazes. Perhaps encouraged by this, many ceramists who create utilitarian ware work at cone 9.

Useful glaze types at cone 9 include those containing significant amounts of calcium/magnesium, which encourages hard-surfaced glazes, some of which are highly

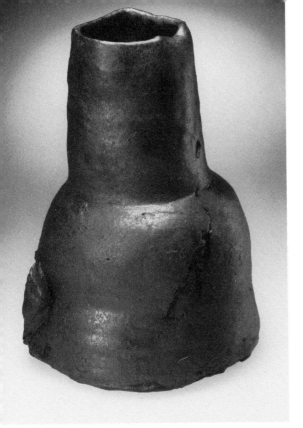

FIG. 6–13   Robert Turner. USA. "Form I," 12 inches. Fired at cone 9 reduction. Photo: Brian Oglesbee.

figured, and some, such as celadon, that are smooth surfaced. Other useful glaze types include those containing titanium, lithium, wood ash, and bone ash, all of which encourage highly figured glazes.

Glazes for Porcelain Bodies
Cone 9 is the firing temperature of true porcelain. Owing to the brilliant white ground of the porcelain clay body they rest upon, porcelain glazes have a rich character. The same glaze applied to stoneware and porcelain bodies will take on a very different look. Glazes applied to porcelain are more brilliant in color and more aristocratic in character.

Porcelain may be fired in either oxidation or reduction; often the differences are not great. Color can be quite similar (except in the case of copper, which is green in oxidation and red in reduction), and the black spots that we associate with reduction do not appear here because porcelain bodies contain such a small percentage of iron.

Some famous glaze types are strongly identified with reduction-fired porcelain. Among them are celadons and copper red glazes. While both glazes may be applied over stoneware bodies, they are at their best over porcelain. When applied to porcelain, the celadons can take on a watery, cool blue-green marked by a feeling of depth, and the copper reds produce a rich scarlet red.

FIG. 6–14   Arthur Sennett. USA. Vase, 9 inches. A saturated iron Albany slip clay-base glaze was applied to the stoneware body, then a wax-resist decoration and a white satin-mat magnesium glaze; fired at cone 9 reduction.

CHAPTER 7

Glaze Making, Application, and Testing

GLAZE MAKING

In the following sections specific directions for glaze making and glaze application are given. Readers with a lot of experience making and applying glazes will not need these suggestions, but others may find some or all of them useful. Because they are only suggestions, you should feel free to modify them for your own purposes.

While the process of glaze making is easily mastered, an ordered procedure should be followed: a badly made glaze will ruin the work. Glaze application is also an ordered, step-by-step procedure that requires great concentration. Most ceramists come to feel that glaze *application* exerts an even larger influence over the look of the finished piece than the glaze *recipe*.

You will need:

1. An accurate scale calibrated in grams (see Appendix C).
2. A clean pan or bucket for weighing the glaze materials (your scale may come with a pan). This is the measuring container. Stainless-steel salad bowls in various sizes make excellent measuring containers.
3. A clean bucket large enough to hold the entire recipe. This will be the mixing container.
4. A good dust mask.
5. Water for suspending the glaze.

6. A fine sieve, either 50 or 80 mesh (50 or 80 strands to the inch). If you are making up a large amount of glaze (over 2,000 grams), you will also need a coarse sieve (the kind you can buy in the supermarket).
7. A clean bristle brush for pushing glaze through the sieve.
8. A waterproof marker for labeling the glaze container.

The Process

1. Put on the dust mask. Assemble all the materials you will need for the glaze and make sure that you have enough of each.
2. Make sure that the scale is clean and properly balanced before you begin work.
3. Place the measuring container on the scale and make sure that with no materials in the empty measuring container the scale weight is at zero point. If not, adjust the tare compensation of the scale so that it reads zero. (See Appendix C).
4. Weigh each material and place it in the mixing container.
5. Add enough water to make a mixture that is as thick as cream. Use a propeller mixer if you have one. (Once the glaze is properly mixed with water, you can take off the dust mask.)
6. Force the glaze mixture through the sieve with a stiff brush to homogenize the mix-

ture and break up any lumps. If you have made up a large amount of glaze (over 2,000 grams), force the mixture through a coarse sieve before using the fine sieve.

7. Thin the glaze with water to the appropriate consistency. For single-layer applications, the glaze should be the thickness of heavy cream. For multiple-layer glazing, the glazes should be thin and milky.

8. Label the completed glaze with its name, color, firing cone, the amount mixed, and the date. In a classroom or group situation, include your initials to identify the glaze.

GLAZE APPLICATION

Beginning ceramists often make the mistake of confusing glazes with paints. Glazes are not paints, nor do they act like paints in the fire. During the firing, they will change considerably; thus an area that seems smoothly covered with glaze before the firing may, after firing, reveal a busy, broken texture. This transformation is unsettling at first and beginning ceramists often need some time to get used to this phenomenon. Learning to apply glazes is exciting but demanding and will call for imagination and persistence.

Dipping

Dipping is the easiest and most common glaze application method and may be used alone or in combination with other glazing methods.

The Process
1. Fire the piece to bisque.
2. Wet or wax the base.
3. Grasp the piece at the top and dip the bottom half in the glaze.
4. Wipe away the glaze from the bottom.
5. Let the glaze dry.
6. Grasp the piece at the bottom, being care-

ful not to smudge the glaze, and dip the top half in the glaze.

Dipping with Glaze Tongs

Glaze tongs look like a set of metal claws and are useful for glazing small and medium-sized pieces.

1. Fire the piece to bisque.
2. Wet or wax the base.
3. Grasp the piece with the tongs and dip it in the glaze.
4. Wipe away the glaze from the bottom.

Spraying

Spraying is an effective glazing technique that can produce beautiful results with only a small amount of glaze. It is especially useful in the oxidation fire of the electric kiln because it tends to soften the glaze effect, which otherwise in oxidation is often characterized by a harsh quality.

Sprayers can be used to apply glazes over large or small areas of the piece. Ceramists who spray their glazes usually own a large "spray gun" and a smaller "air brush" for detail work. Always wear a good dust mask and use a spray booth when using a sprayer.

The Process
1. Place the piece on a revolving turntable.
2. Spray the glaze over the whole surface of the piece. Keep the sprayer moving over the piece so that no one area receives too much glaze.

Intaglio Glazing

An intaglio image is one that has been incised or engraved. Many ceramists like to combine it with "sprigged" or added clay ornament. Once the piece has been fired to bisque this kind of imagery can be glazed in a way that accents the intaglio imagery.

The Process
1. Fire the piece to bisque.
2. Daub the glaze in the incised areas.
3. Wash off the excess glaze, leaving glaze

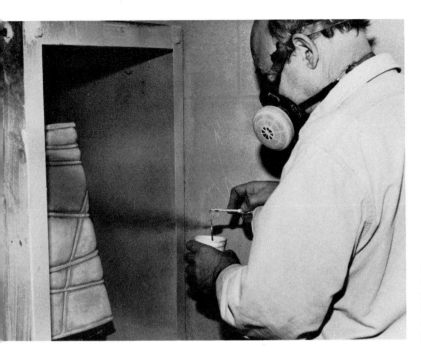

FIG. 7–1 Applying a glaze with a sprayer. Note the dust mask the potter is wearing and the spray booth, which safely evacuates the oversprayed glaze.

only in the interstices (the corners and grooves that catch the glaze).

At this point the piece can be fired and no more glaze applied, or you may want to apply another stain or glaze. The intaglio glaze will "come through" any other glazes applied over it. For example, daubing a black glaze in the incised areas and applying a light-colored glaze over it will produce attractive, contrasting intaglio imagery.

Splash and Pour Techniques
Splashing and pouring are classic methods of applying glaze. Even though they are simple and direct, the effects can be very pleasing.

The Process
1. Fill a cup with glaze.
2. Suspend the piece over the glaze bucket either by holding it or setting it on two sticks.

3. Splash or pour the glaze over the piece, making sure that the runoff flows back into the glaze bucket.

A piece may be glazed solely with this method, but more often we use it in conjunction with dip or spray application techniques. Splash or pour glaze application may be used under or over another glaze.

Brush Application
The brush is an excellent glaze application tool for creating linear imagery. If you try to "paint" large, unbroken areas of solid glaze color with a brush, however, the results will generally be busy and messy. The only exceptions to this are glazes that have been specially prepared for brush application. These glazes are finely ground and contain glues and binders that aid "brushability." Most of the commercial low-fire glazes are of this type and can be successfully applied with a brush.

Glaze Making, Application, and Testing

TESTING GLAZES

Unlike paint, glazes do not have the same color and character during application as they have when the piece is finished. In fact, the kiln firing profoundly changes the characteristics of the glaze. The best way to track these transformations is to fire glazes first on a test tile, using the tile as a surrogate for the finished piece. If the test works with a glaze or glaze combination works well on the test tile, a piece similarly glazed will work as well.

Making a Test Tile

To get a good idea how the glaze will look on your work, make the test tile fairly large. The tile should be similar in character to your usual work.

For hand-built work, make your test tiles flat only if you work with flat slabs. If you work with curved surfaces, curve the test tile. If you usually use the wheel to make your forms, throw a large cylinder and cut it into three or four tiles; in this way your test tile will have the same throwing lines and form as your normal work. If you employ surface imagery in your work, do so on all or part of the surface of the test tile.

Let the test tile dry. If you apply slips or engobes to the unfired clay, apply them now. If you prepare your work for glazing by first firing to bisque, fire the test tile in the bisque kiln as well. Use your normal glaze application and firing methods. In every way, try to make the test tile just as you make your normal work.

CHAPTER 8

Alternative Surfaces

Most recipes for surface finishes fall into the narrow band of requirements that characterize glazes. Most surface finishes are composed of feldspars, fluxes, and clays. Glazes, however, contain no more than 20 percent clay. Some of our most useful surface finishes do not conform in any way to the normal definition of a glaze. The most common of these are colorant washes, slips, and engobes. These do not run and flow in the fire and the surfaces are not glassy in character.

Some ceramists use surface finishes of this type under glazes to create imagery that would not be possible with glazes alone. Using this combination can produce graphic, hard-edged imagery, and, unlike that from glazes used alone, the imagery will not blur or run. Other ceramists use surface finishes of this type as the final finish for the piece when a normal glassy surface finish may not be appropriate. Many pieces do not require the durable, smooth surfaces that we get from glazes, and some pieces will not be improved by glazes. A number of alternatives are open to us. These alternative possibilities allow us to avoid the trap of using a glaze finish just because "this is the way it's supposed to be done."

SLIPS AND ENGOBES

At times we may create a piece that requires little of the flowing characteristics and active visual textures that distinguish glazes. In these cases, we can use surface finishes with a high clay content. Recipes high in clay will have a high viscosity and will not flow and blur during the firing, nor will they be marked by visual texture. These characteristics ensure that high-clay surfaces look very different from glazes.

Two high-clay surfaces used by ceramists are slips and engobes. Both are high-clay formulations. Because the two can be easily confused, contemporary ceramists define the two according to their clay content:

engobes = 21 to 50% clay
slips = 51% or more clay

Applying Imagery

Because slips and engobes do not flow in the fire, they can be used for complex, graphic images. To take advantage of the imagery possibilities of slips and engobes, we apply imagery in ways that would be inappropriate for glazes. Brushes are used most frequently for applying these surfaces, but airbrushes and airbrush and stencil methods can also be used. Any strategy that can create complex, graphic imagery is appropriate for slips and engobes.

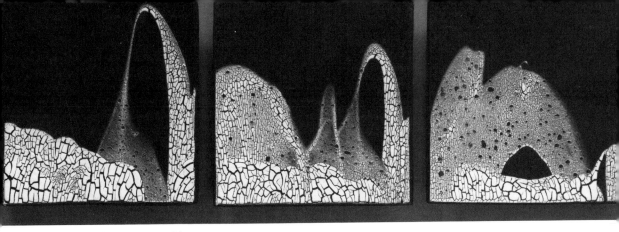

FIG. 8–1 Robert Sperry. USA. "Panels," 16 × 16 inches. Stoneware with a white slip applied over a black glaze. In this photo and Fig. 8–2 we see what happens when a slip is applied over a glaze. Sperry is adept at exploiting these effects. Photo: Robert Schreiber.

FIG. 8–2 Robert Sperry. USA. "#609," 64 inches square. Stoneware with a white slip applied over a black glaze, fired to cone 6. Photo: Robert Schreiber.

Norman Schulman

I paint my pieces with engobes and apply a clear lead glaze over the engobe. I fire to cone 3 (with no preliminary bisque fire) in oxidation in a fuel-burning kiln. I allow the kiln to cool normally until the fire box is black. At this point I light the kiln for 15 minutes and fire in very heavy reduction. I then turn off the burners, shut the damper and slow, slow cool.

My engobe recipe is:

Kaolin	*10*
Soda feldspar	*20*
Ball clay	*14*
Ground silica (325 mesh)	*15*
Whiting	*25*
Zirconium opacifier	*10*
Calcined kaolin	*5*

This is colored with prepared stains, 5—15 percent.

Norman Schulman. USA. "Innocence and Dark Forces."

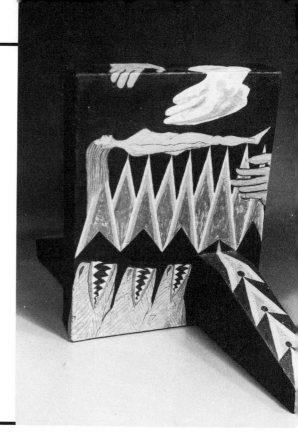

FIG. 8—3 John Maltby. England. "Small Harbour," 12 × 8 inches. Slab-formed dish with painted slips and sgraffito linear imagery; stoneware fired in oxidation.

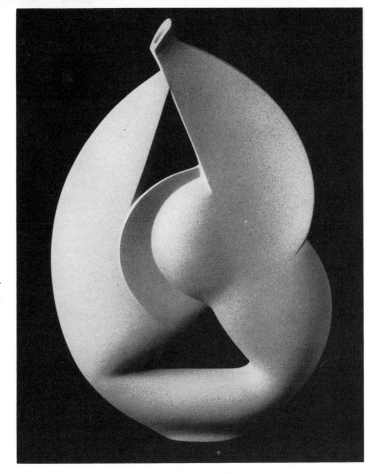

FIG. 8–4 Linda Gunn-Russell. England. "Untitled Vessel," c. 22 inches. "My vessels are made of grogged red earthenware clay. I cut out the basic shapes on the flat and then, using different-size spoons, beat and tap the clay into shape. When leather-hard, the parts are joined. After a low bisque firing (930° C), I use lapidary stones and wet and dry paper to smooth down surfaces and sharpen edges. Before adding color I mask out areas of the surface with a latex masking material. I use commercially prepared engobes to which I add small amounts of transparent glaze. These are applied by spraying and stippling to give a slight texture. I fire (and often refire!) the work to 1060° C. Courtesy Michaelson & Orient. Photo: Brian E. Rybolt.

FIG. 8–5 Larry Elsner. USA. "Mizuhiki," 27 × 50 cm. Hand-formed with a slip applied over the whole piece, then fired to cone 6 in oxidation. After firing, the piece was partially ground, which revealed the lighter body color. Photo: Don Clark.

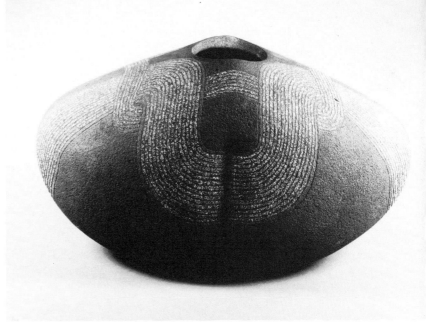

Glazed Slip Techniques

Often slips and engobes are covered with a glaze to protect their surfaces, which otherwise tend not to be durable. Ceramists have turned this to their advantage by developing image-creation strategies in which they apply a transparent or translucent glaze over a slip or engobe. The results combine advantages from each type of recipe.

In the two pieces by Michael Casson (Figs. 8–6 and 8–7), we see the kind of imagery that can be created using slips under glazes.

FIG. 8–6 Michael Casson. England. "Swimmer" pot, 15 inches. Wheel-formed, wood-fired, salt-glazed stoneware, cone 10 reduction. The imagery of the swimming figures was created using paper-resist methods.

FIG. 8–7 Michael Casson. England. "Jug," 18 inches. Wood-fired, salt-glazed stoneware, cone 10 reduction. The slip imagery on the surface was applied with gestural strokes made by a cut kidney, sponge, fingers, etc.

Vitreous Engobes

Vitreous means "glasslike," so a vitreous engobe is an engobe that has a glazelike surface. However, it will still have the smooth surfaces and nonflowing character of a normal engobe. The principle behind vitreous engobes is simple—the refractory quality of these high-clay recipes is offset by powerful melters. Vitreous engobes are hybrid formulations: they do not act like glazes in the fire, nor do they look very much like glazes, but they do have the shiny surface and the durability of glazes.

Like normal engobes, vitreous engobes should contain from 25 to 50 percent clay. The rest should be frits, feldspars, and fluxes. Make sure that these materials encourage strong melts at the firing temperature you are using (for guidance, see the fluxing power notations in the section on intuitive glaze analysis in Chapter 10).

These surfaces will rarely be successful if they are applied exactly like glazes. Indeed they will seem flat and lifeless. If, on the other hand, they are applied like an engobe or a slip, perhaps with a brush or a painting knife, they most likely will be lively and successful. (A painting knife looks like a miniature trowel and is used to apply heavy layers of paint.)

Susanne Stephenson

VITREOUS ENGOBES

In my work I want surface and form to be interdependent. My goal is to make color express three-dimensional form, for color actually to be perceived as that form. I throw and alter soft clay forms to begin the development of the expression. To help bring color and form a step closer together, I began working with vitreous engobes. With the single application of a vitreous engobe on greenware, I can achieve the rich color and thickness of a slip, but, unlike the slip, it will also develop the gloss or sheen of a glaze.

I have arrived at two base recipes that work for most colors. The percentage of stain added to each base varies from color to color; for instance, 20 percent for blacks, 25 percent for greens, yellows, and blues, and 30 percent for crimsons, peach, and pinks.

Of the hundreds of tests I've made, I use about thirty-six for studio use. I have evaluated these tests for color quality, for surface, and for the way the vitreous engobe fits on several different clay bodies. At one point I was also looking for vitreous engobes that would be practical for single-firing application. An unexpected discovery as the result of this research was that some of the same vitreous engobes could be used on already-fired bisqueware and also as an overglaze.

When a vitreous engobe is applied thick, it has a shine; when it is applied thin, it has a dry appearance. Working with applications of varying thicknesses therefore produces surfaces of rich variation but without the complication of the two-step process of slipping and

Susanne Stephenson. USA. "Mountain Crevasse IV," $25\frac{1}{2} \times 9\frac{1}{2}$ inches. Terra-cotta with thickly applied white, black, yellow, and red slips. Photo: Suzanne Coles.

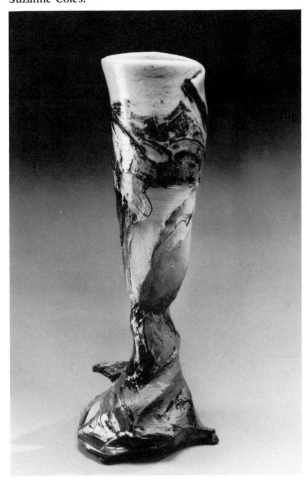

glazing. Testing and combining engobes has expanded my understanding of what is possible in ceramic surfaces, and I have also been able to expand my palette of color.

In order for the surface and form to be interactive, I rely on clay slips (not engobes) in high relief. Thick applications produce a surface in high relief that ranges in contrast from blacks to grays to whites. I use vitreous engobes to produce intense hues such as yellows, reds, greens, and blues to suggest certain light qualities and strong contrasts in a landscape context. These hues are used in the low-relief areas. Since I have been working with more intense color, I have focused more on vertical forms. It has been exciting to discover the flexibility I get in a painting medium as I use these engobes.

VITREOUS ENGOBE RECIPES: CONES 04–03

	Recipe 1	Recipe 2	Recipe 3	Recipe 4
Ferro frit 3124	38	44	50	22.60
Nepheline syenite	12	11	10	11.55
Tenn ball clay (0M4)	31	28	25	16.95
Flint	19	17	15	14.30
Ferro frit 3195				5.75
Talc				.90
Gerstley borate				9.80
Cornwall stone				4.85
Pioneer kaolin				7.70
Bentonite				1.40
	100	100	100	95.05

Pinholing and Crawling

Vitreous slips and engobes are prone to pinholing and crawling. Pinholes are tiny openings that appear on the surface of the glaze or engobe and reveal the clay body. They are artifacts of reactions at the height of the fire; they are openings in the surface that have not melted and healed. They are far less likely to heal in high-clay vitreous slips and engobes than in glazes because of clay's high viscosity. To prevent pinholing, use low-viscosity fluxes in the recipe. Both sodium and boron frits and Gerstley borate are effective for this purpose.

Crawling is caused by shrinkage. During the early stages of the firing, high-clay recipes shrink a great deal. As the clay shrinks, fissures occur on the surface coating and pieces of it may flake away. There are two ways to deal with this problem: (1) apply the slip or engobe to an unfired clay body or (2) modify the recipe.

If a recipe that shrinks is applied to a clay body that also shrinks—in other words, an unfired clay body—crawling and bare spots will not be a problem. If the recipe is applied to bisqueware, a good part of the clay in the recipe should be calcined (fired to bisque temperatures). For example, if the recipe contains 35 percent clay, 25 percent of it should be calcined. The calcined clay is compatible in shrinkage with the bisque-fired clay body. Calcined kaolin can be purchased from ceramic supply firms or you can do it yourself by placing clay in a bowl and firing it to cone 010 or 08.

Unglazed Slips and Engobes

Many ceramic forms do not lend themselves to glazed surfaces and at times the dry, mat surface of an unglazed slip or engobe may be preferable to the shiny surface of a transparent glaze or even the satin surface of a

Walter Ostrom. Canada. "Flower 'Brick' with Tz'u-Chou Pot and Leaves," $11\frac{1}{2}$ inches high. Wheel thrown with hand-formed elements. Majolica glazed with resist techniques. Cone 05 oxidation. Photo: Elaine Dacey Ostrom.

Aurore Chabot. USA. "Fingers Like Pitted Tombstones, II," $25\frac{1}{2} \times 24 \times 45$ inches. Mixed media including low-fire earthenware. Bisque fired to cone 04, glaze fired to cone 06. "This piece has a specially shaped and painted base to enhance the clay parts precariously poised on top." Photo: Steven Meckler.

Roy Strassberg. USA. "Jazzman Torso #5," $31\frac{1}{2}$ inches high. Slab formed, low fire, bisque fired at cone 04, glaze fired at cone 06. Finished with a thin layer of acrylic medium over the entire piece to intensify the color and protect the surface from abrasion.

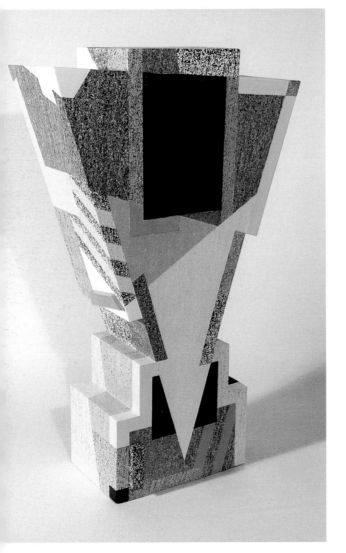

Georgette Zirbes. USA. "Pani X," 18 inches high. This piece was thrown and assembled. Entire surface was covered with a black slip, imagery created with colored slips. A sgraffito line reveals underlying colors and the clay body. A transparent black stain and a black glaze pencil were used to further refine the imagery. Finally, a clear glaze was sprayed over the entire piece, and it was fired to cone 6 in a neutral atmosphere (neither oxidation nor reduction).

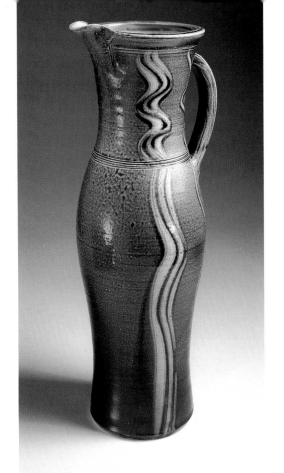

Robert M. Winokur. USA. "Geometric Wrap: Ceramic Table I," 30¼ × 12½ × 10 inches. Stoneware clay body; slips, engobes, and glazes applied to the surface. Fired in a salt glaze kiln.

Michael Casson. England. "Crane Jug," 18 inches high. Wood-fired, salt-glazed stoneware, cone 10 reduction. The slip imagery on the surface of the pitcher was applied with gestural strokes made by a cut kidney, sponge, fingers, etc.

Angelo di Petta. Canada. Platter, 16 × 16 inches. Mold formed. Twice fired, once at cone 03 and then at cone 06. Painted with prepared glazes, some altered with additions, such as lithium carbonate. The Toronto potter Angelo di Petta trained in Faenza, Italy; both places have strongly influenced his work.

Victor Babu. USA. Platter, 28-inch diameter. Wheel-formed porcelain. Snake image created using multilayered stencils and numerous colored glazes; this was covered with a liquid wax resist, the platter dipped into the base glaze, which adhered except to those areas painted with resist. The completed piece was then single fired to cone 10 in a reduction atmosphere. Photo: E. G. Schempf.

Curtis and Susan Benzle. USA. "Moon Glow," 4 inches high. The Benzles use multiple layers of a low-clay porcelain, laminated and compressed while the clay is still wet. While the low-clay porcelain body is extremely difficult to work with and to fire, its color responses are rich.

(Below left) JoAnn Schnabel. USA. "Transmuter," 27 inches high. Hand-formed, cone 04, fired in oxidation, in an electric kiln.

(Below right) Val Cushing. USA. Lidded jar, thrown and altered, hand-formed finial, 22 inches high. Cone 9 reduction fired. Val Cushing is trying to make very "pure" pots. In his work it is hard to separate idea from image or surface from form.

Michael Simon. USA. "Covered Jar," 15 inches high. Thrown and altered, salt fired. This piece was made with a good deal of Avery kaolin, a kaolin with a slight orange blush. This is emphasized by the action of the salt fire.

David Pendell. USA. "Ha-Ha-Ha I'm Crazy, Wall Piece," 28 × 20 inches. Earthenware finished with underglaze, overglaze enamels, and luster. "This is my latest piece, a triumph of determination over the morass of uncertain glaze colors and surfaces. Fired far too many times—'Della Robbia, eat your heart out.'"

Jeff Oestreich. USA. "#2 Teapot," 9 inches high. Wheel-thrown and altered form, finished with a wood fired crackle slip under an amber glaze. Courtesy Pro-Art Gallery, Saint Louis, Mo. Photo: Michael Holohan, Pro-Art.

John Glick. USA. A tray form, 15 × 31 inches, made in an extruder. Stoneware, cone 10 reduction fired. The piece was decorated using a multiple slip technique applied to the wet clay. Multiple glazes were also used along with wax resist, glaze painting, and washes.

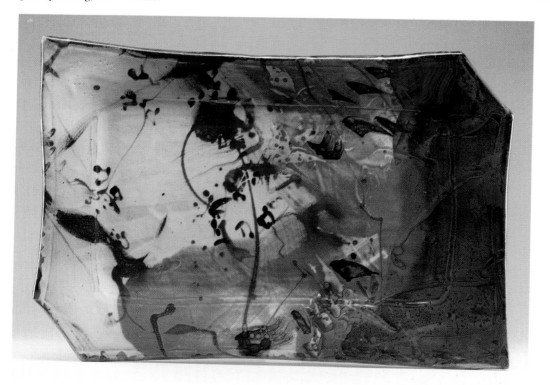

Barbara Frey. USA. "Coconino County Found Objects," 20 × 14 inches. This wall piece is hand-formed from an earthenware clay body. The imagery is hand-formed and carved. Color is derived from slips and commercially prepared glazes. This piece is fired to a low temperature in an electric kiln.

Virginia Scotchie. USA. "Orbiting Forms" wall sculpture, 29 × 19 × 27 inches. Low-fire earthenware, with press-molded and hand-built elements.

translucent glaze. Though slips and engobes are not as durable and abrasion-resistant as glazes, materials can be added to harden them. Especially useful is the flux titanium. When used in additions of 2 percent, titanium will harden and strengthen the recipe. While such recipes are still not as durable as glazes, they are more durable than most other engobes or slips. Titanium's only drawback is that it bleaches the color of some of the brightest stains. An alternative, to prevent this, would be to use 2 percent additions of zinc or tin instead of the titanium. Both will enhance durability, though neither is as effective a hardener as titanium.

Gritty Slips and Engobes
The surface of slips and engobes tends to be smooth and mat. Gritty slips are formulated with coarse clays and have a rough surface. They can be formulated easily by substituting a coarse fire clay for other (finer) clays in a slip recipe. This kind of coarse surface is particularly appropriate for sculptural pieces.

COLORANT WASHES
Colorant washes are made from dark-colored clays, stains, or coloring oxides. Even though they are very thin, they are quite durable and reveal a great deal of the character of the clay upon which they have been applied. Their surface tends to be mat (sometimes with a barely discernible sheen) and their color tends to be darker than the body they are applied to in a manner similar to wood stains.

Finishing with a Glaze and Colorant Washes
A useful method for finishing a piece with a surface ornamented with intaglio or relief imagery is to apply a glaze in the interstices of the piece and spray a colorant wash over the surface. This is an especially useful method

for beginners because what you see before firing is pretty much what you get after firing.

You will need:

1. A piece whose surface has been modified with scratched or impressed or relief imagery and fired to bisque
2. A small amount of glaze
3. A colorant wash
4. A sponge
5. A sprayer
6. A turntable for spraying the piece

The Procedure
1. Glaze the inside of the piece
2. Dip a sponge in the glaze and daub the glaze in the interstices created by the intaglio or relief imagery
3. Allow the glaze to dry for a few minutes
4. Wash off any excess glaze from the surface
5. Let the piece dry for half an hour
6. Place the piece on the turntable and spray the colorant wash over its surface
7. Clean the foot of the piece
8. Fire the piece

TERRA SIGILLATAS
Terra sigillatas have been used extensively by potters in the past, from the potters of Corinth and Athens in Ancient Greece, the Etruscans and Romans in Italy, to the pre-Columbian potters in the New World. As glazes were developed, the terra sigillata process was abandoned and the principles of the process forgotten. At the beginning of the twentieth century, however, there was a great effort to duplicate the look of Classical Greek pots. The method was rediscovered by ceramic scientists in the late 1920s and early 1930s and now is used by many contemporary ceramists (see Figs. 8–8 through 8–13).

Terra sigillatas are highly refined clay slips, in which all sediments above one micron in size have been removed. This desedimentation process is accomplished by defloccu-

FIG. 8–8 David MacDonald. USA. Hand- and press-mold formed, painted with terra sigillatas and highly polished, then fired in a low-fire electric kiln. This piece was strongly influenced by the work of African potters.

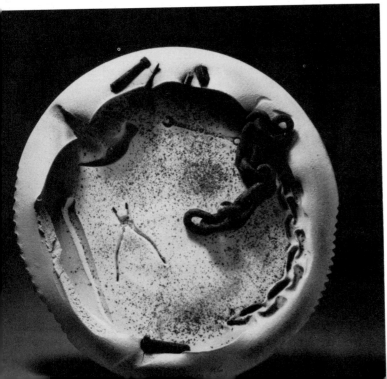

FIG. 8–9 Neil Tetkowski. USA. "Buy American." This piece was fired in a large gas kiln to cone 06–04 in a reduction atmosphere. The kiln was reduced for about 15 minutes toward the end of the firing. Then a small amount of salt (less than a pound) was added to modify the terra sigillata surface.

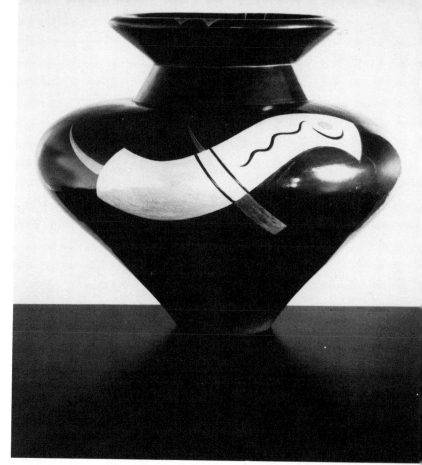

FIG. 8–10 Fiona Salazar. England. Earthenware clay body, coil-formed, then painted with terra sigillatas and burnished. The interior of the piece was treated with glaze; the exterior was waxed after firing. Salazar is interested in pottery from the past painted with terra sigillatas.

FIG. 8–11 Richard Zakin. USA. "Ornamented Vase," 10 cm. Low-fire hand-formed body with terra sigillata and sgraffito imagery, fired to cone 03 in an electric kiln. Photo: Thomas C. Eckersley.

FIG. 8–12 Nina Höle. Denmark. "House Piece," 40 cm. "The top of this piece is a roof with two wolf heads on each side showing how difficult it is to make a decision. Which way to go? It is finished with terra sigillata, stains, and a bit of glaze rubbed in." Photo: Copyright Henning Skov.

FIG. 8–13 Anna Calluori Holcombe. USA. "Homage to the Southwest," $21\frac{1}{2} \times 18\frac{1}{2}$ inches. Earthenware clay, terra sigillata, wood, and low-fire glaze. Photo: Richard Margolis.

lating the slip, which, in turn, is achieved by adding alkaline materials. Deflocculated clays lose much of their viscosity and the cruder and heavier particles sink to the bottom of the container. The mixture is then decanted; the fine particles are saved and the crude particles are discarded.

Creating a Terra Sigillata

First weigh the clay, then the water and deflocculant (usually sodium silicate). Most red clays need 0.5% sodium silicate by weight (multiply by .005) and three times as much water as clay to deflocculate them. Most white clays need 0.3% sodium silicate (multiply by .003) and four times as much water as clay to deflocculate them. Place the clay in a container, then the water and deflocculant; stir the mixture thoroughly and pass it through a sieve (30 mesh or finer). Wait about half an hour, then pour the slip from its container into another. As you pour the slip, note the coarse sediment in the bottom of the container. This sediment is grainy in texture and somewhat darker than the rest of the slip.

Roberta Kaserman

My sculptural pieces are made from porcelain with other materials—dowels, driftwood, wood, metal, gouache, wax—added as needed. The surface on the porcelain is terra sigillata made from Grolleg clay, stained with Mason stains, and single fired to cone 1. The recipe for the clay body is:

Kaolin	30
Ball clay	20
Custer spar	25
Silica	25

I find that this clay is suitable for throwing or hand-building without adding any fiber or grog or other filler. While I single fire to cone 1 to achieve the surface I want, this firing also helps to eliminate the stresses that the clay would undergo at higher temperatures. (I use the same clay body for cone 10 functional pottery.) At cone 1, the clay surface is warm and inviting, and the work has reasonable strength to withstand the rigors of shipping. At cone 10, porcelain has a hard coolness that would not be appropriate for this work.

Much of my work is done using press molds. I find that after I have refined a form to my own satisfaction, if I make a press mold to work from I can free up my decision-making time and energy to focus on surface imagery, its content, composition, color, and relationship to the form.

Roberta Kaserman. USA. "Souls May Travel in Odd Vessels," 24 × 13 inches. Hand-formed clay (painted with terra sigillata) and nonclay elements. Photo: David L. Brown.

Elyse Saperstein

One of my earliest exposures to terra sigillata was while I was taking a summer ceramic course at a university. I remember spending a lot of time in the school library, which was a gold mine of ceramic knowledge. One day I came upon a graduate thesis dealing with simply worked vessels and terra sigillata. Although the forms caught my attention, what really attracted me was this new surface; it had a richness, softness, and elegance that seemed almost primal. I was totally absorbed by what I saw.

Not until years later did I come in direct contact with terra sigillata again. Actually, it was in graduate school during a critique. The conversation had turned to surfaces and someone threw out terra sigillata as a suggestion. It jogged the cobwebs loose and off I went to dig up info and run tests. That was about ten years ago. I have been using terra sigillata in my work ever since.

Terra sigillata is a great surface for my work because it allows the texture beneath to show; it fits like a thin skin, is opaque, and has a wonderful subtle sheen. Initially, I sprayed the terra sigillata on to bone-dry greenware and buffed it with a chamois. For a number of years, I applied it in this fashion. However, the tasks of masking off areas, buffing those areas, and removing the masking was time-consuming and tedious, to say the least. I modified this arduous method by applying the terra sigillata with a soft brush and firing the piece a little hotter. By expediting its application, the method, as well as the results, are more satisfying.

Elyse Saperstein. USA. "Even Keel," 62 × 21 inches. Slab-built terra-cotta, finished with terra sigillata and slips, fired to cone 02, then glaze-fired (using commercially prepared glazes) at cone 07. Photo: John Carlano.

During the decanting process, allow the sediment to remain in the bottom of the container until you have poured off all the fine material; then discard the coarse material. Continue the process by pouring the slip back and forth between the two containers (wide-bottomed containers work best). Allow a short rest period between each pour, perhaps twenty minutes.

As the process continues, the sludge becomes finer and lighter in color. Finally you will have removed all the dark, coarse particles. At this point stop the desedimentation process and test the sigillata. Apply it to a tile, allow it to dry, and rub it lightly. If the sigillata is good, it will take on a perceptible shine and little, if any, will come off on the finger. On the other hand, if it is mat as it dries and if it leaves a layer of clay on the polishing cloth, it is not yet a true terra sigillata. It is a good idea to test-fire the terra sigillata in a small test kiln.

The first few times you try to make a terra sigillata, you may have difficulties with under- or overdeflocculated mixtures. If you have little sedimentation, you need more deflocculant; if you have *no* sedimentation, you have used too much deflocculant.

A wide range of color can be obtained using only a red and a white terra sigillata plus colorants and stains. If white sigillata is added to red sigillata, the result is a pink orange; if cobalt is added to the red sigillata, the result is a brown or black. If cobalt is added to a white terra sigillata, the result is a blue color. Stains added to the sigillatas are used to create the rest of the color spectrum. Stains will look pretty much the same in the unfired state as the fired and can be added by eye, which obviates the need for complex measuring procedures.

Local clays can make excellent terra sigillatas, but their defloculant requirements vary. To determine the proper amount of deflocculant, set aside a few hundred grams of the slip as a test batch. First, try no deflocculant, then add deflocculant to the slip in increments of .1 percent. Wait twenty minutes each time and check the mixture. One of these mixtures should produce more sigillata than the others. This indicates the best percentage of deflocculant.

Terra sigillatas made with too little water will not desediment. Therefore most mixtures will initially be quite thin. This excess water must be evaporated either by exposure to air or by simmering (do not allow the mixture to boil). Do not let the terra sigillata get too thick; these fine-particled surfaces crack and flake off when applied heavily.

Terra sigillatas are low-fire surfaces fired in the range of cone 08 to cone 03. They lose their smooth surface and unique waxy quality when fired above cone 1. They will show every detail of the clay surface and look as if they are bonded to the clay rather than constituting a distinct coating as glazes often do. It is best to apply terra sigillatas to fine-grained low-fire clay bodies, especially red-colored terra-cotta bodies.

Applying Terra Sigillatas

Terra sigillatas are best applied to greenware. They can be applied by brushing, spraying, dipping, and pouring. Because of their stability in the fire, sigillatas lend themselves especially well to brush application. With care and practice, you may apply even broad areas of flat color.

Terra sigilattas are high in alumina and do not flow or blur in the fire, so it is possible to develop strategies for producing complex imagery that would not work well if used with glazes. Terra sigillatas are often used with sgraffito (scratched) imagery on greenware pieces, a technique used by the ancient Greek vase painters. They also lend themselves to multiple-fire and refire techniques, which are possible but difficult when used with glazes.

Terra sigillatas may be hardened by adding 3 or 4 percent of sodium silicate to the recipe *after* deflocculating the slip. They may be finished after firing by burnishing or waxing. Low-fire glazes (cone 04 or 03) work well with terra sigillatas and the two different surfaces will compliment each other. The velvet, mat, or semi-mat surfaces of the sigillatas also contrast nicely with the glassy surfaces of low-fired glazes.

CHAPTER 9

Ceramic Color

One of the things that we notice first about a ceramic piece is its color. The person unfamiliar with ceramics will compare ceramic color to paint. While there are some similarities, the differences between the two are significant. Unlike paint, ceramic color must pass through the rigors of the kiln fire, where it will be transformed in ways that are not fully predictable, and in fact at times are wildly unpredictable. While this is a problem, ceramic color has a great advantage as well: once the piece is fired, the color will be durable and unchanging.

Few coloring materials can withstand the heat of the fire. For millennia ceramists had to rely solely upon a limited group of naturally occurring minerals that needed only to be refined. In the eighteenth century, the color possibilities were extended when ceramists discovered new, naturally occurring coloring minerals. They also learned how to create a new group of compounds in which oxides were added to colorants to alter their color. These "ceramic stains" added a whole new color palette for the ceramist.

Contemporary ceramists now have ready access to both coloring minerals and manufactured colorants. Each has advantages: natural minerals are powerful and relatively inexpensive, whereas stains are less economical and less powerful but offer a wide choice of unusual colors.

THE PHYSICS OF CERAMIC COLOR

All ceramic materials have specific color characteristics when fired in the kiln. These reactions can be (and often are) modified by other materials in the glaze and by the atmosphere and firing temperature of the kiln.

The physics of color is complex. Scientists who have studied the physics of color suggest that there may be as many as fifteen ways in which colors are created in nature. Most ceramic color, however, is created by the presence of minerals that react in a characteristic way to light energy. When thinking about ceramic color, it is best to think of light as individual units of energy, or quanta. These units vibrate at different frequencies. Ceramic color is produced because the clay, slip, or glaze absorbs most of these vibrations and reflects only a narrow band of light energy back to the viewer. The vibration that is reflected back to us is perceived as a color.

COLORANTS FOUND IN NATURE

Chrome—A strong grass green. In stains it is also used for chrome tin pinks. (Note that all chrome-containing compounds are potentially toxic.)

Clays—High-impurity clays will encourage creams, browns, rusts, and burnt oranges.

Cobalt—Blue.

Copper—Green in the oxidation fire, but often blood red in the reduction fire.

Iron oxide—Red to earth yellow (with calcium), bright red (in a pure oxidation atmosphere), brown, rust, brick red, soft green celadons (reduction fired), or black (saturated iron glazes, up to 12 percent iron, reduction fired).

Black iron oxide: Black to grays and browns.

Manganese—Soft browns and pinks. (Note that all manganese-containing compounds are potentially toxic.)

Nickel—Greens, blues, browns, and pinks. (Note that all nickel-containing compounds are toxic.)

Rutile—Tans and browns.

Vanadium—Bright yellows. (Note that vanadium-containing compounds are potentially toxic.)

A note on toxicity: Colorants that are potentially toxic—chrome, manganese, nickel, and vanadium—are much safer if compounded with other materials to form a stain. They should never be used in their naturally occurring form. Even when they are compounded with other materials, however, there is danger during firing—make sure that the kiln area is well ventilated so that dangerous gases cannot concentrate in the kiln area during firing.

CERAMIC STAINS

Many materials in a normal glaze recipe will significantly modify colorants: for example, tin will cause a chrome green to turn a brilliant pink or crimson, and cobalt will create purples and royal blues in the presence of magnesium. When ceramists began to understand the mechanisms underlying these changes, they realized that they could combine the naturally occurring coloring minerals and their modifiers to create ceramic stains. Today there are many suppliers of these specialized coloring compounds, typically offering a list of twenty to fifty colors.

Stains differ from one manufacturer to another, at least in detail. Certain broad types, however, are fairly common:

Chrome/lead—bright red

Chrome/tin based—burgundy, pinks, and crimsons

Chrome/alumina based—pinks and crimsons

Manganese/alumina—pinks

Alumina/chrome/iron compounds—browns and ambers

Titanium—yellow

Praseodymium—yellow

Vanadium/zirconium—greens and blue-greens

Chromium—greens

Cobalt/chrome/nickel/iron—grays and blacks

Stains can be very sensitive to their environment. Below is a listing of a number of popular stain types and the way they react to other materials in a ceramic recipe.

Chrome/tin based—burgundy, pinks, and crimsons
Use: calcium, alumina, and silica tin
Use little: alkalies and boron
Do not use: zinc, phosphorus, titanium, or magnesium. Oxidation fire only

Chrome/alumina based—pinks and crimsons
Use: zinc
Use little: calcium and boron
Do not use: lithium

Manganese/alumina—pinks
Use: alumina in high percentages
Do not use: zinc

Chrome/iron compounds—browns and ambers
Use: zinc and high clay
Use little: calcium
Do not use: tin

Titanium—yellow
Use little: calcium
Do not use: tin

Praseodymium—yellow
Use: zirconium and perhaps zinc

FIG. 9–1 Angela Fina. USA. "Six Cup Teapot," 8 inches. The imagery was created with a slip colored with underglaze stains painted on the bisque. The piece was glazed with a translucent mat glaze fired in an oxidation atmosphere to cone 11 in a gas kiln.

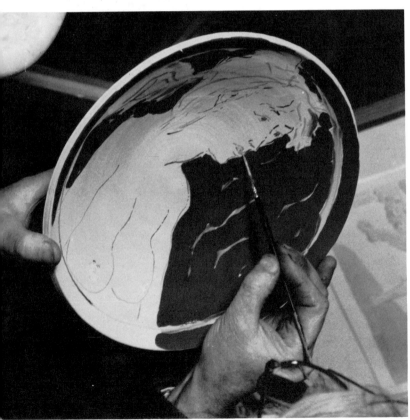

FIG. 9–2 Eric James Mellon. England. Painting oxides onto the bisquit pot. All the coloring oxides are painted onto the bisquit ware. A bush-ash glaze is then poured over the ceramic using a two-pint jug. The work is fired to 1300° C (2372° F) either in an oxidizing electric firing or in a gas kiln reduction firing.

Vanadium/zirconium—greens and blue-greens

All materials seem to work well.

NOTE: Be wary during the firing of the gases from vanadium, which are potentially dangerous.

Chromium—greens
Use: zinc and high percentages of calcium
Do not use: tin

NOTE: The ceramist must be wary of the gases from chrome during the firing, for they are potentially dangerous.

Cobalt
Cobalt's color will change to a violet-blue in the presence of magnesium.

Cobalt/chrome/nickel/iron—grays and blacks
Do not use: titanium or zinc

CHAPTER 10

Analysis of Ceramic Recipes

We make our ceramic recipes, clay bodies, slips, engobes, and glazes from complex compounds. Many are made from naturally occurring minerals that have simply been ground and cleaned. These compounds are relatively inexpensive and contain useful impurities. And perhaps above all, they continue to serve us as well now as they have in the past. Like all compounds, they are made up of elements, some simple and some complex. When we combine three or four complex compounds in a ceramic recipe, it becomes difficult to know what is in the recipe and how it is likely to act in the fire. With molecular analysis, however, we can interpret and understand our recipes.

One approach that can help us is to calculate the various types of molecules in the fired recipe and determine their relationship to each other. The second (and more common) approach is really more of an appraisal than an analysis. We make judgments about the kinds of materials in the recipe and what they contribute to the whole. The first approach is analytic, highly systematized, and accurate, while the second is more intuitive, direct, and not quite as accurate. Each method has its strong points, and each will be discussed at some length in this chapter.

COMPUTED MOLECULAR ANALYSIS

The argument in favor of computed analysis techniques is that glaze analysis is a complex task and cannot be carried out using intuitive methods alone. Because many ceramic materials have a complicated list of oxide ingredients, they can be hard to track. Computational analysis methods are designed to make this easier to do.

Molecular analysis allows the ceramist to convert the weight of a compound in a recipe to a figure that represents the relative number of molecules of an oxide in that compound. An oxide is any element combined with oxygen. Once a ceramic piece is fired, *all* the materials it contains have become oxides. During the firing, oxygen combines with the elements to create oxides. Unfired glaze materials contain either oxygen or carbon. Those that contain oxygen may change little during firing, while those that contain carbon will lose their carbon and combine with oxygen.

Molecular analysis requires some complex procedures that take time to learn, but they provide a useful account of the oxides in a glaze recipe.

To begin, oxides can be divided into three

TABLE 10–1   GLAZE OXIDES CATEGORIZED BY TYPE

Fluxes (RO/R₂O)	Neutral Oxides (R₂O₃)	Glass Formers (RO₂)
calcium (CaO)	alumina (Al_2O_3)	silica (SiO_2)
lead (PbO)	boron (B_2O_3)	zirconium (ZrO_2)
lithium (Li_2O)	iron (Fe_2O_3)	
magnesium (MgO)	phosphorus (P_2O_5)	
potassium (K_2O)		
sodium (Na_2O)		
zinc (ZnO)		

(*Note for advanced experimenters:* Include both RO and R₂O fluxes in your glazes.)

categories: (1) fluxes, (2) neutral oxides, and (3) glass formers. The fluxes have one (or occasionally more than one) atom of the element in question and one oxygen atom (RO). The neutral oxides act as stabilizers. They have two atoms of the element in question, plus three of oxygen (R_2O_3). The glass formers have one atom of the element in question, plus two of oxygen (RO_2). Some examples of glaze oxides are given in Table 10–1.

So that one analysis can be compared with another, the neutral oxides and glass formers are always expressed in ratio to the fluxes. Thus a system is created in which the flux column always is made to total 1. But first we must break down each ingredient of a recipe into its oxide components and organize these oxides into a format that enables us to make this comparison. We will see how this works in a moment.

Analyzing a Simple Recipe

Let's look at a recipe containing only two materials (chosen for its simplicity; it would be of little if any use in actual practice). Both materials are simple and contain only one oxide:

Silica	*50*
Whiting	*50*

We start by finding the molecular weight of the materials in the recipe (see Table 10–2). The molecular weight of a substance is the sum of the atomic weights of a molecule's atoms. We use molecular weight as the tool for converting weight to a number, from the batch weight of a glaze material to the number of parts of the glaze oxides in that substance. For example, using Table 10–2, the molecular weight chart, we find that silica's molecular weight is 60; whiting's (calcium carbonate) molecular weight is 100. To get the molecular equivalent, divide the batch weight by the molecular weight. The *molecular equivalent* is a number that represents the relative quantity of molecules of each oxide in a glaze compound.

The procedure can be formulated in the following equation:

batch weight ÷ molecular weight = molecular equivalent

The batch weight of silica in the recipe is 50, and its molecular weight is 60. And so we determine its molecular equivalent as follows:

$$50 \div 60 = .833$$

The batch weight of whiting in the recipe is 50, and its molecular weight is 100. Thus we can determine its molecular equivalent as follows:

Material	Raw Formula							Molecular Weight
Barium Carbonate	$Ba\ CO_3$							197
Bone Ash	$3CaO\ P_2O_5$							310
Borax	$Na_2O\ 2B_2O_3\ 10H_2O$							382
Cobalt carbonate	$CoCO_3$							119
Copper carbonate	$CuCO_3$							124
Cornwall stone	CaO	.304	Al_2O_3	1.075	SiO_2	8.10		667
	Na_2O	.340						
	K_2O	.356						
Dolomite	$CaCO_3\ MgCO_3$							184
Gerstley borate	Na_2O	.178	B_2O_3	.877	SiO_2	.658		158
	CaO	.822						
Iron oxide (red)	Fe_2O_3							160
Iron oxide (black)	FeO							72
Kaolin	$Al_2O_3\ 2SiO_2\ 2H_2O$							258
Lithium carbonate	Li_2CO_3							74
Magnesium carbonate	$MgCO_3$							84
Nepheline syenite	K_2O	.25	Al_2O_3	1.11	SiO_2	4.65		462
	Na_2O	.75						
Pearl ash	K_2CO_3							138
Petalite	$Li_2O\ \ Al_2O_3\ \ 8SiO_2$							612
Plastic Vitrox	K_2O	.61	Al_2O_3	1.33	SiO_2	13.90		1050
	Na_2O	.34						
	CaO	.05						
Pumice	K_2O	.55	Al_2O_3	1.06	SiO_2	10.49		817
	Na_2O	.45						
Pyrophyllite	$Al_2O_3\ \ 4SiO_2\ \ H_2O$							360
Red Clay (Ohio)	K_2O	.27	Al_2O_3	1.0	SiO_2	6.69		594
	MgO	.125	Fe_2O_3	.275	TiO_2	.08		
	CaO	.025			P_2O_5	.006		
	Na_2O	.04						
Silica (flint)	SiO_2							60
Soda feldspar	Na_2O	.48	Al_2O_3	1.02	SiO_2	5.60		508
	K_2O	.32						
	CaO	.20						
Sodium carbonate	Na_2CO_3							106
Spodumene	Li_2O		Al_2O_3		$4SiO_2$			372
Strontium carbonate	$SrCO_3$							148
Talc	$3MgO\ \ 4SiO_2\ \ H_2O$							378
Tin oxide	SnO_2							151
Titanium dioxide	TiO_2							80
Whiting	$CaCO$							100
Wollastonite	$CaO\ SiO_2$							116
Zinc oxide	ZnO							81
Zirconium silicate	$ZrO_2\ SiO_2$							183

$$50 \div 100 = .50$$

We next have to see how many atoms of silica are in silicon oxide. Looking at the silica formula we see that there is no number in front of the silica: SiO_2. If no number is given in the formula, it is understood that there is one atom present; that is, there is one atom of silica in the silica molecule. The formula for whiting is similar: $CaCO_3$. There is one atom of calcium in the formula for whiting.

At this point we must multiply the molecular equivalent of silica by the number of atoms in a silica molecule:

$$1 \times .50 = .50$$

We now do the same for whiting:

$$1 \times .833 = .833$$

This procedure will be very important as we move on to analyze complex oxides which have a number of atoms in one molecule or which must be represented as having parts of atoms in a molecule.

We can organize our data in a table:

Flux (CaO)	Glass Former (SiO₂)
.50	.833

Now we must bring the formula to "unity." We begin by totaling the flux column. In this recipe we have only one number—.50. (In most recipes we would be adding several figures to determine the total fluxes.) We will use this number, .50, as a "factor" and divide each column by it. Thus we divide the first column, fluxes, by our factor as follows:

$$.50 \div .50 = 1$$

(A number divided by itself always equals 1.) The oxides in the other columns (in this recipe only one other column) can now be expressed as a ratio to the first column. Thus, for the silica column,

$$.833 \div .50 = 1.66$$

Thus there are 1.66 molecules of silica for every molecule of calcium.

Analyzing a More Complex Recipe

In the recipe just analyzed, both materials were simple and contained only one oxide. In the real world, however, our glaze recipes generally include some materials that are complex and contain more than one oxide. For example, nepheline syenite is a complex material composed of four oxides: potassium, sodium, alumina, and silica, in the following ratios:

Fluxes		Neutral oxides		Glass formers	
K₂O	.25	Al₂O₃	1.11	SiO₂	4.65
Na₂O	.75				

This next recipe, which includes nepheline syenite, is a bit more complex:

Nepheline syenite	*90*
Kaolin	*10*

For the analysis procedure, we start with nepheline syenite (see Table 10–2). Then, to find the molecular equivalent, we divide the batch weight of the nepheline syenite (90) by its molecular weight (462):

$$90 \div 462 = .194$$

Now multiply the oxide figures in the nepheline syenite molecular formula by the molecular equivalent. If the tabular format was handy before, it is absolutely necessary for this complex step.

On the left we list the nepheline syenite and kaolin with their batch weight. Next is a column for the molecular equivalent. Then, to the right, are the columns in which to list the oxides (see Table 10–3).

The amount of potassium in nepheline syenite's formula is .25. Multiply this by .194, the molecular equivalent of nepheline syenite:

potassium $.25 \times .194 = .048$

Follow the same procedure for the other oxides in nepheline syenite:

TABLE 10–3   FORMAT FOR ANALYZING OUR RECIPE

	Batch Weight	Molecular Equivalent	Fluxes		Neutral Oxides	Glass Formers
			Na_2O	K_2O	Al_2O_3	SiO_2
nepheline syenite	90					
kaolin	10					

sodium $.75 \times .194 = .145$
alumina $1.11 \times .194 = .21$
silica $4.65 \times .194 = .90$

Follow the same steps for the kaolin, taking the batch weight, 10, and dividing by its molecular weight, 258, to find its molecular equivalent:

$10 \div 258 = .038$

You will remember that if no number is given for an element in the formula, it is understood that there is one atom present. Looking at the kaolin formula we see that there is no number in front of the alumina molecule and a 2 in front of the silica: Al_2O_3 $2SiO_2$ $2H_2O$. This indicates that in kaolin there is one atom of alumina for every two of silica.

The molecular equivalent of kaolin, .038, is multiplied by $1 = .038$ (alumina) and is multiplied by $2 = .076$ for silica.

Our table can now be filled in (see Table 10–4).

At this point we must bring the analysis to unity. First, we total the flux column:

$.145 + .048 = .193$

Thus, .193 becomes our "factor," by which we divide each component. Next, total the alumina column:

$.21 + .038 = .248$

Then, total the silica column:

$.90 + .076 = .976$

Now divide each component by .193 (the flux total):

sodium $.145 \div .193 = .75$
potassium $.048 \div .193 = .25$
alumina $.248 \div .193 = 1.28$
silica $.976 \div .193 = 5.05$

We can now arrange our data in a table:

Fluxes		Neutral Oxides		Glass Formers	
Na_2O	.75	Al_2O_3	1.28	SiO_2	5.05
K_2O	.25				

total = 1

Thus, this glaze contains 5.05 parts of silica and 1.28 parts of whiting for every one part of the fluxes.

Now let's look at a complex recipe composed of four materials. Two of these contain only one oxide, whereas the other two are more complex.

nepheline syenite	65
whiting	19
zinc	2
kaolin	12

TABLE 10–4   MOLECULAR EQUIVALENTS ARE NOW FILLED IN

	Batch Weight	Molecular Equivalent	Fluxes		Neutral Oxides	Glass Formers
			Na_2O	K_2O	Al_2O_3	SiO_2
nepheline syenite	90	.194	.145	.048	.21	.90
kaolin	10	.038			.038	.076

TABLE 10–5 MOLECULAR EQUIVALENTS FILLED IN

	Batch Weight	Molecular Equivalent	Fluxes				Neutral Oxides	Glass Formers
			ZnO	CaO	Na$_2$O	K$_2$O	Al$_2$O$_3$	SiO$_2$
nepheline syenite	65	.140			.105	.035	.155	.651
whiting	19	.19	—	.19	—	—	—	—
zinc	2	.024	.024	—	—	—	—	—
kaolin	12	.046	—	—	—	—	.046	.092
total		.4	.024	.19	.105	.035	.201	.743

The oxides in these compounds are zinc, calcium, sodium, potassium, alumina, and silica. The batch weight of the nepheline syenite, 65, is divided by its molecular weight, 462, to obtain its molecular equivalent.

$$65 \div 462 = .140$$

Then, as in the preceding recipe, the ratio of each component of nepheline syenite is multiplied by the molecular equivalent.

$$\text{potassium} \quad .25 \times .140 = .035$$
$$\text{sodium} \quad .75 \times .140 = .105$$
$$\text{alumina} \quad 1.11 \times .140 = .155$$
$$\text{silica} \quad 4.65 \times .140 = .651$$

Whiting is a simple material and its most important ingredient is calcium. The batch weight of whiting, 19, is divided by 100, its molecular weight, to obtain its molecular equivalent:

$$19 \div 100 = .19$$

The batch weight of zinc, 2, is divided by its molecular weight, 81, to obtain its molecular equivalent:

$$2 \div 81 = .024$$

Kaolin is a bit more complex. The batch weight of the clays, 12, is divided by 258, its molecular weight:

$$12 \div 258 = .046$$

This gives the molecular equivalent of .046 for the alumina atoms in the formula. Double that, .092, for the silica atoms. These data have been entered in Table 10–5.

Complete the procedure by totaling all the fluxes (zinc, calcium, sodium, and potassium) in the analysis.

$$.024 + .19 + .105 + .035 = .354$$

Thus .354 becomes the factor by which the components are divided:

$$\text{sodium} \ .105 \div .354 = .296$$
$$\text{potassium} \ .035 \div .354 = .098$$
$$\text{calcium} \ .19 \ \div .354 = .536$$
$$\text{zinc} \ .024 \div .354 = .067$$
$$\text{alumina} \ .201 \div .354 = .567$$
$$\text{silica} \ .74 \ \div .354 = 2.09$$

The results of our analysis can be put in table form:

Fluxes		Neutral Oxides		Glass Formers	
Na$_2$O	.296	Al$_2$O$_3$	.567	SiO$_2$	2.09
K$_2$O	.098				
CaO	.536				
ZnO	.067				

total = 1

In this recipe there are 2.09 parts of silica and .567 parts of alumina for every 1 part of fluxes.

Once we have completed an analysis, our real work has only just begun. Now we must interpret the data.

Interpreting the Molecular Analysis

The unity analysis results are written in a format that may not be easily interpreted by

TABLE 10–6   ROBERT SCHMITZ'S LIMIT GUIDES

1. Cone 09–04 Leadless Glazes: Transparent to Glossy

0.1–0.8 Na$_2$O	0.07–0.6 Al$_2$O$_3$	1.4–5.0 SiO
0.0–0.5 K$_2$O	0.15–1.0 B$_2$O$_3$	
0.0–0.73 CaO		
0.0–0.4 MgO		
0.0–0.25 BaO		
0.0–0.28 ZnO		

2. Cone 09–04 Leadless Glazes: Satin

0.1–0.8 Na$_2$O	0.2–0.6 Al$_2$O$_3$	1.4–5.0 SiO
0.0–0.5 K$_2$O	0.15–1.0 B$_2$O$_3$	
0.0–0.73 CaO		
0.0–0.4 MgO		
0.0–0.25 BaO		
0.0–0.28 ZnO		

3. Cone 09–04 Leadless Glazes: Mat

0.1–0.8 Na$_2$O	0.2–0.6 Al$_2$O$_3$	1.4–3.5 SiO$_2$
0.0–0.5 K$_2$O	0.15–1.25 B$_2$O$_5$	
0.0–0.5 CaO		
0.0–0.4 MgO		
0.2–0.8 BaO		
0.0–0.28 ZnO		

4. Cone 3–5 Glazes: Transparent to Glossy

0.05–0.4 Na$_2$O	0.2–0.3 Al$_2$O$_3$	2.0–3.0 SiO
0.05–0.4 K$_2$O		
0.05–0.4 CaO		
0.00–0.2 LiO	0.0–0.5 B$_2$O$_3$	
0.00–0.1 ZnO		
0.00–0.05 BaO		
0.00–0.05 MgO		
0.00–0.5 PbO		
0.00–0.4 SrO		

5. Cone 3–5 Glazes: Satin

0.05–0.3 Na$_2$O	0.25–0.35 Al$_2$O$_3$	2.0–3.0 SiO
0.05–0.4 CaO		
0.00–0.1 LiO	0.00–0.3 B$_2$O$_3$	
0.00–0.2 ZnO		
0.00–0.25 BaO		
0.00–0.25 MgO		
0.00–0.3 PbO		
0.00–0.4 SrO		

TABLE 10–6   ROBERT SCHMITZ'S LIMIT GUIDES (*Continued*)

6. *Cone 3–5 Glazes: Mat*

0.05–0.25 Na_2O	0.28–0.4 Al_2O_3	2.0–3.0 SiO
0.05–0.25 K_2O		
0.05–0.4 CaO		
0.00–0.05 LiO	0.00–0.2 B_2O_3	
0.00–0.25 ZnO		
0.00–0.35 BaO		
0.00–0.35 MgO		
0.00–0.2 PbO		
0.00–0.4 SrO		

7. *Cone 8–10 Glazes: Transparent to Glossy*

0.05–0.4 Na_2O	0.3–0.5 Al_2O_3	2.5–5.0 SiO
0.05–0.4 K_2O		
0.00–0.05 MgO		
0.00–0.1 BaO	0.0–0.3 B_2O_3	
0.10–0.7 CaO		
0.00–0.7 SrO		
0.00–0.2 LiO		
0.00–0.1 ZnO		

8. *Cone 8–10 Glazes: Satin*

0.05–0.3 Na_2O	0.3–0.5 Al_2O_3	2.5–4.0 SiO
0.05–0.3 K_2O		
0.20–0.7 CaO		
0.00–0.1 LiO	0.0–0.2 B_2O_3	
0.00–0.2 ZnO		
0.00–0.7 SrO		
0.00–0.2 BaO		
0.00–0.2 MgO		

9. *Cone 8–10 Glazes: Mat*

0.05–0.25 Na_2O	0.3–1.0 Al_2O_3	2.0–3.0 SiO
0.05–0.25 K_2O		
0.20–0.25 CaO		
0.00–0.05 LiO	0.0–0.05 B_2O_3	
0.00–0.30 ZnO		
0.00–0.70 SrO		
0.00–0.40 BaO		
0.00–0.40 MgO		

ceramists. Interpreting a molecular analysis can be accomplished in two ways: (1) by comparing one analysis with another and (2) by comparing the analysis to a group of limit guides. These guides suggest upper and lower limits for the various elements in a glaze. Table 10–6 is a group of limit guides developed by Professor Robert Schmitz of the School for American Craftsmen at the Rochester Institute of Technology. He has designed these to help you interpret unity analysis results.

Let's look at the results of the analysis we just performed:

Fluxes		Neutral Oxides		Glass Formers	
Na$_2$O	.296	Al$_2$O$_3$	.567	SiO$_2$	2.09
K$_2$O	.098				
CaO	.536				
ZnO	.067				

total = 1

If we compare this with Schmitz's charts we see that this analysis conforms closely to category 9, a mat glaze for cone 8–10 firing. Thus we see that this glaze would most likely be successful in the high fire and would most likely be mat surfaced.

The molecular analysis procedure was developed by chemists and adopted by ceramists in the nineteenth century. It has the advantage of taking into account the differing densities of oxides. However, some question whether the division of oxides according to their molecular structure is the most useful format for ceramists. For example, this format lumps boron and alumina in the same category when in fact the two are in most ways dissimilar in their action: alumina is refractory and generally serves to discourage strong glaze melts, whereas boron is highly fluxing and encourages strong glaze melts. This is especially important to the ceramist working in the low fire, who must rely on boron as a strong and relatively safe flux.

To make molecular analysis more useful, I recommend that boron be listed somewhat below alumina in the R$_2$O$_3$ column, but be considered almost the same as the fluxes in the RO column.

RO/R$_2$O	R$_2$O$_3$	RO$_2$
	Al$_2$O$_3$	
	B$_2$O$_3$	

In the future we may use a different format for this process. While still working with mass rather than weight, we might write out the results as percentages. In this format alumina would no longer be placed together with boron. This would remove some of the anomalies of the unity system while still retaining its many useful features.

MATERIALS-BASED EVALUATION OF CERAMIC RECIPES

Evaluation versus Analysis

Not all ceramists use calculated analysis procedures; in fact, the majority do not. The noted potter and author Robin Hopper says of glaze analysis: "From my experience over thirty years of teaching and making pots, I can honestly say that I have almost never seen a calculated glaze that was better than those produced by a solid, sensitive, empirical understanding of the materials we use" (*Ceramics Monthly*, September 1988, p. 57).

As Hopper points out, this kind of analysis is based on an understanding of a recipe as a group of materials and their interactions. Most experienced ceramists can and do evaluate glazes in this way. Some see this method as a quick way to assess a recipe before analyzing it; others find that this procedure is the only one they need. They can do a good job of "reading" the recipe and are able to develop an intuitive understanding of its overall character. In this method the ceramist first tries to get a feel for the materials in a recipe and the elements they are contributing. It is these elements that most influence the character of the glaze at any given firing temperature. Materials-based evaluation gives the ceramist a kind of quick "snapshot" of the glaze. It is somewhat imprecise and certainly not state of the art, but it can be carried out simply and is very useful. Owing to its simplicity and ease of learning, this is probably the best method of analysis for the beginner.

While this method, which I call "guided intuitive glaze analysis," has generally been carried out in a wholly intuitive manner, it can be organized in such a way as to be easily learned even by ceramists without extensive experience of glazes. It then becomes a guided approach to an intuitive process and a widely useful method for appraising ceramic recipes, as we will see.

Following are guidelines for glaze recipes—both general guidelines for all glazes and specific guidelines for glazes at each temperature. We will then see how these guidelines can be used to solve common problems such as interpreting, adapting, or developing a glaze recipe.

The Glaze Clays

kaolin	ball clay
stoneware clay	red clay

Clays enhance the viscosity or stiffness of the glaze; they keep it from running off of the piece. The darker glaze clays can also modify glaze color; stoneware clays and red clays have significant impurities and will darken the glaze.

A 2 to 7 percent clay content in a glaze encourages shiny surfaces; 8 to 14 percent, satin or mat surfaces; 15 to 20 percent, mat or dry surfaces.

The Primary Fluxes

feldspars	silicates
frits	flint

The feldspars are soda, potash, and lithium (spodumene and lepidolite).

There are many frits: boron, sodium, and calcium are the most common.

The silicates are talc and wollastonite.

Ground silica (flint) is 100 percent silica.

The primary fluxes contain silica, which is the basis for most glazes. They can by themselves form a glaze although they often need the help of extra melting from the secondary melters. Often more than one will prove useful in the recipe. One of the most important primary fluxes is ground silica (flint). By itself silica is refractory (nonmelting). However, it is readily melted by those materials in the recipe which are not refractory. It is a useful material in amounts up to 20 percent in glaze types that are highly melted, such as transparent glazes.

Recipes high in primary fluxes (65–90%) tend to be shiny; those moderate in primary fluxes (55–64%) tend to be satin; recipes low in primary fluxes (45–54%) tend to be mat.

Secondary Melters

dolomite	titanium
Gerstley borate	whiting
magnesium carbonate	zinc
tin	zirconium

Secondary fluxes contain no silica and cannot in themselves form a satisfactory glaze. However, they are valuable for modifying glazes (this is why they are called secondary fluxes). It is a good idea to use two or three different secondary fluxes in a given recipe to produce a smoother melting contour. Durable, stable glazes cannot contain any more than 40 percent secondary fluxes because greater amounts deprive the glaze of needed silica. Tin and zirconium can be added to the glaze to encourage opacity. Tin melts well even at the low temperatures but is expensive. Zirconium is more refractory but is much less expensive: as a result, tin is most often used in the low fire and zirconium in the high fire. Tin should be limited to 3 percent or less; zirconium to 8 to 12 percent.

Note: Gerstley borate is available only in the United States and Canada

General Guidelines for Glazes of Any Firing Temperature

Suggested Clay Content	2–20%
Suggested Primary Flux Content	40–90%

Suggested Secondary Flux
    Content   10–40%

Guidelines for Specific Firing Temperatures

Cone 04

This firing temperature requires the most powerful melting materials.

Suggested Primary Fluxes. Cone 04 recipes must contain sodium or boron frits (40–90%). A powerful feldspar such as spodumene or soda spar in amounts up to 20 percent may also be useful.

Suggested Secondary Fluxes. The powerful flux Gerstley borate is useful in amounts up to 40 percent in these recipes. Other secondary fluxes are more refractory and are likely to be useful in amounts up to only 5 percent.

Note: Though lead-containing compounds are fine fluxes at cone 04, I do not discuss their use because of their toxicity.

Cone 02

This temperature range is much less demanding than cone 04; it is quite simple to create leadless, durable, formulations at cone 02.

Suggested Primary Fluxes. Cone 02 recipes must contain sodium or boron frits (45–90%); a powerful feldspar such as spodumene, nepheline syenite, or soda spar may also be useful in amounts up to 20 percent. Flint or a silicate may be useful in amounts up to 20 percent.

Suggested Secondary Fluxes. The powerful flux Gerstley borate is useful in amounts up to 40 percent in these recipes. Other secondary fluxes are more refractory but may be useful in amounts up to 15 percent.

Cone 3

This temperature still requires strong melters. Sodium and boron frits, soda feldspars, and spodumene are very useful in these glazes.

Suggested Primary Fluxes. Cone 3 recipes should contain sodium or boron frits (5–

60%) and feldspars such as spodumene, nepheline syenite, or soda spar make up the rest of the primary flux content. Flint or a silicate may be useful in amounts up to 20 percent.

Suggested Secondary Fluxes. The powerful flux Gerstley borate is useful in amounts up to 40 percent in these recipes. Other secondary fluxes are more refractory, but may be useful in amounts up to 25 percent.

Cone 6

Cone 6 has much of the character of the high fire; there can be less emphasis on powerful melters at this temperature.

Suggested Primary Fluxes. Any of the feldspars are useful in these glazes in amounts of 50 to 80 percent. Boron/calcium frits of moderate melting power are useful in amounts up to 50 percent, but more powerful frits may cause overmelting unless used in amounts up to 40 percent. Flint or a silicate may be useful in amounts up to 30 percent.

Suggested Secondary Fluxes. The powerful flux Gerstley borate is useful in amounts up to 40 percent in these recipes. Most of the other secondary fluxes are more refractory, but may be useful in amounts up to 30 percent. Small amounts (up to 40 percent) of zinc and titanium are strong fluxes and are useful in these recipes.

Cone 9

The big difference between cone 9 and cone 6 is the action of calcium/magnesium-containing materials. They become powerful fluxes by cone 8.

Suggested Primary Fluxes. Any of the feldspars are useful in cone 9 glazes in amounts of 50 to 80 percent. Potash feldspars are particularly well suited to this temperature, and most cone 9 recipes contain them. Spodumene is also a useful cone 9 feldspar, not for its strong melting power but because it encourages exciting colors and visual textures. Boron/calcium frits of moderate melting power are useful in amounts under 40 percent, but more powerful frits may cause overmelting. Flint and a silicate may be useful in amounts up to 45 percent.

Suggested Secondary Fluxes. Many of the secondary fluxes are refractory below cone 8/9 and only come into their own at cone 9. They are useful in amounts up to 40 percent. Gerstley borate can encourage overmelting at cone 9 but may be useful in amounts up to 20 percent.

How Intuitive Glaze Analysis Is Used

Interpreting a Glaze Recipe

Often we see a glaze recipe in a magazine or book and wonder if it is worth testing. To find out, we can use intuitive analysis. Note that to use intuitive analysis, we must have a recipe that adds up to 100 percent. Let us take the following cone 6 recipe:

Gerstley borate	*24*
whiting	*30*
titanium dioxide	*6*
soda spar	*30*
ball clay	*10*

Using the guidelines for primary and secondary fluxes we see that this recipe has only one primary flux, soda spar, at 30 percent and three secondary fluxes—Gerstley borate, whiting, and titanium dioxide—totaling 60 percent. Therefore it is much lower in primary fluxes and much higher in secondary fluxes than is suggested in the general guidelines. This would not be a stable glaze.

The following glaze recipe, with the same materials in very different proportions, would work well. It is within the limits for clay and for primary and secondary fluxes.

Gerstley borate	*14*
whiting	*10*
titanium dioxide	*6*
soda spar	*60*
ball clay	*10*

In another example we look at a cone 02 recipe:

soda frit	*66*
ball clay	*12*
whiting	*18*
zinc	*4*

While this glaze conforms to the general guidelines, it does not conform to the guidelines for cone 02—its whiting content is too high.

Adapting a Glaze—Materials Substitutions

The guidelines given earlier can be used as a basis for making materials substitutions. Frits and feldspars are similar in their basic structure and tend to vary mostly in their flux content. Simply substitute any frit or feldspar for the frit or feldspar in the recipe. Clays, too, are fairly uniform in their basic structure, though the amount and type of their impurities may vary. It is useful to substitute one clay for another in the recipe because these substitutions will significantly alter the look of the fired glaze.

Similarly, the secondary melters can be substituted for each other, sometimes to very good effect. This strategy can be used to "tune up" a glaze by exchanging one material for another whose melting power or character is different. It can even be used to adapt a glaze recipe for use with new materials or a new firing temperature.

For example, let's look at the following recipe:

ball clay	*5*
feldspar	*35*
flint	*20*
whiting	*25*
titanium	*5*
dolomite	*10*

You can substitute a red clay for the ball clay and in this way darken the glaze. You can also substitute 10 percent Gerstley borate for the dolomite. The recipe has now been adapted from a light color to a dark one, and the power of its secondary melters has been increased, thereby making it useful at a lower firing temperature.

Developing a New Glaze Recipe

To develop a new glaze recipe using this method, start with an appropriate figure for the clay, the glass-forming, and the melting materials. For example, to build a cone 6 glaze, do the following:

The guidelines allow for 2 to 20 percent clay. For this example we will choose 9 percent clay to encourage a satin shiny glaze surface.

Between 45 and 80 percent primary fluxes are allowed; we will use 72 percent (also to encourage a satin shiny or shiny surface). This can be filled totally with soda feldspar.

The glaze is finished (and brought to 100 percent) by adding Gerstley borate, a strong melter at cone 6, in the amount of 19 percent.

NEW GLAZE #1

ball clay	*9*
soda feldspar	*72*
Gerstley borate	*19*

Although this glaze will not be very exciting (because few materials were used), it will make a perfectly acceptable glaze.

To make this glaze more interesting we can do the following:

The ball clay is allowed to remain as before. The feldspar is changed: 15 percent is subtracted from the soda spar and 15 percent spodumene is added in its place. Spodumene is a fine feldspar in cone 6 glazes because it encourages strong melting and rich visual textures. Five percent is taken away from the Gerstley borate and 5 percent titanium is added, a material that also encourages visual textures. The result is a much more interesting and individualized glaze surface:

NEW GLAZE #2

ball clay	*9*
soda feldspar	*57*
spodumene	*15*
Gerstley borate	*14*
titanium	*5*

COMPUTER-AIDED ANALYSIS

In learning how to do a molecular analysis, you have had to resort to a complex chart and a great deal of arithmetic. Molecular (unity) analysis is a work-intensive process. As a result, most ceramists rarely analyze their glaze recipes. Furthermore, a great deal of time must be spent teaching analysis methods, leaving little time for teaching the ceramist how to interpret the analysis. Now, however, a number of fine computer-aided glaze-analysis programs are available to the ceramist. With the aid of a computer, analysis procedures become fairly easy and take little time.

Whether you use the intuitive or computational strategies, you still must have an overall understanding of how to make a ceramic recipe. There is no substitute for this knowledge—no substitute for the "solid, sensitive, empirical understanding of the materials of the materials we use," to quote Robin Hopper. No computer program will be able to tell you if a recipe is "good." Whatever tools we use, there are no substitutes for knowledge and good judgment, nor should there be.

CHAPTER 11

Ceramic Forms: Vessels, Sculpture, and Wall Pieces

VESSEL FORMS

The vessel is a universally understood object that has been made in myriad forms for about nine thousand years. Potters over the centuries have never exhausted the possibilities of this simple theme. Not all vessels are made from clay; some are made from basketry materials, some from iron or bronze, stone, lacquer, glass, or, more recently, plastics. However, the bulk of all containers until fairly recently were made from clay. The character of the vessel form is complementary to clay. Wet clay is weak and the potter often will have trouble maintaining the form. Vessels, however, are self-supporting and comparatively strong. They can be formed quickly and inexpensively in clay, while those made of basketry, wood, or stone take time to build.

There is space to mention only a few noteworthy examples of work in the vessel format: the feather-light, highly painted coil pieces from the Yang Shao potters of the second millennium B.C. in China, the rich complex imagery of the Nazca and Moche potters of pre-Columbian Peru, the simple elegant Ting-ware bowls from the Sung Dynasty in China, and the elegant carved porcelain vases made by Adelaide Alsop Robineau in the early part of the twentieth century in the United States.

Utilitarian Vessels

Vessels may be utilitarian, ceremonial, or function strictly as art objects. Utilitarian pottery is an integral part of the ceramic tradition and has played an important role in the history of our material. Clay lends itself to many uses and is still the best material for many functional objects. Today we do not need to use hand-crafted pieces in our daily lives, but many of us prefer to do so because they are expressions of an individual sensibility (see Figs. 11–1 through 11–5). The potter of utilitarian objects has the opportunity to create pieces that are at once objects of beauty and truly useful. In a time when so much around us can be seen as frivolous and ephemeral, such artistry is potentially a source of great vigor.

Interesting and useful examples of utilitarian pottery would have to include Japanese and Korean rice bowls, I-hsing teapots, Nigerian village pottery, and the work of Bernard Leach and Shoji Hamada.

Nonfunctional Vessels

A different view of the vessel form is popular among contemporary ceramists, who see it as a pure form with no utilitarian conno-

(Text continues on page 145.)

Dorothy H. Baker

ANALYZING POTTERY FORM

Pots are a specific type of three-dimensional form not addressed in general design courses. Pots have four characteristics to which I pay close attention: lips, volume, surface, and feet. In analyzing pottery form, I ask myself a lot of questions about those characteristics. The most important of those questions follow:

The lip (along with volume) is often the first thing the viewer sees. What does that lip express, and how clearly does that expression come across? Is the lip bold or quiet? Fluid or crisp? Restrictive of the form's volume or open?

Many people think that volume is the most expressive element in a pot, and with good reason. Hollow volume is what identifies an object as a container. To be an expressive container, the volume needs to be expressive. To be a strong form, the volume of the pot needs to be strong and clearly readable. Does the volume express expansiveness or does it seem restricted? Does it look generous or stingy? Is the volume on a vertical axis, expressing upward growth or stability, or is it on a diagonal axis, expressing movement or change? Is the volume strong (based on a basic shape such as a sphere, ellipsoid, ovaloid, hyperboloid, cylinder, cone, pyramid or cube)? Or is it weak (so caved in or convoluted that its form is unclear)? In forms consisting of combined volumes, are the places where one volume ends and another begins clearly defined or confusing?

The surface of a pot is the skin of its volume and therefore holds great expressive potential. What color, texture, or pattern does that skin have? If the surface depicts representational scenes, does it give the illusion of three-dimensional space or does the space remain two-dimensional and therefore continuous with the skin of the volume? Is the surface smoothly glazed, referring to utilitarian pots, or unglazed and rough, referring to clay sculpture? Does the skin express the same thing as the volume (a taut skin on a restrictive volume) or something different from the volume (a loose, relaxed skin on a tight, energetic volume)?

Although the foot is generally the last thing a viewer sees on a pot, it is a major visual element and, like the lip, volume, and skin, can either aid or destroy the unity of a piece. Is the relationship between the foot and the volume clear? Are they expressing similar ideas and utilizing similar visual elements, or are they expressing totally different ideas and utilizing very different visual elements? Feet also determine much of the body language of the pot: How does it sit on the table? Lightly, as if it barely touches, or firmly, as if attached? Precariously or steadily?

Those who have taken a good three-dimensional design course will see that what I am doing here is applying general principles of three-dimensional design to a specific type of

Dorothy H. Baker. USA. Pitcher, 25 × 21 inches. Thrown and altered form fired at cone 9 reduction.

form. When I make pots, I'm like Dr. Jekyll and Mr. Hyde. Mr. Hyde works, emotes, and intuits in a frenzy of right-brained activity. Then Dr. Jekyll takes over and measures what has taken form against the three criteria by which to judge good art. Once I make the necessary design changes, Mr. Hyde reappears to repair any damage done to the expression of the piece. I flip back and forth until the piece is as good as it's going to get, and then go on to the next one.

Dorothy H. Baker. USA. Teapot, 15 × 22 inches. Thrown and altered form fired at cone 9 reduction.

George Kokis

DYSFUNCTIONAL CATEGORIES

As ceramic artists we seem to have accepted a categorical model that I feel is illogical and dangerous. Within this model there are only two categories: "functional" and "nonfunctional." "Function" is held to mean anything that has utilitarian purpose. "Nonfunctional" includes everything else.

Nowhere in my dictionary are the words "function" or "functional" related to or equated with the concept of utility. And yet "function" and "utility" are often used as synonyms. This general acceptance demonstrates the power of the philosophical doctrine of utilitarianism.

Utilitarianism's chief criterion is "the greatest good for the greatest number." Our materialistic, pragmatic society has allowed this to confuse our goals. If we cannot in our own minds reexamine this culturally derived bias, we will continue to be encumbered by a disabling hierarchy of "function" and "nonfunction."

To disqualify nonutilitarian forms and ideas from being inherently functional is to deny art. What becomes apparent is that a utilitarian bias sweeps the field and is in control of the language. My alternative is simple: *everything* functions—and a most fundamental and necessary human need is to function expressively. I propose an alternate model in which there is only one category—function; "nonfunction" is abandoned since everything functions. The questions then become more interesting. What is the nature of the function this object represents? What attributes does it hold that invites our consideration?

I've identified eight functions, and it amuses me to consider my own work relative to them. These functions are: sensory, evocation, utilitarian, psychological, communication, symbolic, contemplative, and aesthetic. My list is imperfect and probably incomplete. There may be redundancies. Several that appear distinct at first may prove to converge or connect in some way. It may be that the aesthetic function is simply how well it all comes together, how simultaneous purposes and meanings join artfully in an integral image.

The pot/vessel has always been a powerful archetypal metaphor for the human body with its multifunctional capabilities. This is the origin for my model. In application, interesting dynamics surface: functions may or may not be exclusive. In a given case they can be compatible or they can confound one another. A thing can function very well in terms of one attribute and be dysfunctional in terms of another. For example, a Styrofoam cup is quite operable in its utilitarian function but might be held aesthetically dysfunctional, whereas a Cardew teapot may be admired for its strong and sensitive blending of several functional attributes.

We need new models that are based on polyfunctional realities. For example, a pot with a strong utilitarian functional attribute should not be disqualified from serving other functional purposes; its attributes may include both aesthetic and symbolic functions. We give birth to our own vision, and our objects are as our children. They are in our care and we nurture them, give them the best form we can, present them to the world and then—then they are on their own! If we have been successful, the work will reflect, in its attributes, the functional concerns that captivated us and directed their making. Such human gifts always invite human response.

Lewis Mumford wrote, "Art uses a minimum of material to express a maximum of meaning." In that spirit every pot is a small miracle of communication. I hope that the communication I've tried to form here conveys my

George Kokis. USA. "Herme." Hand-formed and sawdust-fired. Photo: Tom Kearcher.

deeper purposes. My proposal is not just a nifty shift in conceptualizing. It is intended to support a truth that every child and artist is in possession of; that through our creative imagination new (or forgotten) unities are revealed. That is our true work. By expressing our small but integral vision, we advance the sensitive relationship among all living things. We give example to form in "agreement." Every pot is designed to hold more than itself—some foodstuff or a bit of space or an idea, and sometimes it can beautifully contain all at once. It is time to reawaken to our potential completeness and give up the short-sighted, exclusive term "nonfunctional."

Ceramic Forms: Vessels, Sculpture, and Wall Pieces

Mary Law

I am primarily a functional potter, and have been for over twenty years. Function continues to provide me with that vital "spark" that makes me want to go into the studio week after week. Sometimes being a potter seems anachronistic, but I know there are many people out there who are moved by the feel of a handle on a cup or the way a plate rim frames a meal—and who want well-made, inspired pots around them on a daily basis. They, and my own similar appreciation of my friends' pots, keep me going!

Mary Law. USA. "Geometric Jar," $11\frac{1}{2}$ inches. Wheel-formed and altered stoneware, salt-fired to cone 9. Photo: Richard Sargent.

Walter Ostrom

My pots are made to function in the everyday complex world of the home rather than in the one-dimensional world of the gallery or museum. A pot should never stop working. In use,

Walter Ostrom. Canada. "Two Vases." Wheel-formed and decorated with slips, underglaze stains, and sgraffito; fired to cone 04–03 in an oxidation atmosphere.

137

it should contain, present, and enhance both its content and its context. A pot comes with all sorts of cultural information—social, economic, aesthetic. I try to keep in mind both the utilitarian and informational roles.

The amount of resistance put up by museums, gallery owners, and the media to actually showing a pot in use is indicative of a culture where objects are validated by their visual role alone. I don't think that flowers in a vase are a prop; these days it is appropriate to be reminded that "use-value" is central to the tradition of Craft.

Earthenware is versatile; it works in the kitchen or the living room. Although both slip/glaze and majolica are traditional earthenware techniques, they differ widely in terms of process and historical association. For holding and garnishing the food we prepare and serve, I choose sturdily potted forms that emphasize material. The flower vases are made for the living room. Their potting is more "refined" and their form and decoration refer to aspects of the history of ceramics. Majolica seems appropriate.

Too many potters follow the model of uniform treatment and decoration of the object regardless of its intended function. When I make a pot, I proceed by clarifying differences.

FIG. 11–1 John Neely. USA. "Black Faceted Teapot," 10 inches. Thrown and faceted, unglazed; reduction-fired. "I have three bodies at work on-going—wood-fired, salt, and reduction cooled. None is glazed in the traditional sense. Surfaces are generated by the interaction of clay and the firing process."

Ceramic Forms: Vessels, Sculpture, and Wall Pieces

FIG. 11–2 Jeff Oestreich. USA. Teapot, 7 inches. A wheel-thrown and altered form finished with a wood-fired Shino glaze. Collection of Sandra and Gerald Eskin, Iowa City, Iowa. Courtesy Pro-Art Gallery, Saint Louis. Photo: Michael Holohan, Pro-Art.

FIG. 11–3 Paul Rozman. Canada. Coffee pot. Wheel-formed majolica, cone 3 oxidation.

FIG. 11–4 Sarah Walton. England. "Lidded Jars," 7 inches (left) and 4 inches (right). Thrown and altered with hand-formed additions; decorated with slips and fired in a light reduction in a salt firing (1280° C). Photo: Mc-Neil.

FIG. 11–5 Valda Cox. USA. Vase, c. 14 inches. Wheel-formed, cone 9 reduction. Photo: Richard Zakin.

Ceramic Forms: Vessels, Sculpture, and Wall Pieces

FIG. 11–6 M. J. Edwards. USA. "Mixed Media Vessel." Wheel-formed with mixed-media additions.

FIG. 11–7 Gordon Baldwin. England. "Bowl Form."

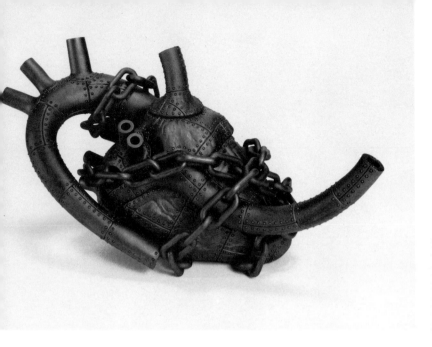

FIG. 11–8 Richard T. Notkin. USA. "Heart Teapot: Ironclad Hostage," 6¼ inches, Yixing Series." Cast-formed stoneware. Courtesy of Garth Clark Gallery, New York and Los Angeles.

FIG. 11–9 Antonella Cimatti. Italy. "Tulipière," 40 cm wide. Slip-cast, low-fire majolica with lusters and glass beads. This piece was created at the Cooperativa Ceramica di Imola (Italy).

FIG. 11–10 Marisa Recchia. USA. Hand-formed, low-fire white earthenware, $10 \times 17\frac{1}{2}$ inches.

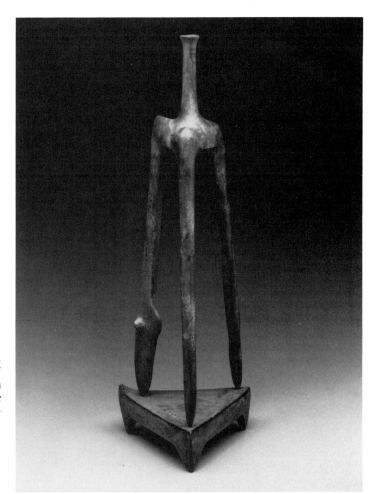

FIG. 11–11 Richard Hirsch. USA. "Vessel and stand #15," $22\frac{1}{2}$ inches. Orange and red terra sigillatas and a cupric sulphate spray were applied to this raku-fired piece.

FIG. 11–12 Angus Suttie. England. "Jug," 38 cm. Hand built, low fire. Angus Suttie has no drawing or idea of what the finished piece will look like when be begins to make it. He first makes a selection of abstract shapes, then joins them together to form the pot. He invents the form as he goes, gradually refining the joined shapes in order to achieve a workable and expressive solution. Decoration is also important to him. Here, too, he refines the result over a period of time. He applies the glazes in a highly improvised way, then refires to alter the color or its tonality, or the shininess or matness of the glaze. Photo: Tim Hill.

FIG. 11–13 Georgette Zirbes. USA. "Pani X," 18 inches. White stoneware, thrown and assembled, with colored slips covered with a clear glaze. The piece was fired in a neutral atmosphere at cone 6.

Donna L. Nicholas

STUDYING POTTERY IN JAPAN

In 1959, as soon as I graduated from college, I went to Japan to teach English. After the first year I decided to study ceramics. I worked for two years in the studio of Morino Kako of Gojozaka, studying under his son Hiroaki. Hiroaki was a stern teacher. I learned partly by imitation (he'd say, "Make a hundred of these"), partly by searching ("It still doesn't look right; work on it some more"), and partly by research (he had me make most of my glazes from scratch). In addition to the basic hand-building and throwing skills, I also learned about loyalty to my teacher and to the school of ceramics to which he belonged.

In 1962 Hirokai went to Chicago to teach for a year and I became if not a full-fledged potter at least a half-fledged one, renting a tiny studio in Kyoto's far southeast side. For just over two years I took part in the neighborhood's monthly routine of making the work, bisqueing, glazing, carrying it all to the kiln, firing, unloading, and hauling it all back. I made a lot and broke a lot.

I never remember a day of homesickness during those five years. I set out to live independently in another culture and to participate in it fully. It has been a powerful influence on my life and work. I now think of myself as an American artist with spiritual roots on both sides of the Pacific.

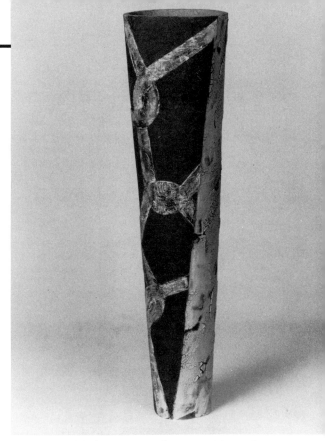

Donna L. Nicholas. USA. "Binary IV," 25 × 7 inches. Low-fire clay body and glazes. Photo: Howard Goldsmith.

---

tations (see Figs. 11–6 through 11–13). They see this attitude as a break from the past, a past in which most pottery was made to be used. In truth, however, in many cultures the best work was nonutilitarian. It is a common phenomenon to find pottery that has been unearthed from gravesites whose sole purpose was the religious veneration of the dead.

SCULPTURE

"Sculpture" is a term that is hard to define. Traditionally the subject of sculpture was the human figure. When U.S. Customs officials were confronted in the 1930s with the import of an abstract sculpture by Constantine Brancusi, they could apply none of the traditional definitions of "sculpture" and were forced to place the piece in the category of "scrap metal." Our definition of sculpture has changed since then and today there is broad agreement that the term "sculpture" can be applied to any art object that is three-dimensional and is neither a vessel nor an architectural structure.

In many ways clay lends itself well to sculpture. Unlike most sculptural media, clay

Itsue Ito

My ceramic sculptural work focuses on "YUME TO SORA," or Dream and Sky. These works are manifestations of my personal experiences as a Japanese who has been in America for seven years. My Japanese experience was permeated by a long history of tradition and the philosophy of Zen, whereas my time in the United States has involved the idea of working free from tradition. I plan to blend and synthesize these influences in my ceramic sculptures.

In my earlier works creativity and freedom of expression were limited because I was producing only utilitarian vessels. However, the imagery of a vessel always inspires my work since Japanese culture centers attention on the beauty as well as the function of a vessel form. At present, my work extends beyond this emphasis and attempts a synthesis of the sculptural elements in the vessel form. This synthesis has become an important way to express my concept of unified harmony among the elements of vessel form and sculpture.

Conceptually, the nature of the sky became my starting point and the emotions that exist in dreams followed. Endless numbers of colors that exist in the sky, with gradations of tone to represent dreams, dominate my imagery. Though natural beauty and dreams are impossible to duplicate, I attempt to express a harmony rather than duplicate natural phenomena throughout my work.

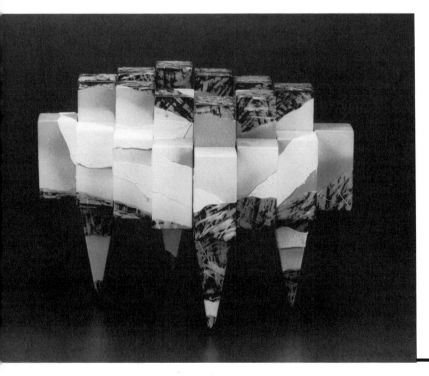

Itsue Ito. Japan. "Shū So," 12 × 12 × 10 inches. "I use the slip-casting technique to create units or modules. I use multiple-firing techniques; each unit is fired a number of times at 1040°C (1800°F) with commercial glazes. I also luster-fire some of the pieces at lower temperatures. After the final firing I assemble the individual units to create the final finished piece. The total piece usually takes about a month to complete."

Doug Kaigler

Much of the work that has evolved from this project has been the product of wondering "What if I try this?" and following the act of placing two or three blocks next to or on top of each other so that forms become new forms, forms become pattern, pattern becomes field, and field becomes form.

These pieces are composed primarily of three modular blocks that were designed to be treated in an incremental manner; beginning with 4-inch-square equilateral pyramid, then an 8-inch-square, then a 16-inch-square pyramid. They were fired separately and attached after the firing.

Doug Kaigler. USA. Mold-formed modular pieces.
Low-fire talc body.

offers a valuable kind of freedom and immediacy. A piece that might take months to carve in marble, or a piece that might require the resources of a large foundry if it were to be cast in bronze, can be built inexpensively in a few days in clay. On the other hand, sculptors who want to work on large-scale pieces or use attenuated, drawn-out forms will have difficulty working with clay. Prob-

lems of size and scale can be dealt with by pushing the forming and firing process to its limits or by segmenting the piece and firing it in sections. Formal limitations often can be dealt with by working around them or by combining clay with other media.

Some important examples of ceramic sculpture are the intense and elegant figural *(Text continues on page 154.)*

John H. Stephenson

TWISTING FORM AND SPACE INSIDE OUT

I often wonder if it was the rotation of the potter's wheel that first attracted me to a scientific drawing of a helix where a single line snaked in equal arcs over and under the horizontal center line. You have noticed the potter's overlapping throwing marks, which leave the impression of a vertical helix as it records the path of the clay in its upward climb. Throwing marks must leave a strong psychological impression on the potter as well as strong impressions on the clay. Sometime after being impressed with the drawing I became the owner of a rusted bit of auger blade pulled from the trash. I was attracted by the auger as a form, but I was also attracted by a metaphor that might be drawn between the iron auger, a tool for moving clay, and a clay auger, which could be a ceramic art form. At this point I liked the form as a horizontal, and more important, I liked the visual push and pull into and out of the axis of the form. The three-dimensional auger form is an extension of the visual energies of the two-dimensional spiral. These forms energize space in a dynamic way. There is nothing passive about them.

On construction sites I saw some larger-scale augers that are used to dig holes in the earth. I continued to develop the metaphor of these large augers that dig in the earth and an auger form made from clay and the materials of the earth. I seemed to hold onto this dynamic horizontal twisting form as a clay form. It was a clay form that seemed to exist in a horizontal space where there was no force of gravity. Or was it so energized that it overcame that force?

But the auger proved to be a difficult form to make horizontally in clay. Small vertical versions can be thrown on the potter's wheel, but this was not what I had in mind. I decided to work the auger form using an armature that could be removed when the piece was firm enough to stand on its own weight. As I started working the auger form in clay, what had been the horizontal center line in the drawing became a horizontal piece of aluminum pipe suspended at each end by a vertical two-by-four. It looked and functioned like a rotisserie. This was my first use of an armature in the clay-forming process. The pipe would become the center of the piece from which I would start working the clay. Holes were drilled at inter-

John H. Stephenson. USA. "Twisted Earthscape #14." Low-fire ceramic sculpture. Photo: Dirk Bakker.

vals perpendicular to the pipe through which aluminum rods were placed. The straight rods, while they were perpendicular to the center pipe, were placed in such a way that they described the twist of the auger form.

The center pipe was wrapped and tied with newspaper. Then clay was worked around this center of the form. Like a rotisserie, the auger form could be rotated as I worked on it. Working from the center toward the outer extremities, the piece was completed without a sense of bottom or top. The clay auger was being supported on the center pipe. As the clay became stiff enough, it was allowed to rest on the form itself. First the aluminum rods were removed and finally the center pipe was removed.

The process of working with the armature worked successfully and it would allow for form variations. The mind is capable of stretching the form concept in many different directions. These variations permit a change of expression in the form. Working with the helix concept, I envisioned and completed a series of twisting horizontal clay augers. From complex concepts I moved to a reductive, simplified concept of a single twist of a two-dimensional plane.

Conceptually compressing the auger form, it closed somewhat like an accordion. Then as I studied the end view of the auger, I noticed that it was circular like the plate form on the wheel, but that the form pulled inward in a continuing form involvement. Because the auger form as it eventually developed had a different feeling from the pot thrown on the wheel, I moved the concept to five-foot vertical forms

that twist somewhat like a greatly enlarged, twisting blade of grass. Then the question came, "What would happen if the form twisted in a circle on itself to become a clay Möbius?" For this form a thrown-clay donut became the axis through which a wooden stick could be stuck to describe the form. In this case the axis didn't need to be removed like the metal one on the straight horizontal augers.

The artist's role at its best connects reality or outer vision and fantasy or inner vision in such a way that it reflects the culture of a given time and place. I enjoy evolving ways of working clay, but technique and process are only important as they meet the needs of visual expression, which must come first. For instance, in doing yoga I personally felt the twist of the auger form in my own spine. It was more than an intellectual concept; it was something physical that I could feel. It became a part of an inner vision, which in turn became connected to an outer vision of my world.

For me the plastic nature of clay has been a perfect match for the mind as it conjures up form largely from an inner vision. The mind instructs the hands as the clay takes shape before the eyes. The mind also instructs the entire process and expects some aesthetic experience in return. As we look at historical ceramics we are carried back in time and get a sense of what was important to the inner vision of earlier clay workers. Something undeniable expresses itself to us in the object. There are times when the mind seems capable of turning form and space inside out.

John H. Stephenson. USA. Armature for the Auger Armature Series. The center axis is rotated so that the form may be worked from every angle.

Nina Höle

The Danish arts and crafts can be traced back to the old apprenticeship traditions, and it is

Nina Höle. Denmark. "Sculptural Piece," hand formed. "I am using underglazes and a wide range of low-fire glazes, oxides, and washes and then raku fire at 99°C–1000°C (1814–1832°F) in an electric kiln. The work is then reduced." Photo: Copyright Henning Skov.

this direct line that our only school for ceramics faithfully followed until recently. A typical piece from this period would be a small, quick form glazed in subdued colors and decorated with delicate patterns, often herringbone, and always with a quality of fine craftmanship. Now we have new schools and competitions.

In the past it was difficult for anyone other than painters and people from the outside to find acceptance of anything experimental. The new generation is much more versatile and more aware of the world around them. They look to America, England, and the rest of Europe.

My feeling is that something new will come along, perhaps based on American technology and freedom, but rooted in the old European art traditions. By that time, it will be interesting to see if something typically Danish emerges.

I began my education in Denmark by studying painting and graphic arts. In the 1970s I went to the United States and became involved with ceramics and I have stayed with it ever since, specializing in the raku technique. I am fascinated with the possibilities that clay and glazes give, and the raku technique provides the elements with which I am most at home. The fast firing provides experimental possibilities, a quick result, using low-fire colors and lusters. My work is constantly changing; curiosity and realization of a thought are my motivations.

I work out my ideas on paper, making a lot of drawings before I am certain which way I want to go. I continue to go back to the drawings throughout the process of building. I use a white low-fire clay with 30 percent grog. I build my pieces out of slabs, working on the floor by throwing the clay against the floor to strengthen and make the shapes from which I form my construction. I try for a spontaneous, not overworked appearance where form and color work as one.

Roy Cartwright

One of my most important experiences was working with Frans Wildenhain. While I was a graduate student with the School for American Craftsmen at Rochester Institute of Technology, I was his apprentice for the 250-foot-long mural at the National Library of Medicine in Bethesda, Maryland. I came to know Frans as an artist, not just as a teacher and "charming fellow." He was relentless in his pursuit of the truth. Reading poetry, discussing current events, listening, arguing, drawing, painting, sculpting, potting—it was all very intense and done in the pursuit of making connections and trying to see the big picture. He worked himself harder than he worked his students. He saw life anew each day, and he remained fresh to his version. These are values he passed on to me.

At one point in my career I made a decision not to use the wheel as a tool for sculpture. This decision was not based on vessel-oriented versus non-vessel-oriented work. It was based simply on discovering sculptural-form possibilities. If I worked more slowly, I felt there were more small decisions to be made along the way.

My large mosaic pieces are constructed from red earthenware:

red art	40
grog	30
ball clay	20
nepheline syenite	10
barium carbonate	1

Cone 1 is the maximum temperature. There is nothing special about the building process except that I work thicker than normal, about 1-inch thick for a 4-foot-tall piece and 1 1/2 to 2 inches thick for large pieces. I make and glaze the slabs of clay and break them into tiles, which I attach to the piece with a paste-type epoxy and grout with an exterior grout.

When I'm working on smaller sculpture, I work for short periods of three or four weeks at a rather frantic pace. I feel like I'm trying to eliminate as many conscious thoughts as possible—trying not to think before I act, trying not to worry about making a mistake, trying not to care if others would approve or disapprove. I make decisions based on intuitive feelings and a gut-level aesthetic response to the material as it shapes and forms in front of me.

Often I will put stains or slips on pieces while I'm working. These are not meant to be final finishes, but they help to set up a situation later, after the firing, that I can react and respond to while I'm painting the piece.

After I've made ten or twelve pieces, it may be a long time before I get back to them to finish the surfaces. Then the struggle to make correct but intuitive decisions begins all over again. Often a piece will sit in front of me, ready to be painted, for weeks. Sometimes I can do three a day. When it works, I really enjoy the sense of "rightness" that these pieces have.

Roy Cartwright. USA. "Flower of Death," 27 inches. Slab- and coil-built earthenware, fired to cone 1, then painted with oil paint and smoke-fired. Photo: Jay Bachemin.

Robert L. Wood. USA. Building "Forgotten Oculus."

1. Paddling an element of the form—an arch.

2. Moving an arch element into position.

3. Placing the element on a work support.

4. Both sides of the arch in place.

5. Working on the central "keystone" element.

6. Refining the central "keystone" element.

7. Setting the "keystone" element in place. The assembly is complete.

8. Finishing the work.

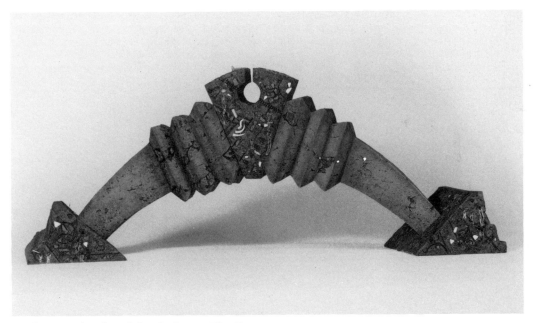

9. The completed and fired piece: "The Forgotten Oculus," 26 × 63 × 33 inches. Earthenware clay, miscellaneous kiln parts, pottery shards, glass, and oxides. Photos: Steven E. Kennedy.

Robert L. Wood

REFLECTIONS ON HAND-BUILT SCULPTURE

For my large, hand-built sculptural pieces, first slabs are rolled out to about 1/2–3/4″ and textured with an array of collected objects. Sometimes using a template, the slabs are cut to size with the edges mitered so that no seam will be apparent after they are joined. The slabs are slipped and scored, then joined, pressing until the slip oozes out the joint. Next a coil is inserted down the interior seam and welded into both sides for extra bond strength.

Each section is constructed separately with an internal support system mainly consisting of slabs or extruded tubes that allows for the almost leather-hard sections to be assembled. This also cuts down on warping or cracking during drying and firing and gives strength to the overall structure. All of the sections are built hollow. I like to work on the form after it is assembled, making alterations and additions. Usually I try to keep the clay in an pre-leather-hard state so that the clay can still be bent, pushed, crushed, or manipulated.

When the piece is finished, I allow it to dry together as much as possible so that the sections will shrink evenly. Any section that will rest on a kiln shelf in the firing is placed on thin slabs with sand to ensure even drying and firing. This helps prevent the corners from warping or cracks developing along the bottom. It also makes loading the kiln easier as each section can be pushed into the kiln on the slab. In this way I never have to lift the actual piece into the kiln or touch the surface. The piece is allowed to dry slowly, usually for up to two weeks.

When the piece is dry, I spray it with a frit and oxide mixture or with terra sigillata. Then areas are rubbed off for highlighting. I once-fire the pieces to cone 3 in a gas kiln with a medium to heavy end reduction.

For the highly textured areas of my pieces, I embed rolled slabs with an array of collected objects that are fragmentary yet give clues as to the meaning within the form. Using the surface of the clay like an Abstract Expressionist painter uses paint, I push, gouge, poke, scrape, and beat objects into the surface of the clay. To embody the ceramic process of transformation by fire, I use fragments of kilns and kiln parts to create a vigorous surface that is embedded with broken pieces of bricks, kiln posts, kiln shelves, stilts, electric kiln coils, shards of common dinnerware sets, glass, and cone packs. Common objects of construction of machines, of industry, such as gears, nuts, bolts, steel shavings, wire, and grids, all add texture to the clay. Often only the impressions of objects are left in the clay, while other times the objects themselves are actually fired into the clay. Glass and oxides melt and run, steel oxidizes, and plastics disintegrate with only trace elements remaining.

pieces of the Haniwa period in Japan; the complex, threatening figural sculpture of Pre-Columbian Mexico; the elegant dancing figures of Leonard Agathon von Weyenfeldt, made at the turn of the century in France; the ceramic collages of Joan Miró and Lorens Artigas, and the brilliantly painted figural work of the contemporary ceramic artist Robert Arneson.

Modular Forms and Mixed Media

The ceramic sculptor may decide to make modular forms separately and assemble them after firing. These assembled pieces can be held together with wire, bolts, or other fasteners or cemented with mastic or glue. This technique allows the ceramist to build a large, difficult piece from small, easily handled

Deborah Horrell

THE WHY OF MIXED MEDIA

Clay was the medium I was reared on. The marriage came hard, fast, and blinding. The complexities, complications, and limitations of clay later became evident. I began to "stray" into pencil and colored pencil on the clay surface. Purism dissipated, and I freely explored other materials to enhance my clay sculpture.

Once liberated from the tortures of ceramics, I began to recognize the benefits of working in other materials, such as wood, glass, and paper, which offered immediate results.

Scale, too, played a role in my sojourn with mixed media. My ideas demanded a larger format, and clay, unless one has incredible facilities or is fortunate enough to be working in an environment of great capacity, is limited. So alternative materials again made it possible for me to make dynamic jumps from ideation to realization.

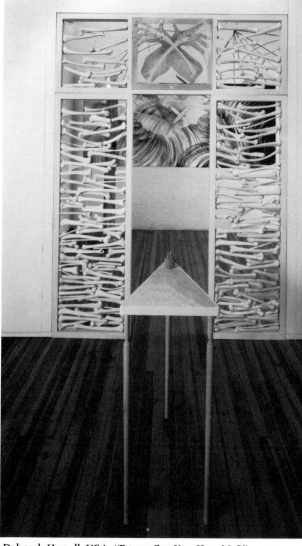

Deborah Horrell. USA. "Poppa Can You Hear Me?" 8 × 10 × 15 feet. Mixed-media installation of porcelain, glass, and wood. Photo: Stephen Satori.

155

Zorin Katarenovski

"Alfred" is one of a group of four portraits of friends that are intended to be viewed together. In this project I am trying to depict the intellect and spirituality of friends without any concern for their physical appearance or relationship to one another. I am attemping to reveal a symbiosis of the bizarre and the formal, which is so beautifully evident in the original model.

In this piece the clay body is white earthenware with grog, vermiculite (an expanded mica product used in ceramics as a filler), and glass crystals. The surface of the piece has been stained with a blue stain and various oxide colorants. The piece has been finished with a modified commercial glaze: Duncan Ultra Clear modified by the addition of equal parts of a high-soda frit and Gerstley borate. It was fired in oxidation to cone 04. After firing, chicken wire, tar, sand, and tinted epoxy were used to further modify the imagery.

Zorin Katarenovski. Canada. "Alfred," $14\frac{1}{2} \times 12 \times 14$ inches. Photo: Peter Brickell.

Katherine L. Ross

"Vessels in the Landscape" is from a new series concerned with the impact of mass production on the individual and its residue as the future artifacts of our culture. Contemporary containers (vessels) in popular culture, as experienced by the masses, are the multitudes of industrially produced plastic detergent bottles that line row after row of grocery store shelves. These are functional objects that every person experiences personally. We each use our own brand, so to speak.

As a ceramist, I have chosen to work with this form because it is truly the contemporary vessel, and like ceramic shards from the past, will remain for thousands of years as an ingredient in our landscape. Through these we will remember, evoke, and experience our own past.

Chain-link fences are a device to control and contain portions of the landscape. I use them to construct containers to hold and control clay images of discarded contemporary vessels. These vessels have the color and surface of the landscape.

Katherine L. Ross. USA. "Vessels in the Landscape," 24 × 94 × 14 inches (each piece 24 × 24 × 14). Mixed media with steel and ceramic elements. The slip-cast ceramic elements are low fire, finished with terra sigillata and saggar fired.

Linda Mosley

This combination of montage and pottery is an expression of how my life is made up of many layers of interests and activities. The montages illustrate my feelings and goals in compositions of symbols, such as the hands lovingly wrapping and tying knots as for a gift, an ordered grid falling into random order, Fibonacci's Golden Mean and the spiral representing growth, the snail living within a spiral, and the turtle being strong and wise.

In looking at the work, the challenge is to decipher whether images are carved, drawn on, or printed on the clear plastic wrapper. Of all the forms that can be made on the potter's wheel, the inverted cone was chosen because its straight sides are similar to curved planes of paper, and its closed form allows the greatest outer surface area to view. It is also the greatest challenge to activate because it is extremely stable and symmetrical. I found that by making my montages into long rectangles they could be arranged in spirals, creating an organic counterpoint to the geometry of the cone.

Linda Mosley. USA. "Toss & Wrap," 9¾ inches high. Porcelain clay body, wheel-formed and carved, wrapped in a mylar photocopy of a collage and two layers of fabric tied with cord and thread. © Linda Mosley 1986.

Linda Mosley. USA. "Pointing It Out," 7½ inches high. Porcelain clay body, wheel-formed and carved, wrapped in a mylar photocopy of a collage and Japanese paper tied with cord and thread. © Linda Mosley 1986.

forms. It also allows materials such as wood, plastic, or metal to be used with clay. Using other materials can maximize the positive characteristics of clay as a material for sculpture while minimizing its limitations.

Technical Problems with Ceramic Sculpture

A ceramic sculpture is difficult to build and fire because the walls of the piece are likely to vary a great deal in thickness. In fact, it is much more common for sculptural pieces to crack or explode during the firing than vessels. These problems, however, can be minimized. The clay body can be altered by adding materials that will make it more robust. Two materials, grog and chopped nylon, are especially useful for this purpose (see pages 15–16). Sculptural pieces also tend to be particularly vulnerable at their joins, and often sculptural forms have a great many joins. During the building process, the joins can be carefully cemented with slip and reinforced with additions of clay.

During the drying period, sculptural pieces should be carefully wrapped so that they will not dry unevenly or too quickly. During the early part of the firing, the kiln should be heated slowly. At this stage of the firing, pieces are particularly vulnerable to cracking and exploding. In an electric kiln, the heat should

(Text continues on page 169.)

FIG. 11–14 Bruno La Verdiere. USA. "Temple Guardian," 50½ inches. Hand-formed stoneware fired to cone 6 in a fuel-burning kiln. This is solid construction, modeled and carved; assembled with steel pins after firing. Photo: © Joseph Levy.

159

FIG. 11–15 Nancy Selvin. USA. "Still-Life." Hand built, low fire. The vessel is intended as an emblem rather than a container form. Photo: Charles Frizzell.

FIG. 11–16 Robert L. Wood. USA. "Loss of a Friend," 74 inches. Hand-built and thrown forms finished with a frit/coloring oxide surface or terra sigillata; single fired at cone 3 in a gas kiln with a medium to heavy final reduction. Collection of Martin and Joan Messinger, New York City.

Ceramic Forms: Vessels, Sculpture, and Wall Pieces

FIG. 11–17 Robert L. Wood. USA. "A Matter of Semantics," 32 inches. Earthenware clay, miscellaneous kiln parts, pottery shards, glass, and oxides.

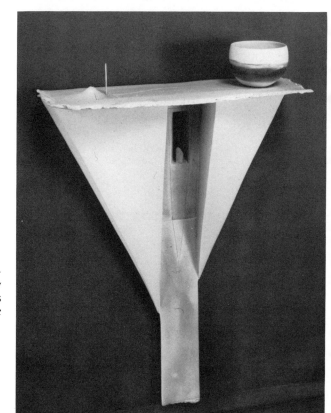

FIG. 11–18 Paula Winokur. USA. "Architectural Remnant II," 34 × 25 inches. Porcelain clay body constructed from slabs (the bowl form is thrown); finished with sulfate colorants and glaze pencils. Photo: Stephen Fiorella.

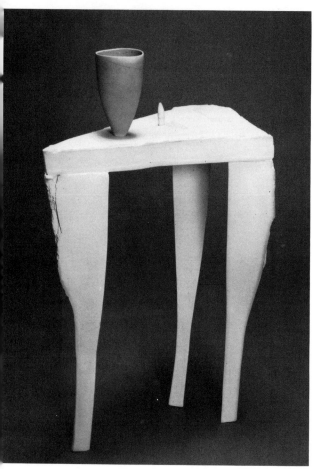

FIG. 11–19 Paula Winokur. USA. "Table: Triangulation #1," 26 × 10 inches. Porcelain clay body constructed from slabs (the bowl form is thrown); finished with sulfate colorants and glaze pencils. Photo: Stephen Fiorella.

FIG. 11–20 Bill Stewart. USA. "First Pueblo," 65 inches. Hand-built terra-cotta made in two parts; finished with commercially prepared glaze fired to cone 04. Pieces of this sort require a very strong clay body. Stewart's clay body recipe, fired at cone 06–04: red art 33, ball clay 26, nepheline syenite 7, barium carbonate 1, coarse grog 17, mullite 16. Photo: Earl Cage, Museographics.

FIG. 11–21 Deborah Black. Canada. Dining Room World View—Still Life," 60 inches. "The sculptures are made from pieces of clay pressed into molds of body parts (mine) and attached to a hand-built core made from chunks of clay. The red earthenware clay with 30 percent grog is painted with colored terra sigillatas, burnished, and fired once to cone 04."

FIG. 11–22 Sally Michener. Canada. "Inside Out—Terracotta Still Lifes," life size (detail). Fired clay with acrylic and/or oil paint. Photo: Trevor Mills.

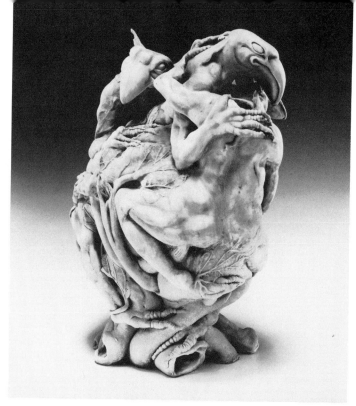

FIG. 11–23 Ruth Barrett-Danes. England. "Predator Birds," 30 cm. Porcelain clay body, unglazed except for the eyeball.

FIG. 11–24 Ruth Barrett-Danes. England. "Dancing Swine," 36 cm. Porcelain clay body, unglazed except for the eyeball.

FIG. 11–25 Robert Shay. USA. Hand-formed, multifired stoneware and mixed media. "This work was multifired over a wide variety of temperatures and atmospheres. Some of my pieces contain parts made of fused glass and many have cast bronze appendages held under tension with greenhide (gut). The pieces, generally small and hopefully artful, are a quirky amalgamation of Anasazi/Viking, primeval/prehistoric, vessel/implement, utilitarian/ritual, fetish/decorative art objects."

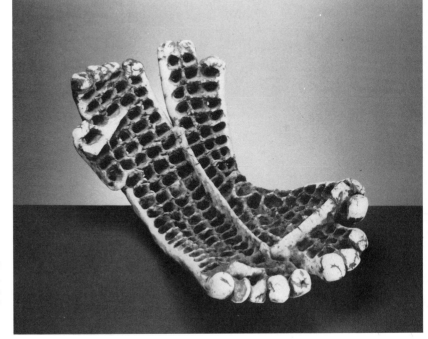

FIG. 11–26 William D. Parry. USA. "Net V," 30 × 20 inches. Hand-formed sculpture. "I use a downdraft, forced-air car kiln fueled with propane and fire to cone 6." Collection of Henry Bauer. Photograph: Brian Oglesbee.

FIG. 11–27 Hiroaki Taimei Morino. Japan. "Work 87–27." Slab construction, fired to cone 9 in a reduction kiln, then fired with brightly colored glazes in a low-fire oxidation kiln. Photo: Takeshi Hatekeyama.

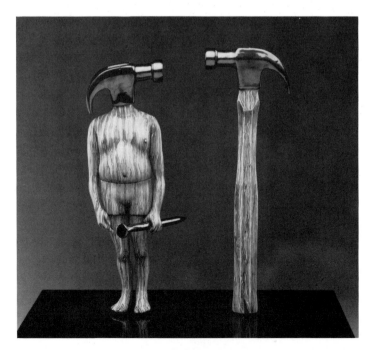

FIG. 11–28 Patti Warashina. USA. "The Imposter," 21 × 17 inches. Mold-formed and altered with hand-formed additions; low-fire talc body finished with commercially prepared lusters and glazes. Photo: Roger Schreiber.

FIG. 11–29 Patti Warashina. USA. "A Step Out of the Dark," 27 × 25 inches. Low-fire talc body finished with underglazes; mixed-media elements. Photo: Roger Schreiber.

FIG. 11–30 Hana Bibliowitz. Colombia. "Sculptural Environment." Low fire, hand built. Ms. Bibliowitz built this elaborate installation in her home in Bogotá. She has studied in Colombia and in the United States.

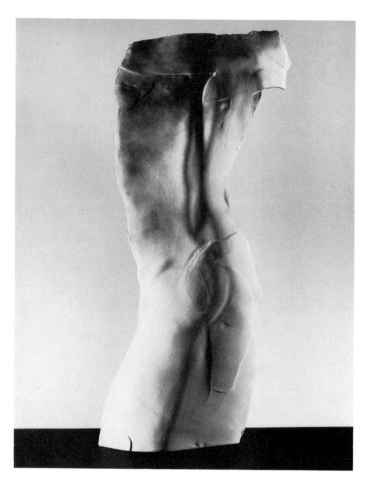

FIG. 11–31 Christie Brown. England. "White Male Figure," 32 inches. "My figural work is slab built, modeled, painted in vitreous slip, fired at 1160° C (2120° F), and smoked and waxed." Photo: Tim Imrie.

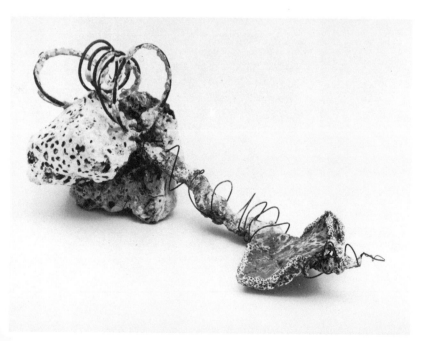

FIG. 11–32 Gillian Lowndes. England. "Collage with Bathroom Tile," length 35 cm. Sand-coated Egyptian paste. Clay-covered chain spring and tile with nichrome wire. Firing temperature 1260° C.

be turned to a low setting and the door left open for a few hours. In a fuel-burning kiln, the damper should be left open and either the pilot burners used or the normal burners turned on low. When firing thick or complex pieces, keep the rate of heat rise very low for an extended period, perhaps overnight or even longer. (Sculptural pieces are shown in Figures 11–14 through 11–32.)

CERAMIC WALL PIECES

Ceramic wall pieces are clay constructions which are meant for wall placement (Figures 11–33 through 11–52). The ceramist who makes wall pieces has great freedom and can employ complex and rich imagistic strategies.

In the past most wall pieces were intended for public places where they would be seen by large numbers of people and would be strongly communicative. Some of the best contemporary wall pieces are still done in this way. On the other hand, pieces can be private and personal and be created in the same way an artist creates a painting on canvas. The only difference is the medium—clay.

Single- and Multiple-Element Formats

Wall-piece imagery can be created from a single element or from many elements. Ceramic panels, for example, are created from a single element, whereas mosaic and tile compositions are made up of multiple elements. In a piece composed of multiple elements, no particular segment has an individual identity; only when they are assembled is an image created.

Ceramic Wall Panels

Pieces made from a single element, such as panel compositions, are uncomplicated, easy to place in a home or gallery, and are intimate in character. In addition, the artist need not worry about the demarcations between each element. In some cases ceramic wall panels may be reminiscent of paintings; in others the artist may have exploited the dimensional characteristics of clay. Panel pieces may be permanently mounted on the wall or hung like a painting.

Mosaics and Tiles

Wall pieces made from multiple elements also have advantages, the main one being size. This is an important factor, for usually no single ceramic piece can be more than 65 cm (25 inches) in its largest dimension. Using multiple elements, whole walls, buildings, and even complexes of buildings can be ornamented with tiles or mosaics.

Mosaics are assembled from small fragments called tesserae. The tesserae are arranged in such a way as to create an image. Tiles, like mosaics, do not have an individual identity. Tesserae and tiles may be made from colored clays or covered with a slip, wash, or glaze.

When a group of tesserae or tiles is placed together, the interstices between each element may be obtrusive. Is the artist to ignore these demarcations and ask us to pretend that they do not exist? Or should the artist work with the demarcations and integrate them with the imagery of the piece? As a practical matter, in pieces that are meant for large (often public) spaces and are to be seen from a distance, the artist may choose to ignore the demarcations. From a distance, the imagery will seem to blend together and each individual segment will become part of the whole. In pieces meant for smaller spaces where they will be viewed up close, the artist often acknowledges the demarcations and designs them into the imagery.

The wall-piece format offers the ceramist many advantages and a wide range of possibilities. In recent years there has been a heightened interest in this format, encouraged by an enthusiasm for sculptural and nonutilitarian work. From a technical standpoint, wall pieces can free the ceramist from

(Text continues on page 179.)

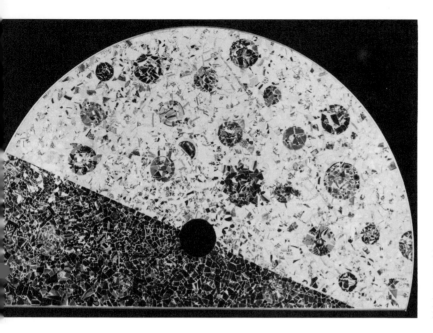

FIG. 11–33 Susan Tunick. USA. "In the Middle," 48 × 72 × 18 inches. Fired clay (some shards from broken pieces of commercial ware) mounted on wood.

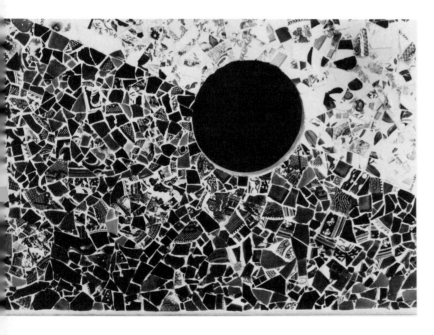

FIG. 11–34 Susan Tunick. USA. "In the Middle" (detail).

Ceramic Forms: Vessels, Sculpture, and Wall Pieces

Jerry L. Caplan. USA. Building "The Wall of Caring," Ceramic Mural, New Kensington General Hospital, New Kensington, Pa. Photos: Donnie Pomeroy.

FIG. 11–35   Pieces finished and polished before firing.

FIG. 11–36   Mapping the placement of the pieces on a plywood support.

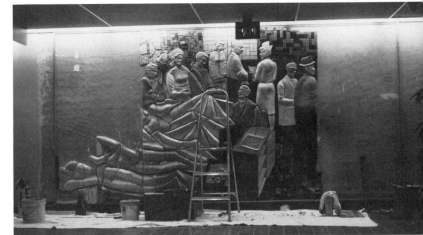

FIG. 11–37 Mounting the pieces on the installed support panels.

FIG. 11–38 The finished piece. Cone 05–02 satin mat glazes.

FIG. 11–39 Henry H. Lyman, Jr. USA. "Merlin's Advice," 35 inches. Porcelaneous whiteware fired at cone 6 oxidation in an electric kiln. Photo: Rick Singer.

FIG. 11–40 Ann Mortimer. Canada. "Interior Space," 15¾ × 17 × ⅝ inches. Hand-formed low-fire wall piece. Photo: Randy Bulmer.

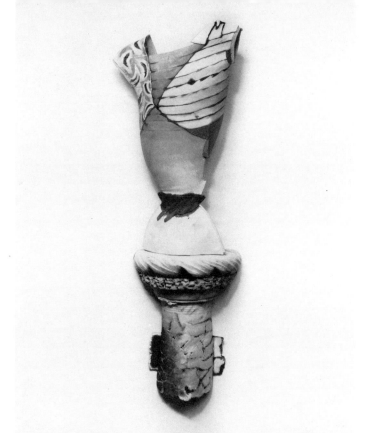

FIG. 11–41 Nancy Jurs. USA. "Kychyna," 65 inches. Wall-hung pedestal in stoneware and acrylics. Photo: Richard Margolis.

FIG. 11–42 George Mason. USA. "Travel Notes." One of five relief tiles (each 16 × 22 inches). Courtesy The Maine Arts Commission.

FIG. 11–43 Angelo di Petta. Canada. "Mural." Made for the C.I.L. Corporation of Canada; mold-formed tiles and additions; cone 04 prepared glazes, some of which have been altered with additions of such materials as lithium carbonate. Photo: Ron Vickers.

FIG. 11–44 Barbara L. Frey. USA. "Coconino County Vista," 19 × 15 inches. Hand-built ceramic wall piece: earthenware, slips, glazes. Photo: Richard Margolis.

FIG. 11–45 Ruth Duckworth. USA. "The Creation," 14 × 16 feet. Stoneware mural for Congregation Beth Israel, Hammond, Indiana. Photo: Thea Burger Associates, Inc.

FIG. 11–46 Elizabeth MacDonald. USA. Segmented wall piece, 29 × 29 inches. Photo: Bob Rush.

FIG. 11–47 Richard Zakin. USA. Terra sigillata wall piece, 45 cm high. Low-fire body, hand-formed, terra sigillata and sgraffito imagery; fired to cone 03 in an electric kiln. Photo: Thomas C. Eckersley.

FIG. 11–48 Kathryn Holt. USA. "Bien," 16 × 16 inches. Piece formed from fiberfax rectangles, painted with slips, glazes and terra sigillatas; fired to cone 06 in an oxidation atmosphere; salt is sprinkled on the tiles to create a fumed imagery.

FIG. 11–49 Barbara Strassberg. USA. Wall piece, 14 inches square. Commercially prepared glazes applied with a brush; low-fire, bisqued at cone 04, and glaze-fired at cone 06; finished with a fixative spray.

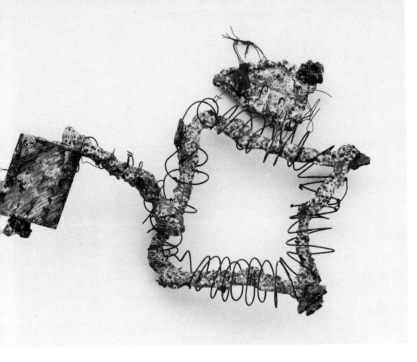

FIG. 11–50 Gillian Lowndes. England. Wall piece, 25 cm high. Gillian Lowndes's pieces are collages made from metal objects such as chair springs, steel and nichrome forms, ceramic materials (Egyptian paste and recycled clay objects, broken cups, and bathroom tiles (all coated with sand, coarse molochite, or alumina to produce granular surfaces). After the firing, resin-coated metal objects may be added to the piece. Some of the clay elements are fired to 1260° C (2300° F); others are low-fire Egyptian paste. Many of the pieces are deliberately smashed before or after firing and then reassembled.

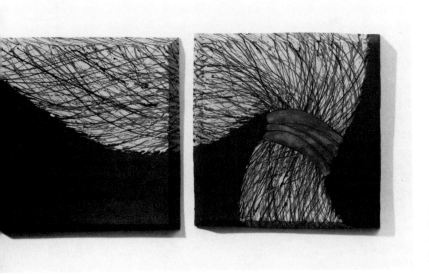

FIG. 11–51 Donna Nicholas. USA. "Shimenawa II," 19 × 40 inches. Low-fire clay body and glazes. Photo: Richard Margolis.

Ceramic Forms: Vessels, Sculpture, and Wall Pieces

FIG. 11–52 John H. Stephenson. USA. "Table Partners," 42 × 39 inches. Pit-fired clay fastened to a painted and welded aluminum armature.

certain formal constraints because the wall or the backing in effect supports the form. This gives an artist the opportunity to use elements that otherwise would not work in clay.

After a period of relative neglect, a period in which we thought of clay only in terms of vessel or sculptural forms, we are now beginning to see a great deal of varied and highly original work in this genre.

CHAPTER 12

Clay Forming

Among the many choices we have to make as ceramists is the method we will use to create our forms. We have a number of strategies to choose from: we can use hand-forming methods, throw our forms on the potter's wheel, or use mold-forming methods.

The descriptions and illustrations of these methods in this chapter are by necessity limited, general, and very basic. They are only a starting point—a foundation. The ceramist builds on this foundation over a period of time through self-examination, identification with the medium, and hard work.

PREPARING CLAY FOR WORK

To prepare clay for work, the potter wedges (kneads), cuts, and seasons the clay. In the wedging or kneading process, the potter forces one lump of clay into another. Rolling and kneading forces much of the air out of the clay and encourages a uniform moisture content. Either the whole lump of clay may be wedged or only one section at a time (see Figs. 12–1 and 12–2).

In the cutting process, a lump of clay is cut into slices and slices forcefully thrown onto a wedging table and onto each other. The slicing action breaks down lumps and the throwing action forces the air out of the clay body. In a variation of this process, the

ceramist who works with slabs may form them by throwing them against the worktable. While the slab is being formed, air is forced out of the clay body (Figs. 12–3, 12–4).

In the seasoning process, the ceramist stores the clay after an initial preparation. The potter who works on the wheel will prepare lumps of clay of the appropriate size and shape and then store them for a time (even a day or two is useful) in a closed container in which they will not lose their moisture. Seasoning is useful to the slab builder as well: after the clay is kneaded or wedged and formed into slabs, the slabs are stored for a day or two under plastic.

These three processes create a dense clay body with a uniform character. Acidic bacterial growth occurs in the watery areas between the particles and helps them slide past each other. The result is a clay body that is highly workable. Both the thrower and the hand-builder find that these processes allow them to work with much more assurance and control

CERAMIC FORMING METHODS

Throwing Slabs

Slabs are sheet-like forms that are easy to make in clay and can be used as the foun-

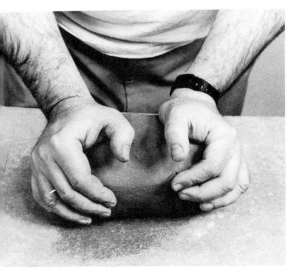

FIG. 12–1 Wedging a small lump of clay. When the potter's hands are in this position, the whole lump is wedged at the same time. This method is often referred to as "dog's head" wedging because of the shape the lump takes during the process.

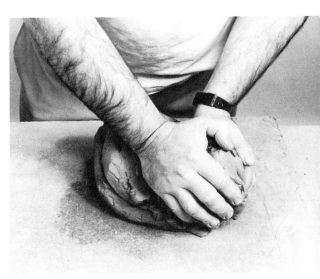

FIG. 12–2 A large lump of clay is wedged one section at a time. This method is often referred to as "spiral" wedging because the clay is turned in a spiral pattern as one section after another is wedged.

FIG. 12–3 The lump of clay is cut into slices to break down lumps and air bubbles. The slices are then thrown against each other to force air out of the clay.

FIG. 12–4 Forming a large slab by throwing it against the table helps the potter make slabs quickly and easily, at the same time forcing out air and breaking up air pockets.

dation for many different forms. Slab-building techniques offer a good introduction to clay forming. Beginning projects are simple and easy to learn, yet slab building can present the experienced ceramist with challenges that are as demanding as any in ceramics.

Clay slabs can be formed in many ways, but the method that follows is quick, makes no great physical demands, and requires no expensive machinery. All that it requires is a plywood or composite work board and a lump of wedged clay about the size of a grapefruit.

Roy Strassberg

Roy Strassberg. USA. "Tunnel House with Guard Dog (Moses)," 18 × 12½ × 26½ inches. Low fire, slab built. Photo: Linda Williams.

Roy Strassberg. USA. "Tunnel House with Jazzleg," 22½ × 13 × 22 inches. Low fire, slab built. Photo: Linda Williams.

I construct my pieces from a relatively nonplastic, low-temperature, white clay body. I construct the pieces when the slabs are quite stiff and then draw directly upon the form when construction is completed. Each piece has a complex matrix/support system. The pieces are heavy, so I dry them for a few months before bisquing to cone 04. Color is then applied using commercial underglazes and a few glazes. Sometimes I also use a crusty-looking volcanic ash glaze with about 10 percent black stain to achieve a textural surface. The glaze firing is at 06. I finish the surfaces by applying a thin layer of acrylic gloss medium over the entire piece to intensify the color and protect the surface from abrasion.

The pieces have to do with my reaction to architecture, the figure, music, and my own ego. I sometimes pay homage to earlier pieces I have made, as well as to historical precedent in architecture.

Flatten the lump of clay until it takes the form of a bun. Pick it up at one corner with both hands. Stretch out your arms as far as possible. Snap the lump of clay toward your torso and let the clay hit the board in a kind of skidding motion. Repeat this process until you have a slab that is 1 centimeter thick. Transfer the slab from the board to a piece of fabric. Smooth it with a wooden roller or with a rib tool and a sponge.

Making a Cylinder
Trim the slab into a rectangle. Pinch down the ends on the right and left sides of the slab so that they end in a sharp edge; leave the top and bottom edges straight. Stand the slab on its bottom edge and bend it into a "U" shape. (The "U" shape will support itself.) Wet the two pinched ends of the slab and join them. Smooth the join. You now

have a clay cylinder, the basic shape for many pottery and sculptural forms. (See Figs. 12–11 through 12–16.)

Joining Pieces with Slip
In some situations you will need to join pieces of clay together securely. This is best done with "slip," a sticky mixture of clay and water. Score the surfaces to be joined and paint them with slip. Then join the two surfaces. You may have to tug and adjust them a bit to make a good contact. It is also a good idea to add some clay to the join to fill in and strengthen it.

Turning the Cylinder into a Vessel Form
Place a slab on one end of a cylinder to form the base of your piece. Trim the slab so that the edge of the base is flush with the walls

FIG. 12–5 Ken Eastman. England. Hand-formed grogged white stoneware clay body, 31 × 44 cm. This piece, formed from slabs, was painted with numerous layers of colored slips and oxides and fired several times to 1180° C (2156° F). Photo: David Ridge.

FIG. 12–6 Roberta Griffith. USA. "Dōtaku Shrine," 31½ inches. Hand-formed, low-fire with acrylic post-fired finish. One of an installation of seven similar pieces placed on an oblong of raked white sand. Photo: Lawrence Mirarchi.

FIG. 12–7 Ruth Duckworth. USA. Slab-formed sculptural form. Courtesy of Thea Burger Associates, Inc.

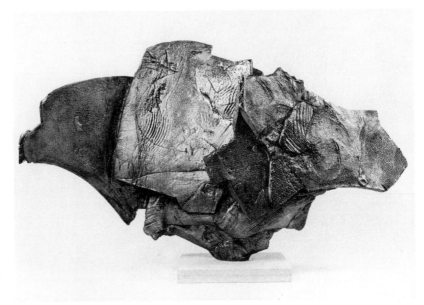

FIG. 12–8 Paul Soldner. USA. "#8826," 23½ × 42 inches. Thrown and altered, stacked tightly with shards to create resist patterns, and unglazed salt-fumed with bronze patina; low-fired (cone 010), fired with a reducing flame but an oxidizing chimney.

FIG. 12–9 Judith Salomon. USA. "Orange Vase," 18 × 10 × 9 inches. Hand-built from cast slabs of low-fire whiteware. Bisque-fired to cone 04, then glaze-fired to cone 05 or 04. (There is usually more than one glaze firing.) Salomon says, "My work is focused on vessels with lots of attention to interior/exterior combinations. Most of my influences are from different types and styles of architecture and my interpretation of the way they might work on a pot form."

FIG. 12–10 Hiroaki Taimei Morino. Japan. "Work 85–5." Slab construction, fired to cone 9 in a reduction kiln, then fired with brightly colored glazes in a low-fire oxidation kiln. Photo: Takeshi Hatekeyama.

Making a Cylindrical Form

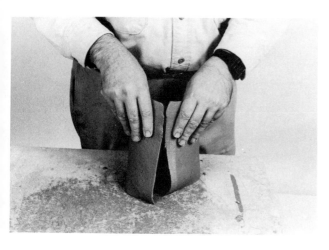

FIG. 12–11 The potter has formed a slab whose edges have been pinched to a sharp point. The slab (which has been allowed to dry a bit) is picked up and formed into a horseshoe shape. Note how the potter's hands support the piece as much as possible but still retain freedom of movement. Once the slab is curved into the horseshoe shape, it becomes self-supporting. Both ends of the slab are brought together to create a cylindrical form. The pinched ends create a long surface area that encourages a strong join and a smooth seam.

FIG. 12–12 For this closed form, both ends of the cylinder are capped.

FIG. 12–13 Trimming and paddling the form.

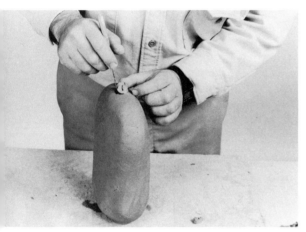

FIG. 12–14 Creating the opening.

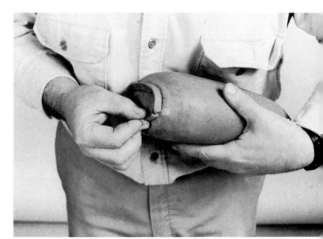

FIG. 12–15 Adding a foot and molding it into the form.

FIG. 12–16 The trimmed piece ready for firing.

of the cylinder. Paddle the base until it is well integrated with the form.

Turning the Cylinder into a Closed Form
Place a slab on each end of a cylinder and assemble the form. Trim the edge of each slab to make it flush with the walls of the cylinder. Paddle the capped cylinder until it takes on a rounded, closed form. Open a section of the form to create the lip. This also allows gasses to escape during the firing.

Making a Triangular Form
Make three slabs and pinch the corners of each one to form a 30-degree angle. Let the slabs partially dry until they are somewhat stiff—the condition ceramists call "leather hard." Paint slip on the corners of the slabs, then assemble them. You now have a triangular form. Join and smooth the corners.

To strengthen the form, place thin coils of clay at the corners where the slabs are joined. To make the base, place the triangle on a slab of clay. Join, trim, and smooth the edges. (See Figs. 12–17 through 12–21.)

Making a Four-Sided Form
To make a four-sided form, use the same techniques you used to make the triangular piece. The only difference is that you will start with four slabs, and the angles of the corners should be 45°.

Creating Irregular and Asymmetrical Hand-built Forms
There is no reason why the walls of a hand-built piece must be uniform in size and shape. Using irregular shapes and sizes is one way to ensure that your forms will not be completely predictable. The character of your slabs is also important. Crisp, geometrical work requires flat, rather stiff slabs, whereas more organic imagery suggests slabs that have been turned and bent. Twisting the slabs can produce interesting forms that reflect the plasticity of the clay.

Coil Building
A "coil" of clay is what we get when we roll a lump of clay on the table. A typical coil will be about a centimeter thick and 20 centimeters long. Coils are placed one layer upon another to create a form.

Coil building can be slow compared to other building methods because each successive layer must be joined firmly to the one before. Even though it is slow, its great advantage is that it can be used to create complex and unusually large forms.

Starting a coil-built piece is best done with a slab form (Fig. 12–25). A piece is likely to crack if coils have been used to form the base. Cylinders or bowl forms are often used for the base, with the coils placed on top. During the building process, the potter must smooth or "weld" the coils on one or both surfaces of the wall (Fig. 12–26). This will obliterate the coil pattern but will ensure that the coils will not crack or open.

As the wall of the form begins to attain some height, the soft coils may begin to sag. The potter must stop until the walls have had a chance to set up. Because of this waiting period, coil builders often work on more than one piece at a time.

Throwing on the Potter's Wheel
For many people, ceramics and the potter's wheel are synonymous. The image of the potter at the wheel always springs quickly to mind. The wheel is a wonderful clay-forming method because it is quick and produces strong, visually satisfying results. Its symmetrical forms speak at once of movement and of that center point where everything is still.

The potter's wheel is really a tool for creating a group of basic shapes that can be used in a variety of ways and allow the ceramist great opportunities for formal invention. Even though created from a limited number of shapes, the products of the potter's wheel are surprisingly diverse.

Learning how to throw on the potter's

(Text continues on page 194.)

Making a Triangular Form

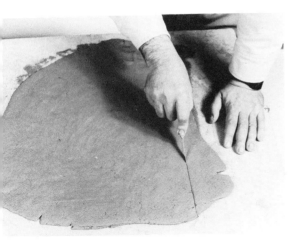

FIG. 12−17   Cutting the slabs.

FIG. 12−18   Forming and shaping the slabs.

FIG. 12−19   Assembling the cut slabs to form the triangular piece.

FIG. 12−20   Refining the form with a rib.

FIG. 12−21   The almost completed piece.

Sue Abbrescia

I begin each vessel with a slab base and progress with layer upon layer of small coils, each rolled out in the palm, pinched and twisted onto each other, smoothed on the inside, and delicately paddled on the outside until reaching a form that is pleasing to me. Following a slow, lengthy, thorough drying, the piece is fired in an electric kiln to 1800° F, after which I apply stains, oxides, and/or colored slips by hand. Additional firings complete the vessel.

Sue Abbrescia. USA. Coil stoneware pot with stains, 7 × 15½ inches.

Mary Barringer

My pieces are made with coils, then scraped and paddled into their final form, and drawn upon with tools, scrapers, and my hands. Layers of slip are then brushed on, rubbed in, built up, and selectively removed to achieve a surface that enriches the form. The pieces are fired to cone 6 in an electric kiln.

Mary Barringer. USA. Coil pot, 12 × 14½ × 8½ inches. Fired to cone 6 in oxidation in an electric kiln. Photo: Wayne Fleming.

While the methods I use are not complicated, I'm interested in the way technique can act as a catalyst, a means, or a limit to form. Working with coils means that the pots evolve slowly, from the ground up. This suits the way my ideas unfold—incrementally, rather than dramatically.

Mary Barringer. USA. "Platform Jar," $11\frac{1}{2} \times 11 \times 7$ inches. Fired to cone 6 in oxidation in an electric kiln. Photo: Wayne Fleming.

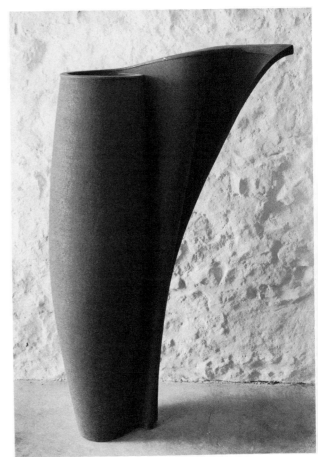

FIG. 12–22 Monica Young. England. Coiled clay form, 60×36 inches. This piece is coil-built using a heavily grogged clay. Young uses thick coils (about $1\frac{1}{2}$ inches) so that she can carve away some of the clay to accentuate the form. She also paddles both the inside and outside of the piece to refine the form. Her work is then fired in a reduction atmosphere to 1300° C, at which point it takes on a deep toasted color. Photo: Roger Murray.

FIG. 12–23 Steve Buck. England. "Self-Aware." Coil-formed piece. Photo courtesy of Michaelson & Orient.

FIG. 12–24. Nancy Angus. England. Coil-formed vase, 38 cm. Painted with slips, glaze, and body stains and fired to 1200° C.

Making a Coil-Formed Vessel

FIG. 12–25 Starting the first coils on the slab-formed base.

FIG. 12–26 Welding the coils together using a knife.

Walter Keeler

I was trained at Harrow School of Art by Victor Margrie and Michael Casson. My first workshop was established at Bledlow Ridge in Buckinghamshire in 1965. I made oxidized stoneware functional pots and an assortment of nonfunctional pieces that reflected the plastic pleasures of thrown pottery. During the 1970s I concentrated on functional pots in reduced stoneware and salt glaze. In 1976 I moved to Penallt in Gwent, but within a couple of years the profit and the joy went out of my down-to-earth domestic ware. To stimulate my interest I recalled my early nonfunctional pieces (rejected as an indulgence ten years before) and brought some of their tactile qualities and a more sculptural attitude to my functional pots. A whole range of possibilities revealed themselves, which, combined with a return to salt glaze, regenerated, and now sustains, my enthusiasm.

Walter Keeler. England. "Pitcher," 20 cm high. Wheel-formed and altered, salt fired at cone 9.

Throwing is my primary technique and the inspiration for my pots. They all begin on the wheel, though most are altered in some way, or assembled from various components. Pots released from their base no longer remain circular. Rims are cut away to leave raised pouring lips, or a vessel is set back on its base, as if affronted by something in its path. Handles may be pulled and sensuous, growing from a rim, or extruded with metallic accuracy, appearing to just rest on the pot. Spouts, whether thrown and altered or pressed in a mold, contribute their peculiarities to the assembled pot. The goal in this complex process is a finished pot which, while performing its commonplace function, becomes a surprising object.

---

wheel with skill and ease takes time, often several years, but for many ceramists the effort is worthwhile. An accomplished "thrower" not only can make a wheel-thrown piece quickly, but can make numerous pieces nearly effortlessly.

The basic wheel-formed shapes are the cylinder, flat disk, hemisphere, and sphere. These basic shapes are used to create vases, bottles, plates, bowls, covered bowls, and closed forms.

The Process

Trying to describe what happens on the potter's wheel is a real challenge. (See the technical photo series, Figs. 12–27 through 12–41, and the finished pieces, Figs. 12–42 through 12–54.) You sit in front of a whirling turntable, upon which is fixed a lump of clay. You must now brace your body, your arms, and your hands, and by a kind of controlled pressure "persuade" the clay to take on a symmetrical cone-like solid form. Water is essential here, and periodically you should moisten the form with a water-soaked sponge. Once you have created this symmetrical cone-like form (this is called "centering"), your next step is to pierce the center of the form with your hand and open it up to make a thick-walled cylinder. Then you will bring a ring of clay from the bottom of the cylinder toward the top. This action is repeated a few times until the walls of the piece are fairly uniform in thickness. The whirling cylinder is then shaped and the piece finished.

Altered Forms

One way for the potter who throws on the wheel to assure diversity is to alter the form after completing the throwing process. Thrown forms can be altered by subtracting parts of the form, by adding to the form, or by changing the shape of the piece. A teapot, for example, can be made with subtractions and additions. In another kind of manipulation, the vessel wall can be altered by squeezing or molding or by pushing out from within. These modifications may be subtle or radical. The underlying principle is that a clay form may be shaped with energy and spontaneity on the wheel and then modified to create an image that has characteristics of both throwing and hand-building.

Extruded Forms

An extruder shapes clay by forcing it through a form or die. Small extruders are given their thrust by a hand-operated lever. More complex versions are mechanically powered. The simplest extruded forms are solid, while more complex ones are channel-like or tubular. The tubular forms are created using an arched support that bridges the outer wall of the die and an inner core. In this way a bisected tube is created by the clay, which passes through the support and between the outer wall and the core. The clay then passes through the extruder. The bisected tube is forced together as it travels down the lower part of the mechanism. Complex forms can

(Text continues on page 205.)

FIG. 12–27   A lump of wedged clay is placed on the wheel head and secured to its surface.

FIG. 12–28   When the wheel is started, the wheelhead with its lump of clay begins to turn rapidly. The potter moistens the lump of clay and braces his arms and steadies his hands, placing them in a way that will force the clay into a symmetrical shape.

FIG. 12–29, 12–30   The lump of clay is pushed up and down a few times to fully center it.

FIG. 12–31 A depression is created in the middle of the centered lump of clay.

FIG. 12–32 The depression is enlarged and deepened.

FIG. 12–33 A cutaway view of Figure 12–32.

FIG. 12–34 The opening is further enlarged and its base is widened.

FIG. 12–35 A cutaway view showing a bulge of clay above the fingers.

FIG. 12–36 The bulge is raised gently, smoothly, and firmly. This act is the core of the throwing process.

FIG. 12–37   A cutaway view of Figure 12–36.

FIG. 12–38   The bulge, which is now much smaller, is again pulled upward.

FIG. 12–39   Cutaway view of Figure 12–38.

FIG. 12–40   What was once an anonymous lump of clay is now a vessel form, ready to be smoothed and the form refined.

FIG. 12–41   A cutaway view of the completed vessel.

FIG. 12–42 Tim Mather. USA. "Basket Form," 14 inches. Wheel-formed with hand-built and slip-trailed ornament; reduction-fired to cone 11, then sandblasted. Photo: Mather/McCormick.

FIG. 12–43 Maren Klopp-mann. West Germany. Tray, 7 inches wide. Thrown and altered porcelain fired at cone 10. Photo: Tim Thayer.

FIG. 12–44 Val Cushing.
USA. Pitcher, 20 inches.
Thrown and altered; cone 9 re-
duction-fired. Photo: Brian
Oglesbee.

FIG. 12–45 Val Cushing.
USA. Covered jar, 22 inches.
Thrown and altered; cone 9 re-
duction-fired. Photo: © 1985
Steve Myers.

FIG. 12–46 Georgette Zirbes. USA. "E.C.E. Babies," 61 cm. This thrown and assembled piece was finished by covering the entire surface with a black slip. Zirbes created imagery with colored slips, using a sgraffito line to reveal underlying colors and the clay body. Then she used transparent black stain and a black glaze pencil to refine the imagery. Finally, a clear glaze was sprayed over the entire piece and it was fired to cone 6 in a neutral (neither oxidation nor reduction) atmosphere.

FIG. 12–47 Marvin Bjurlin. USA. Vessel, 14 inches. The textured surfaces and brushed multiple layers of commercial underglaze slips have been partially wiped away with a sponge; wheel-formed and fired to cone 04 in oxidation in an electric kiln. Bjurlin also uses commercial glazes.

Clay Forming
200

FIG. 12–48 Andrew Schuster. USA. Lusterware and steel, wheel-formed.

FIG. 12–49 Warren Mackenzie. USA. Covered Jar. Glazed stoneware, wheel-formed with brushed underglaze slip decoration; fired in a reduction atmosphere.

FIG. 12–50 Chris Staley. USA.
A group of unfired faceted vase
forms. Porcelain body in-
tended for cone 9 salt firing.

FIG. 12–51 Takeshi Yasuda.
England. "Fat Rim Dish," 39
cm in diameter. Wheel-thrown
stoneware forms with three-
color glaze, high-fired in an
oxidation kiln.

FIG. 12–52 Colin Pearson. England. Thrown slab vase with thrown attachments, 45 cm wide. Wheel-thrown and altered with a dark slip under a high-silica, frosty mat glaze; oxidation-fired to cone 7 in an electric kiln.

FIG. 12–53 Colin Pearson. England. Thrown slab vase combed and carved, with attachments, 46 cm wide. Wheel-thrown and altered with a dark slip under a mat glaze; oxidation-fired to cone 7 in an electric kiln.

FIG. 12–54 Walter Ostrom. Canada. "Baker," 12 inches wide. Wheel-formed and decorated with slips and sgraffito; fired to cone 04–03 in an oxidation atmosphere. Photo: Bill Rice.

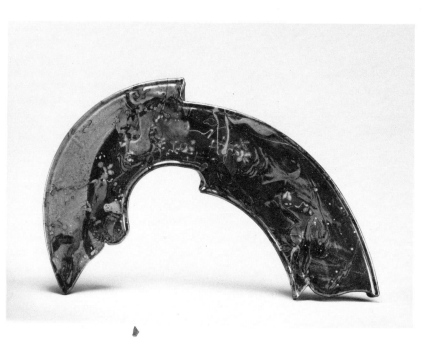

FIG. 12–55 John Glick. USA. Tray form, 26 × 11 inches. Stoneware clay body, cone 10 reduction-fired. Made in an extruder, the form was curved using "diverters" on the extrusion die. The piece was decorated using a multiple slip technique applied to the wet clay. Multiple glazes were also used along with wax resist, glaze painting, and washes. Photo: Dirk Bakker.

FIG. 12–56 Bryan McGrath. USA. Sculptural form, 24 × 26 × 19 inches. Stoneware fired at cone 10. The surface is sprayed with colemanite (a material with some similarities to Gerstley borate) and dusted with ash. "These pieces are constructed of 3"-square stoneware extrusions. They are built up much like a coil pot, then paddled into the finished form. The surface is brought out by spraying colemanite, rutile iron, or a fruit on the bisqued piece. The piece is then dusted with ash."

be created with an extruder: for example, lidded forms, in which both base, lid, and flange have been extruded. It is also possible to produce curved pieces, which turn as they leave the extruder. Extrusions can be of any length but are limited in width to the width of the die.

While extruders have been used extensively in the ceramics industry, their use by studio ceramists has been limited. The extrusion method has been used to make quick handles and decorative elements, but little else. The potter John Glick, who lives in a suburb of Detroit, Michigan, has done extensive work with the extruder as a tool for forming vessels (see Fig 12–55). His experiments have yielded fine work and the promise of new approaches to forming in the future.

Mold Forming

A mold is a matrix—a tool for imparting a new shape to a material. Molds are excellent tools for creating ceramic form. Because clay has no form of its own, it can be made to take the form of the mold quite easily. There are a number of strategies for doing this: the first is the press-mold process, in which clay is pressed into the mold; the second is slip-casting, in which a clay slip—"soup" composed of clay and water—is poured into the mold.

Pressed-Mold Forming

Pressed molding is a simple mold-form process in which the ceramist forces a moist, coarse clay body over or into a mold. As the clay dries, it releases from the mold. At this point it is taken from the mold and cleaned and finished. Large forms can be produced using the press-mold process. Many buildings in our cities are faced with terra-cotta, which often appears to be cut from marble or stone. Actually they are large press-molded ceramic blocks called "ashlars."

The simplest molds often are little more than a volumetric form; a slab is merely draped over or in the form. They are so simple, in fact, that it is perhaps more accurate to call them "forming aids" than to call them molds. Complex press molds, on the other

Aurore Chabot

While in graduate school, I developed what I call a "reverse inlay" process that gave (gives) my pieces a mosaic-like surface reminiscent of fossil-embedded rocks and excavated archaeological layers of earth. I have continued to develop this and other techniques so that my pieces have become somewhat more complex. One side of the piece appears more painterly and two-dimensional, while the other sides seem to grow like roots or stalactites from the back of this surface into three-dimensional, still-living organic forms. Some pieces seem more architectural, while others seem more organic. There is structure versus chaos—a protective, bright shell on the outside and a more vulnerable, writhing interior to the more organic sculptures.

When making clay sculpture, I spend several days painting rolled-out slabs of low-fire white or terra-cotta clay into patterns and stripes of brightly colored low-fire underglazes. These days I prefer Reward underglazes for their intensity of color and easy applicability, but I also use home-made slips and terra sigillata slips colored with Mason stains. I use no special formula at the moment, but try different formulas that come my way. Then I make a variety of small fossil-like parts. This whole period is like a meditative time leading up to the more energetic construction of sculpture. Either I'll sketch a form or have an overall form in mind as I choose a mold in which to construct the piece. The mold might be two hinged pieces of wood (a sharp angle), a plaster mold, leather-hard slabs joined together, or a thick, nontextured material set over a slab of clay set over sausage-like bags of vermiculite, or a bisque mold.

I then break apart the painted slab and lay the pieces, along with fossil-like shapes, upside down against the surface of the mold. Therefore the painted side becomes hidden while I construct the piece. Only later, after the piece is constructed and stiff enough to remove from the mold, can I see what the mosaic-like side looks like. I have built in an additional element of surprise by working this way, and I believe it somehow puts me more in touch with my subconscious.

Over the backs of all the fragments I press soft clay, compressing the clay over and between all the elements. Using hollow, pinch-construction, or slab construction, depending on the piece, I build the form that will later, after firing, be oriented upside down or sideways from the position in which it was built. The forms are then carved into, manipulated, distressed, painted with colored slips, rubbed with powdered oxides and stains, carved again, painted again, until I perceive an intensity of

Aurore Chabot. USA. "Repository for Dreams and Other Schemes." Installation view, first corner. Mixed media including low-fire earthenware; bisque-fired to cone 04, glaze-fired to cone 06. Photo: John Perry.

expression that brings the piece to life. After a bisque firing I further glaze the piece with various textural glazes, both homemade and commercial, to further intensify the surfaces. A piece rarely feels complete until after the glazing. On occasion I will glaze-fire a piece several times if it seems to need it. All glaze firing is done at cone 06, but sometimes I bisque fire to cone 04 to strengthen the clay.

Lately, I have been using nonclay bases for my pieces so that I don't have to worry about how a piece might be diminished by a pedestal. I have also experimented with installations, as in "Repository for Dreams and Other Schemes," where I used white silica sand and Astroturf pathways on the floor along with several sculptures and drawings to create a dream-like environment in a box-like gallery.

---

hand, may have a great deal of detail and function much like a mold used in the slip-casting technique. These molds are made in the same way as slipcast molds.

Slipcasting

The principle underlying slipcasting is simple: plaster will absorb the moisture in a clay slurry or slip (a wet, soupy mixture of clay and water). As the clay next to the mold begins to dry, it creates a form that replicates the inside of the mold. This clay replication becomes the mold-formed piece. (See the technical photo series, Figs. 12–57 through 12–64, and the finished pieces, Figs. 12–66 through 12–70.)

To create a slipcast piece, the ceramist pours the slurry into the plaster mold. A layer of slurry adheres to the mold wall and some of its water is absorbed. In this way a wall of clay is built up on the inside of the mold. In the middle of the mold cavity, however, the slurry remains wet. When the clay wall is of sufficient thickness, part of the wet slurry is poured out or withdrawn. The clay wall that adheres to the inside of the mold is allowed to firm and dry. Once dry, the clay is removed from the mold and finished and fired.

Any fine-grained clay body high in ball clay is appropriate for slipcast work, but it must be deflocculated first. Usually clay slips have a water content of 40 percent or more and will saturate the mold and cast poorly. Deflocculation changes the structure of the clay so that it contains less water (about 30 percent) but is still quite liquid. Defloccu-

lation is a process that requires judgment and experience and is most easily learned under the tutelage of a person who has done it a number of times.

Many ceramists who work with slipcasting, even those with a great deal of experience, use commercially prepared casting slips, which are reliable and inexpensive.

Economic questions often play a big part in ceramics, and this is especially true of slipcast processes. Mold-forming techniques allow for the ready creation of complex form and decoration not available to those who work in other ceramic techniques. In fact, the results are in some ways closer to printmaking than they are to ceramics. If a complex cast piece were made by hand, it would have to be sold at a high price, but since slipcasting allows for the easy duplication of complex forms, the piece can be made economically. We often see this in ceramics from the turn of the century.

MOLD MAKING

Molds for slipcast forming are made from an original model formed either from clay or from gypsum plaster (plaster of paris), which is very effective in absorbing the water in a clay slip. Depending on the form of the piece to be cast, the mold will be a single piece or segmented into two or more parts. Studio ceramists usually work with one- or two-piece molds rather than more complex multipart molds, which are difficult to manage. While the mold-making process sounds

Marek Cecula

I have developed a limited edition series and a small production line in order to escape from the market momentum of one-of-a kind objects. Designing functional and semifunctional ceramics demands a deeper planning of the object and its process. In my work it is critical that I maintain the integrity of originality and the ability to create an impact on a larger group of collectors and clients.

My interest in ceramic design is specifically focused on the process of slipcasting techniques, where models and molds are an important aspect. The investment of time and work are substantial, and this imposes a specific reality and adaptation of the studio.

My work usually does not carry any visible handmade qualities, although it's basically handmade through the assemblage of individual elements, fabrication, and decoration.

My inspirations and influences are basically derived from an urban reality where architecture, environment, and social habits mix in with the aesthetics of today's perception.

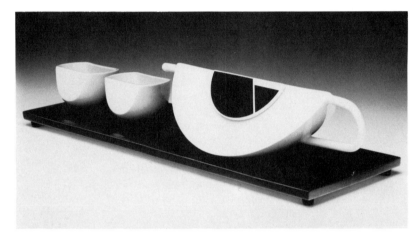

Marek Cecula. USA. "Ceremonial Set II." Slip-cast and assembled porcelain with decal application on the lid, fired to cone 8. The tray is 15×5 inches, the pot is $9\frac{1}{2} \times 3$ inches, and the cups are $1\frac{1}{2} \times 2\frac{1}{2}$ inches.

Marek Cecula. USA. "Design Set." Slip-cast and assembled porcelain, fired to cone 8. The handle and pegs are made from acylic. The trays are 7×7 inches, the teapot is $7\frac{1}{2} \times 5\frac{1}{4}$ inches, and the cups are $2\frac{3}{4}$ inches.

Karen Estelle Koblitz

I began working with the "Still Life Image" in the late 1970s. I would throw platters and bowls and fill them with hand-built fruit, vegetables, and fish. I was living in Kansas at the time, it was February, and I think I was homesick for the warmth and color that appear in the supermarkets and urban landscape of my native southern California.

In 1978 I spent part of the summer involved in a mold-making workshop at the Kohler Company in Wisconsin. While I had played with the use of molds in graduate school, this workshop rekindled my interest in adapting the use of molds in my still lifes. I had been bothered by the "funky" aesthetics the hand-built ob-

jects had given my previous pieces and wanted a more sophisticated and exact feeling to the still-life objects. After the workshop I began using molds exclusively.

In 1982 I expanded on the idea of one platter or bowl as a finished piece to include a number of objects incorporated into still-life tableaux placed on ceramic fabrics. These tableaux, instead of being glazed to mirror the surface of the original object, were glazed with brightly colored patterns. The surfaces have become more and more complicated over the years. For instance, in the beginning I was using underglaze on the surface and putting a shiny clear glaze over the entire piece. As the work progressed I began experimenting with textures on the surfaces. I did this by imprinting the ceramic

Karen Estelle Koblitz. USA. "Still Life: Homage to Della Robbia," $21\frac{1}{2} \times 15\frac{1}{2} \times 7\frac{1}{4}$ inches. Mold-formed wall relief with post-mold manipulation; low-fire underglaze and glaze. Photo: Susan Einstein.

Karen Estelle Koblitz. USA. "Art Deco Still Life in Black & White," $11\frac{1}{4} \times 19 \times 19$ inches. Mold-formed piece with post-mold manipulation; low-fire underglaze and glaze. Photo: Susan Einstein.

fabric slabs with linoleum blocks I had carved. The objects themselves were given texture after they were removed from the molds. I used a sharp object and carved patterns into the surfaces. To give more interest to the colored surface I began using colorful, shiny, transparent glazes on the very textured patterned areas next to flat areas in which an underglaze was fired without an overglaze to give it not only a muted color, but a mat contrasting feeling.

daunting (and can be made so if you wish), it is basically a simple process.

One important aspect to remember about mold making is that undercuts must be avoided. Undercuts are places where the model is formed in such a way as to impede the removal of the piece from the mold. It is also important that the plaster walls be at least two and a half inches thick to permit adequate absorption of moisture in the slip. Once the mold is made, it is allowed to dry for a few days before it is used.

Mixing Plaster

Plaster of paris should be fresh. If it is more than six months old, it will be lumpy and will not set well. Always mix plaster in flexible plastic buckets as it will stick to other types of containers. Also, let plaster set completely before discarding it because wet plaster will clog plumbing.

A successful plaster-to-water ratio is approximately 1.25 to 1 (kilograms to liters). Sift the plaster into the water (never the reverse) until small "islands" of plaster appear above the water. After a few minutes agitate the mixture vigorously. It is now ready to use.

You will need a container to hold the wet plaster around the model. It can be made from four separate plywood walls coated with a thin layer of petroleum jelly. The walls can be adjusted to create containers of various sizes.

Angelo di Petta Casts a Sconce

FIG. 12–57   The two molds ready for the slip. Notice the mold support ready to receive any excess slip.

FIG. 12–58   Pouring the casting slip. The slip is poured to the very top of the mold.

FIG. 12–59   After a suitable interval, the part of the slip that is still wet is poured out of the mold. If you look carefully at the mold opening, you can see a wall of clay adhering to the wall of the mold.

FIG. 12–60   The slip is allowed to firm up inside the mold.

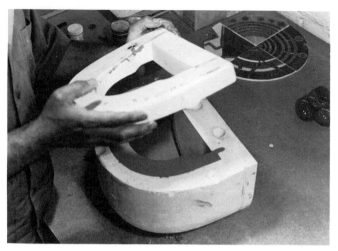

FIG. 12–61 The top segment of the mold is removed.

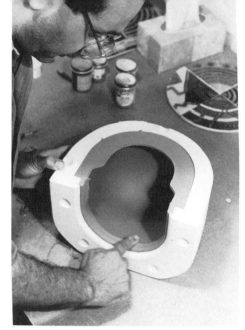

FIG. 12–62 The lip of the sconce is cleaned.

FIG. 12–63 Two sconces ready for drying and bisque-firing.

FIG. 12–64 The completed sconce.

Making a One-Piece Mold

Place the model upside down on a sheet of glass to which petroleum jelly has been applied. Then build a containing structure around the model, leaving plenty of room so that the plaster walls will be thick enough (at least 2½ inches) to absorb the water in the slip. Pour the plaster into the containing structure and allow it to set. Finally, separate the mold from the glass and remove the model from the plaster.

Making a Two-Piece Mold

To keep this process simple, in this version of the mold-making process the model is cut in half. Other strategies would be used in more complex and sophisticated versions of the process.

Place the first half of the model on a sheet of thick glass to which petroleum jelly has been applied.

Next, build a container around the model and pour the plaster over it. Allow the plaster to set. Release the mold from the glass and turn it over to reveal its face, leaving the model embedded in the plaster. Carve two or three inverted domes into the wall on the face of the mold. These will act as keys that will aid you in lining up the two halves of the mold.

Next, place the other half of the model on the half that is still in the mold. Apply petroleum jelly or mold soap (a soapy liquid with "nonstick" characteristics) to the face of the mold. The walls of the container that will hold the plaster for the top half of the mold are built around the bottom half.

Pour the plaster into the container to create the other half of the mold and allow it to set. Finally, separate the two halves of the mold and remove the model.

Clean the completed mold and allow it to dry for a few days. The mold needs to become "seasoned," so the first few casts may not be entirely successful.

Note: for a more thorough examination of the mold-making process, see *Mold Making for Ceramics* by Donald E. Frith (Radnor, Pa.: Chilton Book Company, 1985).

FIG. 12–65 Barbara L. Frey. USA. "Toot Sweet Teapot #5," 8 inches. This piece is constructed from slabs that have been thrown on the wheel. When the slabs had dried to a leather-hard state, Frey used templates to cut the shapes; then she assembled the component parts. The body of the teapot was first constructed as a closed form. The lid was cut from the top plane with a knife held at an angle to create a beveled seat. Attached to the lid is an inner wall that insures the lid will stay in place when the pot is used. The clay body is cone 6 porcelain-fired to maturity in an electric kiln. Only the interior is glazed. Photo: Thomas Eckersley.

FIG. 12–66 Victor Spinski. USA. Mold-formed low-fire sculptural piece. Spinski's work is marked by an interest in humor and irony.

FIG. 12–67 Paul Rozman. Canada. A group of cast-formed pieces. As well as making one-of-a-kind utilitarian pieces, Rozman also produces a line of cast dinnerware.

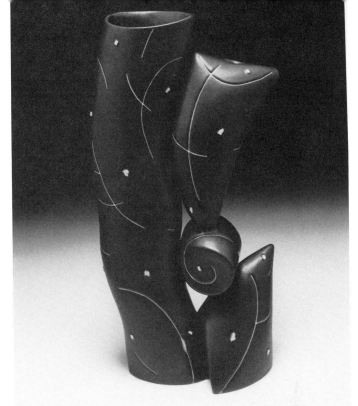

FIG. 12–68 Kurt Weiser. USA. Porcelain pot. These pieces, made from slip-cast forms, are cut up while wet and formed into different shapes. Weiser uses the mold-forming process to create forms that have their own unique identity. They are finished with a stiff, high-viscosity glaze; a sgraffito line has been carved into its surface. The work is fired to cone 10 in a reduction atmosphere.

FIG. 12–69 Kathryn Lawrence. England. Lawrence produces her work using a variation on the normal slip-cast techniques that she calls "strata casting." She places small pieces of stratified clay on the surface of the mold, thereby embedding them in the wall of the pot. After the piece is removed from the mold, she rubs it down with an abrasive pad to reveal the stratified additions. The piece is then fired to its vitrification temperature of 1270° C. After firing, the piece is polished with a fine sandpaper to achieve a crisp imagery and a smooth, stony surface.

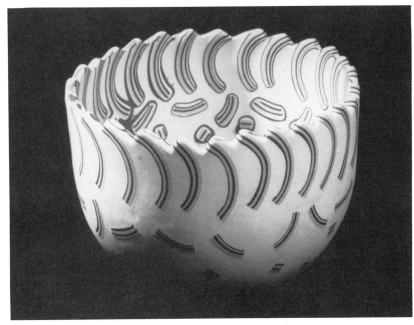

FIG. 12–70 Richard Notkin. Cups from the Yixing Series, from $2\frac{1}{8}$ to 5 inches high. Cast-formed stoneware. Courtesy of the Garth Clark Gallery, New York and Los Angeles.

MAKING CERAMIC WALL PIECES

Making Tesserae and a Mosaic Panel

Roll out a number of thin clay slabs (about a $\frac{1}{4}$-inch thick). If you are using colored clays, prepare them now. Draw lines where the slabs will be broken to form the tesserae. Draw deeply into the slab, but not all the way through. Each tessera should be half an inch to an inch wide. If you are glazing the tesserae, do so now.

Fire the tiles, then break them apart. As-semble the tesserae to form an image and transfer the image, piece by piece, to the mounting board.

Mounting Tesserae

Mounting is one of the most important steps in making wall pieces because this is the time when the piece comes together and many form decisions must be made. The individual pieces are mounted on a panel or directly on a wall with mastic adhesive. The spaces between the tesserae (or tiles) are filled with grout. Coloring the grout can considerably enhance the decorative quality of the piece.

To mount the tesserae, cover a section of a plywood board with a thin layer of mastic cement. Press the tesserae into the mastic, making sure to anchor them securely. When the image is complete, fill in the area between the tesserae with grout.

Note: When working on large mosaic pieces, assemble the tesserae and glue them (from the front) to large sheets of paper. Transfer the sheet to the prepared mounting board. This method provides a way to cover large areas quickly.

Making Tiles

Ceramic tiles are limited in size by the size of the kiln and the character of the clay body. (Large tiles often warp or crack during the firing.) Tiles are often modular, in units of a standard size. To ensure uniformity, mod-

---

Beth Changstrom

PAINT IN CERAMICS

There are few surfaces that totally integrate with the ceramic surface. Wood firing is perhaps the best example I can think of in which the "glaze" or "surface treatment" really gives a feeling of being part of the piece. Applied glazes vary greatly as to how well they integrate with the object itself. I spent years air-brushing realistic landscapes on pots, glazed over with a transparent celadon and fired to cone 12. I have used multiple techniques to get an extraordinary variety of colors and textures on my work. I finally came to the conclusion that I was making a lot of work for myself that didn't really add to the aesthetic value of the pieces.

For the last several years I have been making assembled wall reliefs using both ceramic and mixed-media elements. I use different kinds of glue for different applications.

I use a high-density professional-grade silicone for items that have a large area to be adhered, and where I won't have to touch up with paint. I use epoxies for items that have just a small area to be glued. This offers a harder bond, and one that can be touched up with paint. In both cases, the surfaces should be cleaned and roughed up to ensure a better bond.

Beth Changstrom. USA. "#1–FM 88," 43 × 48 inches. Ceramic wall piece with mixed-media elements. Photo: Mel Schockner.

When I make an object that would normally be glazed to put into one of my pieces—a functional object such as a plate or a cup—I glaze it. Any additional patterning will be done in overglazes. I want the viewer to feel the object is really what it appears to be. Other parts of my pieces are not ceramic at all. The paintings in my recent pieces are actually painted on hardboard and the whole piece mounted on plywood. I use acrylic paint and prepare the ceramic surface with gesso the same way I would prepare hardboard or canvas. In the end, the finish is determined by my own feelings about what I think is most effective for the object represented.

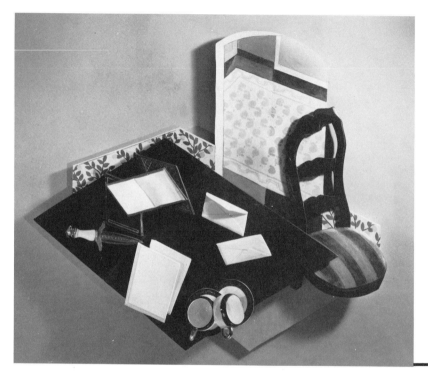

Beth Changstrom. USA. "#4–FM 88," 43 × 48 inches. Ceramic wall piece with mixed-media elements. Photo: Mel Schockner.

ular tiles are best made using a cardboard or sheet-metal template.

Making a Modular Tile Piece or Nonsegmented Panel

Many wall pieces are simple monolithic panels that are easily formed and easy to mount and exhibit.

To make a modular tile piece, begin by wedging wet grog in the clay, from 10 to 20 percent by weight. Chopped nylon may also be used, adding one teaspoon to a hundred pounds of clay. Next, prepare a clay slab. The tiles should be half a centimeter to a centimeter thick. If all the tiles are the same shape and size, cut a template from paper or a thin sheet of metal. Cut out the tiles. If you want to add clay relief imagery, do so now.

Allow the tiles to dry on a rack. Cover the tops of the tile so that they will stay more moist than the reverse side. This will discourage the kind of warping in which the edges of the tile are raised above the middle. Fire the tiles.

David Pendell

My work for the past several years has been entirely out of earthenware, most of it low-relief wall pieces and some cast/fabricated free-standing work. As the complexity and number of firings increased, the need for an appropriate clay body and specific underglaze-like colored surfaces became paramount. I have derived an adequate clay body after a series of tests started from formulas and information given to me several years ago.

David Pendell. USA. Untitled Wall Piece #6, 26 × 21 inches. Earthenware finished with underglaze, china paint, and low-fire enamels. The piece was fired approximately ten times.

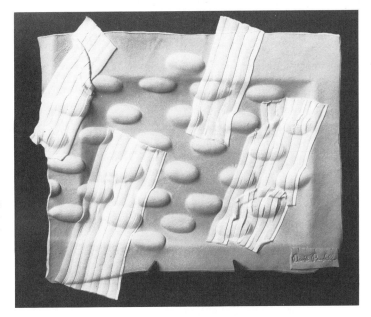

David Pendell. USA. "Jacob's Coat," 16 × 14 inches. Earthenware finished with underglaze colors.

Talc	*30*
EPK	*15*
Ball clay #4	*30*
Wollastonite	*10*
Grog	*15*
Bentonite	*1.5*
Macaloid	*2*
Nylon fiber	*.25*
Shrinkage cone 04	8.5%–9.5%
Absorption	13%

The body can be fired higher, and I often do that for increased strength.

In my fired surfaces I use commercial glazes, underglazes, china paints, enamels, and lusters. Of particular interest to me lately has been a denser, more fused underglaze-type surface. To achieve this I use commercial underglazes mixed 50-50 with low-fire glaze and now have developed simple formulas using Mason stains. Starting with equal parts of stain, clay, and frit (#3134), I now use equal parts of stain and frit with three parts of clay and fire at cone 04. This gives me a wide range of dense and fused yet dry surfaces to contrast my glazed and enameled surfaces.

Mounting Tiles
Prepare a plywood board for mounting the tiles by applying a fairly thick layer of mastic cement to the back of each tile. Tile industry sources advise using two-part mastic cements, which, though less convenient, are more secure than premixed cements.

Press the tiles firmly into the mastic and fill the areas between with grout.

Mounting a Nonsegmented Panel
The panel may be mounted with pins or bolts or with mastic. Pin- or bolt-mounting hardware is set in holes in the panel. It is a very secure method of mounting. At one point mastic could not be relied upon to be as secure, but new varieties have been developed that are quite reliable, and many ceramists feel that mastics are suitable for mounting all but the heaviest tiles. It is common to see nonsegmented panels mounted to another panel, which in turn is hung on the wall in the same way as a painting on canvas or board.

Mold-Formed Wall Pieces
Mold-forming is a good method for making tiles and is especially useful for making modular tiles. Mold-formed tiles are uniform and lend themselves to modularity. If the ceramist wishes, relief imagery can be created in the mold while the tile is being formed.

Either press- or cast-forming methods can be used for creating wall pieces. Both have their advantages: press molding is a simple and fairly direct process, while cast-forming produces a thin, light tile that is not likely to warp in the fire.

CHAPTER 13

Kilns

ATMOSPHERE

The conditions inside the kiln chamber during firing are called the kiln "atmosphere." This atmosphere strongly influences the character of the fired ware.

Fuel-burning kilns allow the ceramist to subject the work to direct flame (called "flashing") and to reduce the amount of oxygen that is allowed to enter the firing chamber (called "reduction"). Work that has been flashed and reduced is valued for its rich and highly individual character.

Flashing

Flashing changes the character of sections of a piece that has been directly exposed to the flame. To accomplish flashing, the ceramist modifies the flame path inside the kiln or strongly reduces one or two burners in a multiburner kiln. In the flashed area color will be deepened and the transition from one color to the other may be marked by unpredictable visual effects.

Reduction

In the reduction process, the ceramist reduces the amount of oxygen that is allowed to enter the firing chamber. Since a fuel-burning kiln demands a great deal of oxygen, it is natural for the oxygen inside the

kiln to become depleted during the firing. This phenomenon is called reduction.

Reduction leaves its mark on both clay bodies and glazes. It modifies color and visual texture. Clay body color is deepened, sometimes moving to rich oranges and reds and somtimes to a grayed color. A strong visual texture is created by dark spots that occur randomly over the surface of the piece. These are caused by particles of iron oxide, which become transformed into black iron oxide in the reduction process.

Glaze texture and color are also modified. The dark spots that mark the surface of the clay come through to the glaze and mark it as well. Glaze color can be strongly marked by the reduction: for example, copper will turn a blood red and white glazes take on warm tones with a broken texture of dark spots. Iron greens and ochres become burnt oranges and brick reds; sky blues become slate blues.

Oxidation Firing

Even in the past, when all kilns were fuel burning, not all firings were in reduction. Although reduction is natural in the fuel-burning kiln, the ceramist can control the firing to avoid it; this is called oxidation firing. With the advent of modern kilns it became easy to fire in oxidation. Fuel-burning kilns, whose burners are fan-driven, lend themselves to oxidation firing. The popular electric kilns not only lend themselves to the oxidation fire, but most are not designed to be fired in reduction at all.

The contemporary ceramist must decide whether to use an oxidation or reduction firing atmosphere. This will dictate the choice of kiln. Neither oxidation nor reduction is superior; both are to be used by the ceramist when appropriate.

FIRING TEMPERATURES

The choice of firing temperatures is important because it has a strong influence on the look and mood of the work. We fire our work at temperatures that range from approximately 600° C (1112° F) to 1360° C (2480° F).

How do ceramists choose their firing temperature? Those who fire with cones choose a cone or group of cones that falls within that part of the range they feel is desirable. This range can be neatly divided into five segments, each 50 to 60 degrees apart on the Celsius scale. These divisions correspond to the nominal firing temperatures of the Orton cones 04, 02, 3, 6, and 9:

Cone 04—low fire 1060° C/1940° F
Cone 02—low/mid fire 1101° C/2014° F
Cone 3—mid fire 1168° C/2134° F
Cone 6—mid/high fire 1222° C/2232° F
Cone 9—high fire 1250° C/2400° F
(See Tables 14–1 and 14–2 for complete Orton cone charts.)

The jump of 60° C is significant, and the character of each section of the firing spectrum has its own unique aspects. The low temperatures are valued for their vivid color and graphic glaze imagery. As we rise in temperature, we have the opportunity to keep most of the rich color and clay bodies become more workable and durable. The midfire temperatures give us the opportunity to work with durable clay bodies and richer glaze surfaces. Color limitations grow more numerous as we move up in temperature.

High-fire clay bodies are even more workable, and work fired in the high fire tends to be even more durable. Glazes have rich textures and are quite stable. At this point, however, the color range is limited.

Cone 04: 1060° C/1940° F

Cone 04 clay bodies tend to have mediocre workability. Durability is not particularly good either. Bodies fired at this temperature cannot develop the mullite crystals needed for strength. Cone 04 glazes often lack durability and many of them contain toxic materials. Most cone 04 recipes rely on the melting power of lead. These deficits, however, are offset by a brilliant color range. Color in fact is the strong point of cone 04. Almost every color in the spectrum can be achieved here using either normal glaze colorants or galze stains.

Cone 02: 1101° C/2014° F

While cone 02 is still in the low-fire realm, it is easy to develop fairly durable clay bodies and glazes for this firing temperature. Cone 02 glazes need not contain lead. Glaze color is quite rich and saturated. Second only to cone 04, most colors in the spectrum can be achieved using either normal glaze colorants or glaze stains. The glaze surface can be quite durable and can have a great appeal. Clay bodies can be easily worked and fairly durable, though not as durable as those for the higher cones. Mullite crystals which strengthen the body are beginning to develop at this temperature.

Cone 3: 1168° C/2134° F

Cone 3 is a temperature used frequently in industry, and with good reason: the resulting color has a look reminiscent of the low fire, while the clay bodies can be quite dense, durable, and fairly nonpermeable. In this part of the firing spectrum mullite crystals have a chance to fully develop in the clay body, thus strenghtening it in a significant way.

Glazes tend to be durable and stable, and while they benefit significantly from a 10 to 20 percent frit content, their other ingredients can be normal feldspars and secondary fluxes. Firings are short, comparatively effortless, and economical.

Cone 6: 1222° C/2232° F

Cone 6 bodies are usually extremely durable as ample mullite crystal growth is assured at this temperature, and so too is fired durability. Cone 6 glazes are durable and their surfaces can be quite rich. Although cone 6 does not offer the extensive range of saturated color available in the lower fire, color is still good. Many glaze stains as well as normal colorants work well at this temperature.

Cone 6 is an excellent choice for high-fire work in the electric kiln, for it does not place a heavy load on the Kanthal coils in the firing chamber.

In recent years a number of ceramists have become interested in cone 6 reduction. The high calcium/magnesium glazes that are the norm at cone 9/10 will not work as expected at cone 6. The rich glaze-flow patterns that are part of the cone 9/10 reduction fire are not available here. If cone 6 reduction could be made to work well, the benefits would be significant, including comparatively short firing schedules and great economy.

Cone 9: 1250° C/2400° F

Cone 9 has an excellent reputation for its extremely rich and durable glazes. The growth of mullite crystals is assured at cone 9. The problems associated with this firing temperature are in good part technical and economic: it can be difficult and expensive to attain these high temperatures.

It is important to differentiate between the effects of reduction and the effects of temperature upon cone 9 glazes. The spots of black iron that we see in reduction will be absent in oxidation and iron colors will be less saturated. Many stains will lose their color in cone 9 reduction but retain it in oxidation. Glaze flow, however, is markedly similar in oxidation and reduction.

Cone 9 reduction glazes combine the patterns of darkened iron oxide spots and rich glaze flow to create textured surfaces that are not available to ceramists who work at lower firing temperatures. Clay bodies lean toward rich grays, buffs, and whites. Cone 9 reduction color, while often subdued, is extremely rich and the colors harmonize well with each other.

While far more work is done in cone 9 reduction than in cone 9 oxidation, oxidation has many adherents, especially among those who fire in the electric kiln. Durability is excellent and the range of glaze color is surprisingly wide. Unfortunately, the coils in an electric kiln are degraded by frequent firings above cone 8. The ceramist who fires to cone 9 in the electric kiln may well have to replace kiln elements every six months or so. Many ceramists have found the advantages of cone 9 so persuasive, however, that they are willing to put up with its minor inconveniences.

TYPES OF KILNS

While clay can be fired in an open fire and does not require a kiln, kilns allow the ceramist excellent control of heat rise and fall and protect the ware during the rigors of the fire. Therefore almost all contemporary potters use them. A kiln must keep its structural integrity over a period of many firings while being efficient and keeping heat loss to a minimum.

Fuel-Burning Kilns

Until recently, all kilns were fuel burning. Even now that we have access to easily fired electric kilns, many ceramists continue to use fuel-burning kilns because this kind of firing has enduring appeal. Very simply, certain kinds of visual effects can be obtained only from a fuel-burning kiln.

Fuels are divided into solid, liquid, or gaseous. Until the late nineteenth century only solid fuels were available, such as animal dung, wood, and coal. In kilns fired with solid fuels, the unburnt ash residue must be removed frequently. Only one solid fuel, wood, is used extensively among contemporary ceramists in the developed countries. Now most ceramists who fire in fuel-burning kilns fire with a liquid fuel such as oil, or gaseous fuels such as natural gas or propane.

While fuel-burning kilns may be simple, most are complex structures designed to create a strong flow of heat around the work to be fired. A number of different designs are employed: the most important of these are updraft, crossdraft, and downdraft types.

In updraft kilns the firebox is at the base of the kiln. The flame moves up through the ware to an exhaust and a chimney at the top of the kiln. In crossdraft kilns the flue is located on the side of the kiln opposite the burners. Here the heat travels through the ware and is then drawn up the chimney. In downdraft kilns the flame begins at a firebox in front or on the sides of the firing chamber; it is then directed upward over the ware and back down again through the ware. The flame is exhausted into an underfloor chamber and from there is drawn up the chimney. Crossdraft and downdraft kiln designs are the most complex and efficient: it is much easier to reach the high temperatures required for stoneware and porcelain temperatures using kilns of the crossdraft and downdraft type.

Most fuel-burning kilns are built by the ceramist rather than a commercial firm. To build them requires knowledge, time, and skill. Many kilns are the result of innovative and creative thinking and have a real impact on the life and work of the ceramist.

Wood-Burning Kilns

Wood is a surprisingly versatile fuel, and in many parts of the world it is the most economical and widely available fuel. It is still used for low-fire work in simple updraft kilns. In the developed countries, however, wood is mostly used for high-fire work in complex downdraft kilns. At high temperatures wood firing leaves an ash deposit on the ware. The richness of these surfaces in fact is the main argument for using wood as a high-fire fuel.

Firing a wood kiln to high temperatures is physically demanding and requires constant attention. It also calls for an instinctual understanding of what is going on inside the kiln. Almost all high-fire wood kilns work on the crossdraft or downdraft principle. They require a firebox in the front or at the bottom of the kiln with supports (made from either clay or metal) to hold the burning wood. There must be an outlet for spent gasses. It is usually placed near the bottom rear of the kiln. The outlet is connected to a chimney rising above the kiln. The draft of this chimney pulls the spent gasses from the firing chamber and exhausts them into the atmosphere.

Oil and Gas Kilns

Liquid and gaseous fuels have become highly favored among contemporary ceramists, in part because they create no unburnt ash residue and thus are fairly easy to fire. These fuels include oil, kerosene, natural gas, and propane. Modern kilns fired with these fuels are flexible and allow the ceramist to use a wide variety of glaze types and rich visual textures.

Oil has many advantages. Pieces fired in the oil kiln are apt to be somewhat richer and more highly reduced than those fired in the gas kiln. On the other hand, an oil flame is difficult to keep lit until the temperature inside the kiln is above 1000 degrees F. Oil-fired kilns must have a burner system to compensate for this characteristic. Oil kilns are also smokier than gas kilns.

Kilns fueled with natural gas or propane (a derivative of natural gas or petroleum) do not have combustion problems and so are used more in highly industrialized areas than oil kilns. The burners used to fire these fuels are quite efficient and have only a moderate impact on the environment. Piped natural gas is popular in the United States and Canada. It is moderately priced, but its availability is limited to populated areas. Propane, while widely available, is more expensive. Because these fuels have little residue and no ash, they do not encourage as much visual texture as do wood kilns or even oil kilns.

Many high-fire oil and gas kilns are downdraft designs usually with a firebox at the front or the side of the firing chamber. These kilns are similar in design to solid-fuel kilns with the exception that since there is no unburnt ash residue, the firebox can be smaller and need not have a door for the removal of ash.

There are gas kilns that are updraft in design and employ powerful blower-driven burners capable of reaching high temperatures. This design type is commonly found in commercially manufactured gas kilns.

Salt Kilns

Salt firings are done in fuel-burning kilns designed specifically for the salt-firing process. They are constructed of refractory materials that are high in alumina (it is relatively unaffected by the salt which covers everything in the kiln). Special ports are built into the side of the kiln. At that point when the kiln is nearing the highest part of the fire (near cone 9 or 10), the ports are opened and salt is forced into the kiln. The salt reacts strongly to the sudden change of temperature and breaks into its component parts—sodium and chlorine. The chlorine is expelled as a gas. The sodium is deposited on the surface of the ware with such force that the silica and alumina of the clay unite with the sodium from the salt to create a glassy surface.

Because chlorine gas is toxic, most salt kilns are installed outdoors and away from habitations.

Electric Kilns

Electric kilns are used by more contemporary ceramists than any other type. Their economy, simplicity, reliability, and relatively benign impact on the environment guarantee their great popularity. They are somewhat limited in the eyes of many ceramists because they do not lend themselves to the rich effects of reduction and fire markings that characterize fuel-burning kilns. On the other hand, they lend themselves to a wide color range, are simple to load and fire, and are reliable and efficient.

Electric kilns are simple structures, essentially closed boxes made from soft, porous, highly insulating bricks. Inside the kiln, running along channels grooved into its walls, are coils made from a special alloy. Heat is produced by forcing electric current through these tightly wound coils. The result is friction and the result of the friction is heat. This

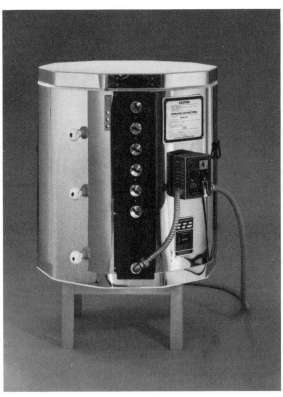

FIG. 13–1 A contemporary top-loading cone 10 electric kiln. Courtesy the American Art Clay Company.

heat is even, easily controlled, and quite reliable.

Electric kilns may be fired manually or with the aid of control mechanisms, which are also used to end the firing when the kiln reaches maturity. Though useful at all parts of the firing spectrum, they are particularly suitable for low- and mid-fire work. They are highly efficient at these temperatures and encourage brilliant color, which is a hallmark of the low and mid fire.

Electric kilns are not as well suited for work at the highest part of the firing spectrum. Coils used for the high fire tend to wear out more quickly than those that have been used only for low-temperature firings. This problem is not insurmountable, however, if careful glazing and cleaning procedures are followed. Manufacturers of coils for electric kilns recommend that they not be fired above cone 8 (1263 C/2305 F), but if cared for properly they will last fairly well even if fired to cone 9 (1280 C/2336 F).

Purchasing an Electric Kiln

Most electric kilns are purchased completely assembled and ready to plug in. Their design and construction varies a great deal, however, so it is no easy matter for the ceramist to make an intelligent purchasing decision.

At one time most electric kilns were front loading. Kilns of this design must be heavily braced. While this is expensive, this design results in a strong kiln that lasts a long time and can be loaded quickly and easily.

Top-loading electric kilns have been popular for years because they are inexpensive. The roofs of these kilns must be carefully designed because they are subject to both mechanical and heat stress. If you choose a top-loading kiln, make sure the roof is replaceable because eventually it will crack under the stress of normal use. The roof hinges, also points of stress, should be designed with strong elongated arms to keep them away from the heat path.

Many newer electric kilns are segmented. The electrical connections between each segment can be a source of problems, so look for connections made with industrial-grade cables or plug-in connections that can withstand the stress that results when the heavy segments are assembled and disassembled.

Look for a kiln that fires evenly. Two designs address this problem—floor mounted coils and fan driven, bottom venting. Originally bottom venting was employed as a way to get rid of fumes from the kiln; their even firing was an unanticipated benefit.

The gutters that hold the coils should be deep and set at an angle to hold the coils securely. The coils should be pinned to the soft brick with refractory metal pins to ensure that they will not come loose and sag during the stress of the high fire. The coils should be made from an alloy that resists high temperatures, such as Kanthal A1; they also should be eaily replaceable, fairly thick (thin coils burn out quickly), and consistently wound to avoid hot spots. The switches, wiring harness, and connecting wires should be heat resistant and of the highest quality. Connections to the power source should be secure: a poorly connected coil will soon burn out. The insulation should be effective and durable.

Electric kilns require special high-quality, high-capacity fuses, cables, and outlets. To install an electric kiln, there is no substitute for the services of a qualified electrician.

Small Test Kilns

Most small test kilns are simply designed and can be built easily or purchased. They are electric-fired and work from normal house current (110 volts U.S., 240 G.B.). They have small firing chambers, usually under a square foot in area, are portable, quick firing, and inexpensive. Because of the quick pace of the firing, pieces fired in these kilns are likely to crack or explode. Furthermore their quick cooling adversely influences the look of the glaze. In a normal firing cycle glazes have a chance to develop a crystalline structure during the cooling period. Most glazes derive a great deal of their character from crystallization, a process that opacifies and modulates their surfaces. A glaze fired in a test kiln will not only lack character, it will also not look the same as a glaze fired in a standard kiln.

To control the firing cycle and encourage rich glaze surfaces, the current flowing to the test kiln must be controlled so that the coil runs only part of the time. This can be done with a reliable and inexpensive device called a "current-interruption" switch. Many companies install these devices on test kilns, so if you buy a kiln, you may not have to purchase this device separately.

The following firing cycle is recommended for test kiln firings: for ten minutes, set the kiln on very low current with the lid open, then close the lid. After twenty minutes, turn up the switch. Continue to turn it up every twenty minutes, switching the current from very low to low, then to medium low, then to medium, then to high. Leave the kiln at the high setting until the cone bends and the kiln has reached the desired temperature.

Now the kiln must be fired down. Turn down the switch every thirty minutes, switching the current from medium to low to very low. At the end of this procedure, turn off the switch and allow the kiln to cool. An hour later open the lid. Then forty minutes later take off the lid and empty the kiln.

You can fire finished pieces as well as tests in these tiny, quick-firing kilns. While you must tailor the form and size of the piece to the limitations of the kiln, in many cases this presents an interesting challenge. Small-scale ceramic objects such as jewelry are perfect for this kind of kiln. Since the kiln is so portable and may be installed anywhere, a ceramist on the move might find it a useful tool.

CHAPTER 14

Loading and Firing

LOADING A KILN

Contemporary ceramists usually place their ware on kiln shelves. In the past, when there were no shelves, they often piled the pieces one on top of another, sometimes touching, sometimes separated by wads of refractory clay. They also placed their work in refractory clay containers called "saggers." Saggers were designed to be stacked one on top of another.

Kiln shelves are more efficient and convenient than saggers. They vary in size but are rarely more than 20 or 25 inches in any dimension and usually are half an inch to an inch thick. The shelves are made from refractory materials so that they will resist warping and cracking.

Alumina shelves are often used for oxidation firing (including electric kiln firings). They are light in color (white or buff) and can withstand heat shock well. Silicon carbide shelves are used for the reduction fire. While not as resistant to heat shock as alumina shelves, they are extremely durable.

Kiln shelves are supported by posts that range in height from three to nine inches. Kiln posts are usually made from a refractory fire clay.

Loading an Electric Kiln

Before you begin to load the kiln, check the height of the ware to be fired to determine what kiln posts you will need. If you need just a bit more height, add kiln shelf fragments on top of the posts. Start with fairly low pieces and keep your tallest pieces for the top of the kiln. Don't waste space by putting low pieces with tall pieces. Instead, keep the height of the ware on each shelf fairly uniform.

Place the posts on the first shelf. Generally three posts are used, though large shelves for the electric kiln (over 1,200 square centimeters or 200 square inches) require four posts. Load the ware on this first shelf. Be careful as you load: a great many pieces are broken at this time.

Place the next shelf on the kiln posts. If you are using four kiln posts for each shelf, check for wobbling. If the shelf wobbles, place kiln wadding (a mortar-like substance made from grog and clay) over the low post.

Place the posts on the newly placed shelf and load this shelf. Continue until the loading is finished. If you are using cones to indicate conditions inside the kiln (a good idea even if you are firing with a kiln controller), leave room for the cone on the shelf that is nearest to the spy hole. Check by looking through the spy hole as you load the kiln.

CONES

Cones are our most accurate indication of the conditions inside the kiln during firing. They are much accurate in fact than electrical or optical measuring devices. This is because cones contain the same materials as clays and glazes and have been carefully formulated to act in the same way during the firing. Cones are merely small elongated triangular pyramids. When the proper conditions occur inside the kiln, they soften and

deform. This deformation tells the ceramist that the firing is complete. Cones indicate a combination of time and temperature, not just temperature alone. For convenience we talk of the firing temperature of a cone, but this is only a nominal figure used for comparison with other cones.

Beginners often find the numbering system for cones confusing. High-temperatures cones are numbered from 1 to 14, with each step indicating a rise in temperature. The low-temperature cones have a zero as their first digit and descend from cone 01 to 020. The numbers increase as the temperature falls. In other words, the numbers fall in value as the temperature rises in the low-temperature part of the firing spectrum; the numbers rise in value in the high-temperature part of the spectrum (see Tables 14–1, 14–2).

FIG. 14–1 The Orton Foundation is a major source for ceramic cones. From left to right: a large regular cone, a large self-supporting cone, a small regular cone. In front: a bar cone (for use with current-interruption devices). Courtesy The Edward Orton, Jr., Ceramic Foundation.

Placing the Cone in the Kiln

Use a cone pack of three or four cones: one or two that are lower in temperature than your desired maturation point, one that will deform at the desired maturation point, and one that will deform at a temperature higher than the maturation point. The lower-temperature cones will let you know when you are approaching maturation temperature, the cone that deforms at your desired firing temperature will let you know that you have reached the desired point, and the final cone will let you know if you have overfired.

Place the cones at a slight angle in kiln wadding and force them into the wadding. The surface of the wadding is pierced to prevent the cone pack from blowing up, and it must be dry before the firing begins.

If you are firing a new kiln or a kiln that is difficult to fire, place the cones in various parts of the kiln to help you troubleshoot after the firing is over.

Kiln Sitters

Many ceramists who fire in the electric kiln use kiln sitters, a mechanical kiln controller

TABLE 14–1   CONE CHART IN DEGREES CELSIUS

Cone number	Heating Rate (Large Regular Cone)		Heating Rate (Small Regular Cone)
	60° C/hr	150° C/hr	300° C/hr
022	579	589	625
021	596	611	646
020	620	634	664
019	671	685	712
018	708	725	755
017	731	752	785
016	764	784	825
015	787	807	843
014	807	831	880
013	837	859	892
012	855	864	900
011	873	884	918
010	887	894	919
09	915	923	955
08	945	955	983
07	973	984	1008
06	991	999	1023
05 1/2	1011	1023	1042
05	1031	1046	1062
04	1050	1060	1098
03	1086	1101	1131
02	1101	1120	1148
01	1117	1137	1178
1	1136	1154	1179
2	1142	1162	1179
3	1152	1168	1196
4	1168	1186	1209
5	1177	1196	1221
6	1201	1222	1255
7	1215	1240	1264
8	1236	1263	1300
9	1260	1280	1317
10	1285	1305	1330
11	1294	1315	1336
12	1306	1326	1355
13	1321	1346	1349
14	1388	1366	1398
15	1424	1431	1430

Courtesy: The Edward Orton, Jr., Ceramic Foundation

that holds a small cone. When the cone deforms, a bar moves upward and activates a solenoid switch, which switches off the current to the kiln. When kiln controllers are kept clean and rust-free, they are reliable and useful. If the controller is not cared for properly, or if the cone is not carefully placed, the switch will not work and the kiln will overfire. Even if you use a kiln controller, it is a good idea to place a large cone next to one of the spy holes as a backup.

One final note: the small cones used in

TABLE 14–2 CONE CHART IN DEGREES FAHRENHEIT

| Cone number | Heating Rate (Large Regular Cone) | | Heating Rate (Small Regular Cone) |
	108° F/hr	270° F/hr	540° F/hr
022	1074	1092	1157
021	1105	1132	1195
020	1148	1173	1227
019	1240	1265	1314
018	1306	1337	1391
017	1348	1386	1445
016	1407	1443	1517
015	1449	1485	1549
014	1485	1528	1616
013	1539	1570	1638
012	1571	1587	1652
011	1603	1623	1684
010	1629	1641	1686
09	1679	1693	1751
08	1733	1751	1801
07	1783	1803	1846
06	1816	1830	1873
05	1888	1915	1944
04	1922	1940	2008
03	1987	2014	2068
02	2014	2048	2098
01	2043	2079	2152
1	2077	2109	2154
2	2088	2124	2154
3	2106	2134	2185
4	2134	2167	2208
5	2151	2185	2230
6	2194	2232	2291
7	2219	2264	2307
8	2257	2305	2372
9	2300	2336	2403
10	2345	2381	2426
11	2361	2399	2437
12	2383	2419	2471
13	2410	2455	2460
14	2530	2491	2548
15	2595	2608	2606

Courtesy: The Edward Orton, Jr., Ceramic Foundation

kiln sitters were not originally intended for ceramic use. They are formulated differently from the large cones and tend to bend earlier. You may find that the equivalent to a cone 3 in a small cone is cone 4 and that a small cone 7 should be substituted for a large cone.

Electric kilns soon will be fired using computers (see Appendix).

Sighting the Cone
During the later stages of the firing, the atmosphere inside the kiln is brilliantly lit and

the cone is visible. When loading, obviously, the kiln is dark, so light up the interior with a piece of burning newspaper or a flashlight. Close the door tightly and sight the cone. Make sure that the kiln shelves are not obstructing the view of the cone. If they are, place shims under the cone to adjust its height and move it to a spot where you can easily see it. This is important because the cone is your only accurate indicator of the conditions inside the kiln.

BISQUE FIRING

Contemporary ceramists usually do a preliminary firing (or bisque firing) before applying a glaze or another type of surface finish to the piece. This makes sense because most surface finishes are suspended in a water medium, which can crack or break an unfired piece. Our finishes are much less likely to peel or crawl during the firing when applied to bisque-fired ware. This is because a glaze with little clay shrinks very little. These glazes are highly compatible with bisque ware, which also shrinks very little.

Bisque firing may be lower in temperature, the same, or higher in temperature than the final firing. Most bisque is fired to a fairly low temperature, usually cone 08–06. Work that is bisque fired in this way will not break down in water, but its absorbent surface will readily accept glaze. After applying the surface finish, the ceramist fires the piece at a higher temperature and the work completed.

On some occasions ceramists fire to higher temperatures in the bisque than in the final fire—for example, porcelain bisque firings and firings of low-fire glazes. In high-temperature porcelain bisque firings, the ceramist fires the unglazed piece to maturity in a container of silica sand, which discourages warping. The piece is then glazed and fired normally, but to a temperature significantly lower than the warping point of the clay body; the body is unaffected by the heat needed to fuse the glaze and does not warp.

FIG. 14–2 Richard Devore. USA. Bowl 13¾ inches wide. Multifire techniques.

FIG. 14–3 Richard Devore. USA. Vase, 13½ inches. Multi-fire techniques.

Glazes applied to such mature bodies need to be thicker and stickier than normal glazes. This may be accomplished by using an oil base rather than water base or by adding glue, a colloidal material, or bentonite (a very fine clay) to a water-base glaze.

Ceramists who work with low-temperature glazes, such as cone 06 or 08, will often fire to a cone 04 bisque. The body is still absorbent at this point but is more durable than it would be if it were fired only to the maturation point of the glazes.

Bisque firing at the same temperature as the glaze is also possible. The advantage in this case is that bisque and glaze pieces may be fired in the same kiln. This method is appropriate when used with low-fire absorbent bodies or if the glazes have been formulated for application on a mature, non-absorbent bisque.

BISQUE FIRING AN ELECTRIC KILN (Cones 010–05)

A Day-Long Firing

First Day

9 A.M.	Start the kiln on a low setting (two switches turned on) and leave the door ajar.
10 A.M.	Close the kiln door.
6 P.M.	The interior of the kiln is now quite hot (around 600° C). Turn the kiln switches to medium or medium high.
7 P.M.	Turn the kiln switches to high.
8–10 P.M.	When the kiln reaches maturation temperature, turn it off.

Second Day

11 A.M.   Open the kiln door slightly.
3 P.M.   Open the kiln door
            completely.
6 P.M.   Unload the kiln.

An Overnight Bisque Firing (Chart 14–1)

First Day

3 P.M.   Start the kiln on a low setting
            (two switches turned on)
            and leave the door ajar.
5 P.M.   Close the kiln door and allow
            the kiln to fire overnight.

Second Day

9 A.M.   The interior of the kiln is
            quite hot (around 600° C).
            Turn up the kiln switches
            to medium or medium
            high.
9:30 A.M.– When the kiln reaches
    1 P.M. maturation temperature,
            turn it off.

Third Day

9 A.M.   Open the kiln door slightly.
11 A.M.   Open the kiln door
            completely.
1 P.M.   Unload the kiln.

THE FINAL FIRE

The final step before the ceramic piece is complete is often the most dramatic. The final firing has a strong effect upon the look

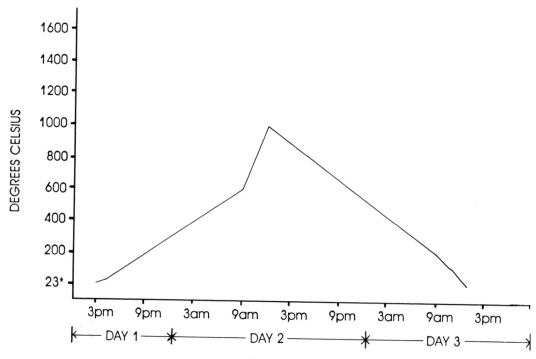

* 23° is a typical ambient temperature in the kiln.

CHART 14–1   AN OVERNIGHT CONE 06 BISQUE FIRING (ELECTRIC KILN)

of the fired piece. In fact in some cases, as in a wood or a salt fire, it may be the single most important influence upon its character. It is here that the piece is likely to undergo its greatest stress, and it is here that the greatest possibility exists for a gratifying success or a frustrating failure.

In some kinds of firing, such as reduction, salt, or wood firing, the process can be extremely time-consuming and demanding. In others, such as an electric fire, the process is far less exacting. Even the electric fire, however, requires attention, especially during the cooling phase.

All firings are demanding, and all end in the moment of truth when the kiln door is opened and the outcome of the work is revealed.

FINAL FIRING IN AN ELECTRIC KILN (Cones 04–9)

A Day-Long Firing

First Day

9 A.M.	Start the kiln on a low setting.
9:30 A.M.	Close the kiln door.
6 P.M.	The interior of the kiln is quite hot (around 600° C). Turn up the kiln switches to medium or medium high.
6:30 A.M.	Turn up the kiln switches to high.
9 P.M.–11 P.M.	When the kiln reaches maturation temperature, turn the heat to low and "soak" the kiln.
1 hour later	Turn off the kiln.

Second Day

11 A.M.	Open the kiln door slightly.
2 P.M.	Open the kiln door completely.
6 P.M.	Unload the kiln.

An Overnight Glaze Firing (Chart 14–2)

First Day

3 P.M.	Start the kiln on a low setting (two switches turned on) and leave the door ajar.
5 P.M.	Close the kiln door and allow the kiln to fire on low heat overnight.

Second Day

9 A.M.	The interior of the kiln is quite hot (around 600° C). Turn up the kiln switches to medium or medium high.
9:30 A.M.	Turn up the kiln switches to high.
2 P.M.—4 P.M.	When the kiln reaches maturation temperature, turn the setting to low and "soak" the kiln.
1 to 2 hours later	Turn off the kiln.

Third Day

9 A.M.	Open the kiln door slightly.
1 A.M.	Open the kiln door completely.
2 P.M.	Unload the kiln.

Cooling the Kiln

Controlling heat loss is especially important during the firing since most electric kilns lose heat quickly. Glazes are especially sensitive to abrupt changes during the cooling process. Crystals form in a glaze as it cools. These crystals strongly influence the look of the fired glaze, encouraging matness, depth, and richness: if the cooling is abrupt, the crystals will not have a chance to form.

To control the cooling process, turn off the kiln in stages. Leave it for an hour at medium heat, then an hour at a low setting, before turning it off completely.

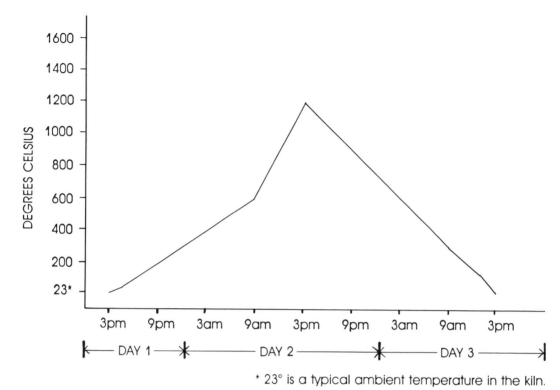

* 23° is a typical ambient temperature in the kiln.

CHART 14–2   AN OVERNIGHT CONE 6 GLAZE FIRING (ELECTRIC KILN)

FIG. 14–4 Bruce Cochrane. Canada. "Elevated Covered Dish," 10 × 8 inches. Earthenware red-clay body, wheel-formed and altered, fired to cone 05, finished with a majolica glaze and overglaze decoration on the bottom and terra sigillata on the top. Photo: Peter Hogan.

Kilns Equipped with a Control Mechanism

An electric kiln can be fired down or soaked even if it is equipped with a control mechanism. Activated by a sensor that is tripped when a desired temperature is reached or by the bending of a cone, these mechanisms shut off all current to the kiln. Reset the controller, turn the coil switches to moderate settings and keep at these settings for an hour or so before turning off the power.

A CONE 9 REDUCTION FIRING IN A GAS KILN (CHART 14–3)

First Day

3 P.M.   Start the kiln with the burners on very low and open the damper wide. Allow the temperature to rise only 38° to 45° C (100–110° F) an hour. Leave the burners on low to fire overnight.

Second Day

9 A.M.   The interior of the kiln is quite hot (around 870° C/1600° F).

As body reduction begins, close the damper slightly. This will restrict the amount of air allowed to enter the kiln. The gas pressure is also raised. Keep the kiln in body reduction for half an hour to an hour.

At this point reduction is moderated. Keep the kiln in this state of moderate reduction for the rest of the firing. If too much reduction is allowed to occur, the work will become muddy in color and will be brittle. If the kiln is allowed to reoxidize, the effects of body reduction will be lost. Closely monitor the rate of rise in temperature and don't allow it to fall. It should rise consistently.

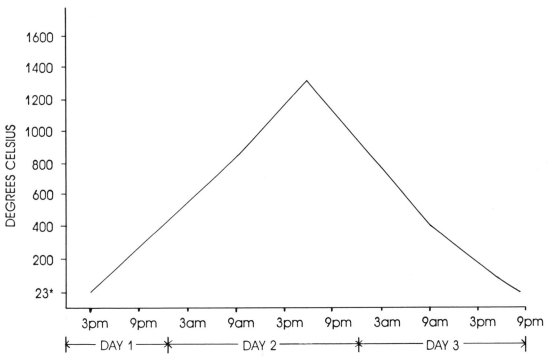

* 23° is a typical ambient temperature in the kiln.

CHART 14–3   A CONE 9 FIRING (GAS KILN)

If the temperature begins to fall, open the damper slightly. If the temperature climbs too rapidly at this point, the kiln may have slipped into oxidation. In this case, partially close the damper.

2 P.M.–11 P.M. The kiln reaches maturation temperature sometime between 2 P.M. and 11 P.M.

At this point many potters terminate the firing. Others, however, "soak" or "fire down" by turning down the gas to low, lowering the amount of air allowed to enter the firing chamber, and partially closing the damper. The soaking period takes a half an hour to an hour.

Controlling Cooling in a Reduction Firing
When the kiln is in reduction, it may stall and there will be little or no heat rise. Since most ceramists put the kiln into reduction toward the end of the firing, heat loss is controlled naturally.

To end the firing, turn off the gas, close the damper, and allow the kiln to cool. In some open kilns, the burner ports may also have to be stopped up; this is usually done with a spun kaolin blanket. The cooling process will take one or two days.

When the kiln is at 400° C (750° F), open the damper slightly. A few hours later open the damper wider. When the temperature reaches 250° C (500° F), open the damper completely. A few hours later you may unload the kiln.

It is difficult to understand what is happening inside the kiln during the firing. Clues as to the character of the atmosphere inside the chamber are particularly important. The traditional indicator is the way the flame comes from the spy hole. A two-inch-long flame indicates a heavy reduction, while a half inch flame indicates a light reduction. Many ceramists use a meter that analyzes the atmosphere inside the kiln; these can be useful tools.

Many ceramists who fire a great deal in reduction feel that the body reduction is the most crucial part of the reduction process and emphasize that it should take place at a point below cone 08 (955° C/1750° F). Beyond this point many of the glaze fluxes may have begun to melt and body reduction will not be effective.

The time at which the kiln reaches maturation temperature depends on its efficiency, the density of the kiln load, and the character of the draft pulling the heat through the kiln. Perhaps the most important factor, however, is the rate which the ceramist would like the temperature to rise. Some ceramists would like the period before maturation to be marked by a swift heat rise; others prefer a long, slow "stewing" process. These preferences seem to depend mostly on the expectations of the ceramist and on the character of the imagery used on the work.

Whether the ceramist employs a soaking process seems to depend in part on the efficiency of the kiln, its cooling pattern, and the character of the glazes used. Here too, however, personal preference seems to play a big part in the nature of these decisions.

MULTIFIRING
Multifiring is the process of firing a piece to different temperatures during successive firings, starting with the highest temperature and then moving down the scale. This process is frequently used in color-oriented work. The guiding theory here is that each part of the firing spectrum is effective for the production of different colors and that multifiring allows the whole range of the color spectrum to be covered.

The process requires great care, patience, and technical skill. The ceramist must be willing to spend a good deal of time and energy on each piece. In addition, multifiring puts the ware in jeopardy because each successive firing increases the risk of cracking. The advantage of multifiring is that the work will be rich and intense.

In the photo essay that follows, the potter Regis Brodie takes us through the steps required to multifire a large porcelain piece.

This photo shows an application of a thickened copper red glaze painted with a large brush. With a finger and a wooden tool, lines were scratched through the freshly glazed piece. The piece has already been fired once to cone 9/10 with underglaze pencils and wax resist and stained with soluble metal salts. Because the surface has already been fired, the glaze must be thick in order to achieve the proper application. Excess glaze at the neck and base are cleaned and the piece is ready to be fired again.

The same piece after it has been fired a second time to cone 9/10. A luster has been applied over the entire surface except for the neck and the base. I use a soft brush and use the potter's wheel as a banding wheel. I try for an even application. Once dry, the piece is ready for a cone 019/018 luster firing.

The final result of the three firings, two to cone 9/10 and one to cone 019/018. The luster changes its color and iridescence depending if the glaze that is applied to is shiny or mat, or, in this case, the piece has areas where the colored raw porcelain is exposed and not glazed. The combination gives the piece a depth and richness. "Lustered Oval Form," porcelain, multifired, 22" high.

Regis Brodie

Over the years I have used many different firing techniques. My explorations were sometimes motivated by the need to alter the results that came from a single firing technique. I did not want to be dictated to by the kiln. Instead, I wanted to work with the many firing options available to any potter wishing to improve a glaze or finish.

I began multifiring as a way of saving pots

Regis Brodie. USA. "Large Oval Form," 30 inches high. White stoneware clay body with porcelain slip, underglaze pencils and chalks, wax resist, and soluable metal salts. Photo: Joseph Levy.

that had good form but whose glazes didn't quite work. I have reglazed high-fired pieces with high-fire glazes and engobes two, three, and even four times. I have combined high-fired pieces with low-fire 06 glazes, enamels, and lusters. I choose the multifiring technique that best suits the particular piece.

Because high-fired pottery is dense and vitreous and cannot take much thermal shock, special care must be taken during the refiring and cooling process. Earthenware bodies are generally open and more resistant to thermal shock because of their porosity and low-firing ranges. However, care in refiring and cooling is still necessary to avoid dunting.[1] "Dunting" is a term used to describe the cracking that occurs in the ware during the firing or cooling cycle. Dunting points are critical temperatures at which the silica inversions take place. The potter must be concerned with the stresses on the clay body caused by the expansion or contraction of the silica inversions.

The two silica inversions are quartz and cristobalite. Quartz is present in all clay bodies, regardless of their firing temperature. In addition to the quartz form of silica, stoneware and porcelain and other pottery bodies fired over 2012° F (1100° C) form varying amounts of cristobalite during their firing. Earthenware, due to its "open" character, can withstand the stress of the cristobalite squeeze.

According to David Green, there are two important dunting points to watch for when firing and cooling *already-fired* pottery.

On Heating:
1. The alpha cristobalite, for ware that was fired over 2012° F (1100° C), inverts to beta cristobalite at 428° F–536° F (220° C–280° C) with a 3% expansion.
2. The alpha quartz, for all pottery, inverts to beta quartz at 1022° F–1067° F (550° C–575° C) with a 1% expansion.

On Cooling:
1. The beta quartz inverts back to alpha quartz at 1067° F–1020° F (575° C–550° C) with a 1% contraction.
2. The beta cristobalite inverts back to alpha cristobalite at 536° F–428° F (280° C–220° C) with a 3% contraction.[2]

When firing, keep these dunting points in mind. The best way to fire is slowly and evenly, much like a biscuit-firing schedule. For tall or open pieces, firing at a rate of 150° F (65° C) per hour up to 570° F (300° C) should avoid dunting. Continue to fire the kiln normally until the desired temperature is reached. The kiln should be allowed to cool as slowly as possible. I wait until the kiln is 250° F (150° C) or lower before opening it.

Kilns that are thicker walled or better insulated can be fired more evenly and will cool more slowly. If I have only one or two pieces to fire, I will fill the spaces in the kiln with extra posts and hard bricks to increase the mass in the kiln. This slows the firing and the cooling and reduces the chances of dunting.

On an already-fired porcelain piece that I had decorated with underglaze pencils and wax resist and stained with soluble metal salts, I applied a thickened copper-red glaze (see photo series). I scratched lines in the wet glaze with my finger and a wooden stick, then fired the piece to cone 9/10. The firing of refires must proceed slowly, especially between 400° F and 600° F, and again between 950° F and 1150° F. Once past these temperatures the firing can proceed normally. After the piece was cooled slowly and the temperature was below 350° F, I removed it from the kiln. I then decided that I needed a third firing. I applied a luster over the whole piece except for the rim and the base and refired it again to cone 019/018. The final result was quite satisfying.

Multifiring has made it possible for me to correct and save some pieces that would otherwise have been mediocre. Refiring provides an opportunity for a different creative solution. I do not give up on my pieces even if it means firing them seven or eight times. I keep firing until the piece is right or the piece dies trying.

1. Frank Hamer, *The Potter's Dictionary of Materials and Techniques.* London: A & C Black, 1975, 91.

2. David Green, *Pottery Glazes,* New York: Watson-Guptill, 1975, 179–181.

APPENDIX A
Ceramics of the Past

As ceramists it is inevitable that we look at pieces from the past in a unique way. We tend to connect with this work directly and identify with certain examples almost as if we ourselves had made them. Which one of us has not looked at such a piece and tried to put ourselves next to its creator during the time of its creation? Looking at these works even has overtones of a detective novel: with a little study we can begin to understand how they were created and why particular methods were used.

ASIA

China

Ceramics developed in China about 220 B.C. Two types of work were developed almost simultaneously: in western China a type called Yang Shao Redware, painted with highly burnished terra sigillatas, and in eastern China a monochromatic blackware known as Lung-Shan ware. Both are low fire. The Yang Shao ware is coil formed, very thin, and constructed and painted with great skill. Its painted imagery is highly patterned and elegantly geometric. Lung-Shan ware is monochromatic. While not as striking as Yang Shao redware, its carefully designed shapes seem to have been formed with the aid of a potter's wheel (probably a "slow" wheel).

These cultures were succeeded by the Shang and Chou dynasties, which are noted for their cast bronze vessels (molded from clay originals). Highly carved ceramics of great refinement were also created during this period. The Han Dynasty (200 B.C.–A.D. 200) was a time of great advances in ceramic technology. Both low-fire lead-glazed and high-fire ash-glazed work was made during this period. The low-fire ware was often mold formed. Its lead glazes, originally a transparent copper green, have evolved over time into an opaque metallic silvery green. The high-fire pieces were thrown with great virtuosity and elegance.

The glaze effects of these early stoneware pieces were derived from wood ash, a natural by-product of the wood fire. The development of high-fire stoneware was brought about by advances in kiln design. During this period a new kind of kiln, a hill-climbing kiln, was developed in which high temperatures could be produced and maintained. (These are long, narrow kilns built on the side of a hill; the mouth of the kiln is at the bottom of the hill and the flame exits at the top. This creates a draft just as a tall chimney would and encourages high temperatures.) This period also saw the production of the clay armies of the Emperors of Ch'in. These unglazed sculptures are striking in their numbers and size.

The next great period of Chinese ceramics occurred during the T'ang Dynasty (618–906). A good deal of this work was thrown, and much of it shows great skill and verve. Most Tang ceramics were low-fire, slip-decorated, and lead-glazed. Because lead bonds with the silica and alumina in clay, lead glazes can be used that contain no clay. The Tang potters seem to have applied glazes composed entirely of lead over their clay bodies and colored slips. Because it had no alumina content of its own, this glaze ran and flowed in the fire. The Tang potters compensated for this strong glaze flow by leaving the lower part of the piece unglazed.

The Sung Dynasty (960–1279) was a time of great brilliance in Chinese ceramics and marks the widespread introduction of porcelain. From northern China came the porcelain called T'ing ware, which is light cream in color and soft and fluid in appearance. In southern China the porcelain is whiter, harder, and more restrained in shape. Most of this work was thrown, some of it over highly decorated press molds, then fired in wood-burning climbing kilns in a reduction atmosphere. The dense white clay bodies enhanced visual texture and glaze color and often were ornamented with carved or drawn imagery.

At the same time in northern China, an oxidized, highly decorated mid-fired stoneware was

FIG. A–1 China. Yang Shao Redware, Kansu Province, 13½ inches, 3d Millennium B.C. Hand-built (probably coil-formed) earthenware painted with terra sigillatas. The Everson Museum, Syracuse, New York Museum purchase. P.C. 86.71. Photograph © Courtney Frisse.

produced called T'zu Chou. It was thrown on the wheel and featured graphically ornamented surfaces. Sometimes slips were partially carved to reveal the clay body and the whole piece was then covered with a clear glaze. Or a dark glaze based on a high-impurity clay might be applied over a lighter body and partially carved.

After the Sung Dynasty came the Yuan period (1280–1368) and the introduction of blue-and-white ware, in which a cobalt decoration was painted over white porcelain and covered with a clear glaze. After the Yuan came the Ming Dynasty, which lasted from 1368 to 1643. The Ming potters continued the tradition of blue-and-white ware but also explored the possibilities of multiple firings, wherein low-fire glazes were first applied to a glazed and fired porcelain piece. In this way the taut forms and durable glazes of porcelain could be combined with the brilliant color and graphic imagery of the low fire.

The potters of the Ch'ing Dynasty (1644–1912) carried on the Ming tradition of high-fire porcelain. The great achievements of Ch'ing pottery took place from 1662 to 1795 during the reigns of Kang Hsi, Wan Li, and Chien Lung. Ch'ing

dynasty porcelains are aristocratic (many of the best pieces were created for the Imperial House), fastidious, technically imposing, and highly inventive. Much of this work was strongly marked by the then-new palette of brilliant low-fire overglaze colors that had originated in France.

During the Ch'ing Dynasty another kind of work was developed that was quite different from the Imperial porcelains. Yi-hsing, which is still being produced, is mold-formed and the clay bodies, which are not glazed, vary in color from light tan to a brick red. In this style, form is important and conveys a sense of care and intellect.

The nineteenth and twentieth centuries were difficult times for the Chinese, at first marked by decay and then by political turbulence. The production of porcelain and Yi-hsing continued, but none of it seems to have attained the high levels of technical skill and aesthetic value of the earlier work.

Japan

The best-known early Japanese work is from what has come to be called the Jomon culture. The name means "cord impressed" and is derived from the characteristic cord markings on the sides of the pots. While some ancient examples of Jomon have been found, most of the great Jomon pots date from around 500 B.C. This work was built with coil-forming methods and fired to low temperatures in open fires. The Jomon potters knew nothing of glazes or slips, yet they were able to make the most of their clay surfaces. These large coil pieces are noted for their exuberant, inventive applied imagery.

The Jomon was an indigenous culture, while the next Japanese cultures reflect the influence of newcomers from Asia. The first was the Yayoi culture, which was strongly influenced by the new technology and form ideas emanating from Korea and China. The Tomb culture followed, marked by the creation of large burial mounds and ceramic sculptures called Haniwa, which were intended for placement upon them. These large, robust, simply modeled figural sculptures are evidence of a real understanding and love for the material.

A period of renewed interest in the creation of vessels and the learning of technical skills followed. At this time the potter's wheel and ceramic glazes were introduced from the Asian mainland. Next came the Kamakura potters (1185–1338), who produced thrown pieces with rich, full forms. Simple geometric designs were often stamped on the surface of these pieces, which were then finished with wood-ash glazes. The pottery of the succeeding Muromachi period is similar but with a greater emphasis on loose, thrown forms and highly textured glaze surfaces, often the result of long firings. Many of the great pieces from Bizen and Shino were created during this period.

The Momoyama period is marked by the desire to create a sophisticated artistic ceramic ware. Oribe ware, intended for use in the tea ceremony, was developed, named after Oribe Furita (died 1615), a Japanese tea master and connoisseur of ceramics. These pieces seem to have been fired in mid- or high-fire kilns in an oxidation or neutral atmosphere. Many of the most important pieces were hand-built, often over muslin-wrapped forms; others were thrown on the potter's wheel.

The Oribe potters employed a complex system of imagery. A single piece might be ornamented with two different colors of clay, a black glaze (used to create linear imagery), slips, and a translucent green glaze.

In the next period, the Edo, two approaches to clay coexisted—a materials-oriented strategy, exemplified by Bizen ware, and an image-oriented approach, which took its cues from painting, fabric imagery, and the Oribe style. The calligrapher Kenzan Ogata (1663–1743) produced work of the second type. While his work was modest in size and the forms were simple, the painted imagery was complex and graphic. Kenzan or his brother Korin did the painting and Kenzan oversaw the glazing and the firing. This ware is low-fire, painted first with a white slip, then with imagery (often created with a simple black slip), and covered with a clear glaze. Kenzan's work is closely related to Kyo-Yoki (Old Kyoto Ware), a highly graphic style with a strong emphasis on color.

The nineteenth century was marked by a great interest in technical skill, precise imagery, and a good deal of work utilizing the multifire techniques of Ch'ing Dynasty in China. In the early decades of the twentieth century the Japanese were ready for a revival of interest in the looser, more materials-oriented strategies of earlier periods. This revival was led by Soetsu Yanagi, its ideologist, and the potters Shoji Hamada and Bernard Leach (for more on Leach, see the section on English pottery). At present, Japanese ceramists seem to be trying to integrate contemporary, international ceramic styles with their own traditions—often with much success.

Korea

The potters of the Silla Kingdom (about 57 B.C.–A.D. 935) produced high-quality tomb ware, particularly ceremonial covered jars with large pierced feet. This work was thrown on the potter's wheel, high fired in a reduction atmosphere, and left unglazed. Its gray color was derived from a heavy reduction with no reoxidation.

During the Koryo period (918–1392), the Korean potters came under the influence of the Chinese potters of the Sung Dynasty. They produced vessels with full and generous forms finished with celadon glazes, the pots often decorated with inlaid clay designs, which became the basis for the Mishima work of the Japanese. The Yi Dynasty followed and was marked by work in a similar vein.

At the end of the 1500s Korea was twice invaded by Japan, and in 1637 it became a vassal state of China. Nothing of note seems to have been produced over the next several centuries. Recently, however, in newly prosperous South Korea, there has been a renaissance in ceramics

FIG. A—2 Korea. Silla ware, 4 inches, 57 B.C.–A.D. 935. Wheel formed and unglazed; fired in heavy reduction with no reoxidation. Private collection.

by potters taking their lead from contemporary Japanese pottery and from a revival of interest in ancient Korean pottery.

THE MIDDLE EAST

The potters of the ancient Middle East are responsible for many of the tools and techniques that are still an important part of ceramics. These include the potter's wheel, terra sigillatas, and glazes. Pottery making began here before 7000 B.C. By 4000 B.C. terra sigillata was in common use. Much of this work was monochromatic, but many of the most interesting pieces were ornamented with painted imagery. The painted ware of Susa, in Iran, is especially noteworthy for its graphic painted imagery.

The potter's wheel and true glazes were developed in Egypt as early as 3000 B.C. During the Achaemenid period in Iran (1533–330 B.C.), large richly colored and glazed brick wall reliefs were created. The Sassanian period in Iran (3d–7th century A.D.) was marked by a decline in interest in ceramics, for its rulers were far more interested in the metal arts. It took the advent of Islam with

its release of new energies to revive interest in ceramics. This revival is noted for the mastery of glaze imagery. Both vessels and tiles were formed using the press-mold process. Many slip and glaze techniques were employed in this low-fire work, the most common being the application of a clear alkaline or lead glaze over painted slips.

Many other techniques were employed as well, including fritted white clay bodies (made in imitation of porcelain), multicolored slip-painted ware, and luster ware. This work is elegant and colorful, with a singleminded concentration on rich surface imagery. Architectural ceramics were especially important, and large quarters of such cities as Isfahan, in Iran, became noted for their tile-clad buildings.

EUROPE AND ENGLAND

Painted wares from Crete and Cyprus (2000–1000 B.C.) were influenced by the work of the ancient Middle East. These wares were richly painted and served as the basis for the painted terra sigillatas of Greece's golden age. Greek pottery was low fired, thrown on the potter's wheel, and often highly decorated by skillful painters working in terra sigillata. Corinth and Athens were the two great centers of Greek pottery.

Corinth, a center of pottery from 700 to 550 B.C., is noted for highly painted work in which little open space was allowed. Animal images surrounded by florettes are most common. Corinth had strong ties to Persia and its potters were strongly influenced by Persian ceramics.

The great period of Athenian pottery was from about 600 to 400 B.C. These skillfully thrown forms seem to be derived from stone and metal as much as from clay. The painted terra sigillata imagery is at once highly stylized and quite realistic. The act of throwing was separated from that of painting. The painters in fact were judged to have more significance, and their deft, stylized imagery, defined by a sharp sgraffito line, is unique in the history of ceramics.

Roman potters used both terra sigillatas and lead glazes, but usually their work was monochromatic. The Romans were pioneers in the art of slipcast pottery. In general, decoration consisted of bas relief formed in the mold. Roman imagery was far less ambitious than that of the Greeks.

Between the fall of the Roman Empire and the beginning of the Renaissance, ceramic work was mostly utilitarian, either unglazed or finished with a simple dusting of lead powder, which formed a thin glassy coating on the surface of the piece. The Renaissance saw a revival of pottery in Italy under the influence of ceramics from the Islamic world. The Islamic tradition was imported to Spain, which was under Islamic rule during this period. It was from Spain that the Italian potters learned to use colored slips and glazes.

The great period of ceramics in France and Germany came with the development of European porcelain in the early 1700s. While the methods used in making and firing porcelain were well known in Asia, these principles were unknown in Europe. The effort to develop a European version of porcelain was carried to its successful conclusion by an unlikely pair, Johann Friedrich Böttger, an alchemist and adventurer, and Ehrenfried Walther von Tschirnhausen, a theoretician interested in creating artificial gems. Von Tschirnhausen had already worked with high temperatures in his experiments in creating gems, and this was a key to the team's success in developing porcelain.

Sometime between 1705 and 1708 the two men were able to make a hard dense red por-

FIG. A–3   Italo-Greek. Lucanian Ware, 21 inches, attributed to the Arno Painter, late 5th century B.C. Earthenware, thrown and painted with terra sigillatas. The Everson Museum, Syracuse, New York. Gift of Mrs. Morton C. Nichols. P.C. 71.17. Photograph © Courtney Frisse.

celaneous clay body, and by 1708 they had begun to experiment with white porcelain. By 1710 they were beginning to get promising results, and by 1720 porcelain making was an established art, first in Dresden and then throughout much of Europe. Though European porcelain looked like Chinese porcelain, it differed from it in its character and ingredients and really was a very different material; it was much less workable, though with fewer impurities. European porcelain work was highly refined, elegant, and aristocratic. While there is little of the sense of vitality that ceramists often look for, these pieces at their best have an inventive quality that can be persuasive.

In the late nineteenth century, experiments with imagery in Europe and England derived from contemporaneous thinking about art led to a whole group of new ceramic movements. These can be placed together in the category of "Arts and Crafts Ceramics," exemplified first by Barbotine ware and later by Art Nouveau ceramics. In general, this work was low fire and lead glazed. Its influence crossed the Atlantic and served as the genesis for the American Art Pottery movement.

In the mid-twentieth century, in reaction to some of the more imagistic characteristics of Arts and Crafts Ceramics, a renewed emphasis was placed on the character of the material. This was exemplified by the work of the English potter Bernard Leach (1887–1979). His influence on English and American pottery was profound, in part through his work and in part through his ideas and his writing. Leach's writing is persuasive and always absorbing. His work was generally thrown, decorated simply, and deftly fired in high-fire reduction kilns. His mission was to bring to potters and those interested in pottery a conception of simple, useful, and intelligently wrought forms made with craftsmanship and a sense of the material and the process.

Contemporary potters in England tend to be vessel-oriented and interested in exploring ceramic materials and processes. There is a strong wish to blend tradition and contemporary attitudes and little interest in importing ideas from the popular arts, which is such a powerful theme in American ceramics.

AFRICA

The work of the village potters of Nigeria is an example of the survival of an ancient tradition. It is fired at low temperatures and finished in a monochromatic, carbon-darkened clay surface. The surface is often ornamented with stamped, drawn, and applied imagery. Most pieces are produced using a coil and paddle technique. In the hands of a skilled potter (always female), this is an effective method for quickly producing objects of beauty and usefulness. The pieces are highly functional and fill a real need in the culture, which continues to support these potters.

PRE-COLUMBIAN AMERICA

The Pre-Columbian potters of the Americas produced high-caliber work that was hand-built and often formed in a press mold; it was usually finished with terra sigillatas.

The Peruvian potters produced work that was intended for tombs and thus imbued with a strong sense of purpose. The ware was made in press molds and painted with terra sigillatas, the favored forming method and surface finish of all subsequent Peruvian potters as well. The first important tomb ware from Peru was made by potters of the Chavin de Huantar culture (1800–500 B.C.). It is highly modeled and painted with a monochromatic terra sigillata. Applied decoration was mold formed separately and luted to the body of the piece. A little later than the Chavin culture and somewhat to the south, the potters of the Paracas culture worked with mold-made forms that they finished with colorful, resin-based, unfired paints.

The Nazca culture (200 B.C.–A.D. 600) followed the Chavin and Paracas cultures and was strongly influenced by them. Its pottery differed, however, in its surface treatment, for the Nazca potters are noted for their use of rich terra sigillata and polychromatic painted imagery. In fact, as many as thirteen colors have been counted on a single piece. In an area to the north, potters of the Moche culture (200 B.C.–A.D. 700) began to produce rich tomb ware strongly influenced by Chavin work. Moche potters often created compound press-mold forms of great complexity and sculptural character. Perhaps because of the emphasis on sculptural form, color was subdued and was limited to tan and cream.

In Central America, the first great work came from the Olmec culture in Mexico. The Olmec potters specialized in a highly stylized imagery. From about 300 to 1500 A.D., in what is now Guatemala, Honduras, and Mexico, Mayan potters created a low-fire pottery with simple and strong form and finished with terra sigillatas. The essentially linear imagery drawn over the surface of the piece tells us a great deal about the beliefs of these people. The imagery is drawn with vigor and intelligence and a flair for characterization. The pottery produced in Central America outside the Mayan culture is influenced by Mayan pottery but is more direct and vigorous in character.

The American Southwest

The Indians of the American Southwest, both before and after the arrival of newcomers from Europe, created a low-fire painted utilitarian ware that was influenced by Pre-Columbian ware from Mexico. The work is highly developed in both form and imagery. Form is developed using care-

FIG. A–4 Mexico. Olmec culture. Funerary urn, $11\frac{3}{8}$ inches. 800–600 B.C. Earthenware, hand-formed (probably coil-formed). The Everson Museum, Syracuse, New York. Gift of Janos Szekere. P.C. 86.87.1. Photograph © Courtney Frisse.

FIG. A–5 Nicaragua. Chortega culture. Funerary urn, 13 inches, circa 1200 A.D. Earthenware, hand-formed and painted with terra sigillatas. The Everson Museum, Syracuse, New York. Gift of Ariberto Guidani and Leonardo Patterson. P.C. 75.92. Photograph © Courtney Frisse.

fully executed coil techniques; the imagery is created with sigillata-like fine-particled slips. The tradition remains vigorous even today.

AMERICA SINCE COLUMBUS

The settlers who came to North America from England and Europe had a very different ceramic tradition from the Native Americans. While it too had a strong utilitarian cast, it was different in character and technology. Some of it was low-fired slipware and some was high-fired, salt-glazed stoneware; all of it was based on European and English models.

As society in North America evolved toward a goal of cultural democracy, new needs developed. A new, more sophisticated type of ceramics known as American Art Pottery came to serve as an indicator of the social status and aspirations of its owners. American Art Pottery began in 1878 with the creation of the Cincinnati Faience style. This work was highly influenced by the European "Arts and Crafts" style. It was fired in low-temperature oxidation kilns, and its imagery was derived from low-fire slip decoration covered with a clear lead glaze. The Rookwood studio in Cincinnati, Ohio, was the foremost studio producing work in this style.

By the turn of the century other methods of creating surface imagery were being employed. Noteworthy are the remarkable pieces of George Ohr and the Grueby studio with its highly influential "Dead Mat" glazes. While some art potters worked alone or with a staff of one or two, the typical American Art Pottery establishments were organized on the factory plan. Many jobs were specialized and mass-production methods were used where possible. Adelaide Alsop Robineau (1865–1929) was one of the most famous individual artists working in this movement. She began to work in porcelain in 1904. Her work is thrown on the wheel and ornamented with excised and carved imagery. It is especially noteworthy for its rich and detailed surfaces and its inventive crystal and flowing mat glazes. Robineau's work conveys a spirit of great intensity and coherence.

In the 1930s ceramic work was constrained by the Great Depression. During World War II, the fuel necessary for firing ceramic work was directed instead to the war effort. After the war there was a renewed interest in pottery. The ap-

proach to clay of the English potter Bernard Leach became the model for American potters. This led to the widespread use of warm-colored, reduction-fired glazes marked by strong visual textures. This utilitarian pottery tended to be emphatically thrown: its mood emphasizes its ties to nature and the earth. For a time this movement swept all other approaches aside.

FIG. A–6 USA. The Rookwood studio. Hydrangea Vase, 14$\frac{5}{8}$ inches, 1904. Painted with slips, covered with a clear lead glaze, and fired in a fuel-burning low-fire kiln in an oxidation atmosphere. With the mark of the painter, Albert Valentien. The Everson Museum, Syracuse, New York. Gift of the Dorothy and Robert Reister Ceramic Fund. P.C. 86.9.4. Photograph © Courtney Frisse.

FIG. A–7 USA. The Grueby Pottery. Vase, 12½ inches, circa 1900. Earthenware, wheel-formed with hand-formed additions. Earthenware clay body with a low-fire "Dead Mat" lead glaze. The Everson Museum, Syracuse, New York. Gift of the Dorothy and Robert Reister Ceramic Fund. P.C. 86.9.2. Photograph © Courtney Frisse.

FIG. A–8 USA. Adelaide Alsop Robineau. The Crab Vase, 7⅜ inches, 1908. Porcelain body, wheel-formed and carved; flowing mat and crystal glazes fired to cone 9/10; bisque fired and glaze fired at the same temperature. The Everson Museum, Syracuse, New York. P.C. 16.4.2. Photograph © Courtney Frisse.

Perhaps in reaction, a movement called Funk or Pop Pottery evolved on the West Coast in the late 1960s. The movement was strongly image oriented and its practitioners borrowed freely from the themes of popular culture but added an irreverent and ironic twist. The technology was also borrowed: the Funk potters used the prepared clays and glazes that had been developed to meet the needs of ceramic hobbyists, a group long held in low esteem. This work was low fire, fired in the electric kiln, and painted with strong (at times garish) colors.

By the early 1980s ceramists had become much more interested in questions of form and color. References to popular culture and to tongue-in-cheek humor were set aside in favor of experiments in strong color and expressive, sculptural form.

APPENDIX B

Safe Practice for the Ceramist

In recent years we have become keenly aware of the danger our materials pose to both ourselves and those who eat or drink from our pieces. Some materials are toxic, and others, though nontoxic, are potentially dangerous irritants. These problems are not insurmountable and should not keep us from working in clay or from making pieces that people will want to use. In some cases, however, we must modify our work methods and materials.

The following materials are toxic and should be avoided:

barium carbonate
all cadmium compounds
all chrome and chromate compounds
all lead compounds
lithium carbonate
manganese dioxide (powdered)
nickel carbonate
all nickel compounds
vanadium pentoxide

Some materials used in ceramics contain toxic elements, but when combined with other materials to create compounds, such as frits and stains, they are fairly safe to use. Note, however, that some highly acidic or alkaline foods may release toxic elements, so never use these compounds in pieces that might be used to hold food. To complicate the problem further, they may produce toxic gases during firing. These compounds include:

lead frits
lithium feldspars
vanadium stains

SUBSTITUTES FOR TOXIC MATERIALS
Titanium dioxide or tin oxide in amounts over 7 percent can be substituted for barium carbonate.

Both of these materials encourage soft, mat surfaces with a rich sheen somewhat reminiscent of barium's mat effects.

Cadmium has no substitutes.

Copper oxide or carbonate will serve as a partial substitute for greens derived from chrome. There are no real substitutes for the pinks and crimsons that chrome imparts or for the brilliant fire-engine red and oranges that are produced from chrome/lead combinations.

Boron and sodium are fine melters and in part can be substituted for lead compounds and lead frits.

The lithium feldspar spodumene is much less toxic than lithium carbonate and can serve as a useful substitute for this material.

Black iron oxide is a fairly close substitute for powdered manganese dioxide.

Nickel carbonate has no substitutes.

Titanium yellow stain is an excellent substitute for vanadium pentoxide or vanadium stains.

MATERIALS CONTAINING SILICA
Until it is fired, any material that contains silica is dangerous to the ceramist. These include clays and feldspars, which are the core materials of ceramics that we must use every day. The problem is made more complex because it is difficult to predict how people will react to materials that contain silica. There is no doubt that these materials can cause health problems, but the problems vary greatly from person to person. Constant exposure to silica over a period of years can cause respiratory damage.

The ceramic materials that contain silica are:

clay
all feldspars

ground silica (flint)
talc (calcium, magnesium silicate)
Wollastonite (calcium silicate)

Other respiratory irritants include:

bone ash
cobalt colorants
all copper compounds
Gerstley borate (calcium, sodium borate)
wood ash
zinc oxide
all zirconium compounds

SAFETY PRECAUTIONS WHEN MAKING CLAY AND GLAZES

Clay body and glaze making can be dangerous because the powders used to make them are dusty and can settle in the lungs. The work room should be well ventilated and dust should not be allowed to accumulate. The studio should be cleaned with a mop. In addition, you should always wear an approved respirator. You may also wish to purchase disposable safety garments.

Bench grinders, which are especially useful for grinding glaze off the bottom of a piece, produce flying ceramic chips that can cut the skin or damage eyes. The rapidly turning grinding wheel can catch articles of clothing or hair and pull you toward the machine. When using a bench grinder, always wear a protective face shield, tie back long hair, and do not wear loose-fitting clothing that easily could become entangled in the grinding wheel.

SAFETY EQUIPMENT

Respirators

Some respirators purify the air of dust, whereas others purify both dust and fumes. In an ideal world, we would not create dangerous dusts and fumes. In a slightly less ideal world, we would be able to filter all airborne impurities and no one would be threatened by toxic dusts or fumes. Since the world is not ideal, we must sometimes filter impure air as it is about to enter our lungs. While such protection may be inconvenient, it is highly efficient because of its localized nature.

Respirators fit over the nose and mouth and contain filters that let oxygen pass through but prevent the inhalation of dust or fumes. Some

respirators are intended to be used once or twice and then discarded. Though they are easy to wear, disposable masks are not that useful to the ceramist.

Ceramists should use respirators that have a reusable facepiece and accommodate disposable filter cartridges. The sophisticated multilayer filters are designed to filter extremely fine dusts such as those produced by ceramic materials. These respirators are modular in design. The disposable filtering cartridges are attached to the facepiece, which is made from a rubber-like material that seals out dust and fumes. Most manufacturers carry a whole line of cartridges, each designed for a specific job. Ceramists should use cartridges that will filter very fine dusts. Occasionally we may need filters that protect against fumes, especially during kiln firing.

Change the respirator filter immediately if you sense irritation or experience an unpleasant smell or taste. Some ceramists place a mark on the filters for every hour the mask is worn and change to a new filter after ten or twelve hours. This commonsense strategy is perhaps as useful as any. When you change the filter, wash the facepiece as well.

Disposable Safety Garments

Disposable safety garments are inexpensive and offer good protection and durability. Some are made from a paper-like material that will last through several wearings. These are especially useful to the ceramist who is working in particularly dusty environments.

SAFETY PRECAUTIONS DURING FORMING

A great deal of clay dust can be created while a piece is being formed. Without care, our work areas easily can become as dusty as the mixing area. The dust should be cleaned with a mop since few vacuum cleaners can cope with such fine dust without clogging.

Wet clay can irritate the skin and cause contact dermatitis. Those ceramists with a predisposition to skin irritations must be especially wary. Clays do not by themselves seem to be particularly irritating. Rather, it is the additions to the clay body that make them so. Clay bodies that contain highly alkaline materials, such as strongly alkaline fluxes and feldspars, are particularly at fault here. Applying a barrier skin cream may be helpful in this case.

Also potentially troublesome are clays in which mold growth has been encouraged. Molds enhance the workability of the clay, but they can irritate the skin and trigger allergic reactions. Some ceramists have reported good results adding yogurt to the clay body. The yogurt mold encourages plasticity in clay but seems not to cause allergic reactions.

PROCEDURES FOR SAFELY PREPARING AND APPLYING GLAZES

When working with dry materials, wear a NIOSH (USA) or WHMIS (Canada) or Factory Inspectorate (Great Britain) approved dust respirator. When working with highly alkaline materials, wear special protective clothing, including headgear; disposable paper safety suits are useful for this purpose.

Add water to dry materials as soon as possible and never sieve dry mixtures. Sieving a wet mixture is far quicker and safer. Once the recipe is wet, it is safe to use unless it contains toxic materials.

Most methods of glaze application are not particularly hazardous. Spraying, however, can be. Always wear a mask while spraying and spray into a well-vented spray booth.

PROCEDURES FOR SAFE KILN FIRING

Kilns can be the source of fires or explosions. Electric kilns carry heavy current loads, and gas kilns need large volumes of gases. The connections to electrical sources or gas lines should be carefully and professionally installed. The same is true for safety mechanisms that interrupt electric current and gas during an emergency.

The ventilation of dangerous gases produced during firing is also a problem and one that is especially serious because it may be hard to connect these gases with their bad effects. Kilns should be placed in a separate room or outside in the open air. Kilns located indoors should be fitted with an efficient exhaust system that vents to the outside. Electric kilns may be fitted with an under-kiln or overhead hood. The under-kiln hood seems to be efficient for venting top-loading kilns. Fuel-burning kilns installed indoors should have an overhead exhaust canopy.

VIEWING THE KILN CHAMBER DURING FIRING

When you fire with cones, you will need to look into the incandescent firing chamber to check the position of the cone. This action can cause eye damage, so you should always wear "tuned" safety glasses during the latter part of the firing. Tuned glasses are readily obtained from a safety supply house; the supplier merely needs to know the temperatures at which you fire in order to supply glasses of the appropriate shade. Dr. Michael McCann in his book *Artist Beware* (Watson-Guptil, 1979) recommends welders glasses with the designation 2–2.5. These glasses are inexpensive and, aside from protecting the eyes, make it easy to see the cone.

ENSURING THAT FIRED PIECES ARE SAFE TO USE

As well as attending to our own health, we also must be attentive to the welfare of those who will use our work. There is no need to use glazes that contain toxic materials on work that may be used to contain food. In theory, toxic materials can be "locked" in the glassy matrix of a glaze; however, they can also be "unlocked" during the firing. We have many alternative nontoxic materials that melt strongly and encourage rich glaze surfaces. The important message here is that with a little bit of rethinking we can produce work that is safe for our customers, and we can work in a way that does not threaten our own well-being.

APPENDIX C
In the Studio

Clay is a demanding material. It is messy and dusty and requires tools for forming, glazing, and firing. Since some of these tools can take up a fair amount of space, ceramists usually create a separate work space. In these sometimes chaotic spaces we spend a great deal of our lives; so we owe it to ourselves and our work to make them as easy to work in and as safe as possible.

THE WORK SPACE

A ceramic studio can be set up in a garage, a separate building, a basement, or an attic. The floor should be washable, either bare cement or covered with linoleum, and have a drain. Good ventilation for dust and fumes and adequate overhead lighting are essential. A sink is useful but not mandatory: the careful manager can do without a sink: ideally this would keep some of the heavy metals which we use as colorants and fluxes out of the water system.

The work table, workstand, and potter's wheels should be designed for safety and should be comfortable. Work tables that are too high or too low or potter's wheels that encourage back strain unfortunately are common. As you design your studio space, keep comfort in mind. The way you arrange your work area can make a big difference in the way you work and your level of fatigue at the end of the day.

Studio planning can be made easier by first mapping your work space on a large sheet of graph paper. On another piece of graph paper cut out scale models of your wheel, work tables, storage areas, glazing areas, and your kiln. Now shift and arrange these models with an eye to safety and convenience. This kind of modeling is fun and will help you design an efficient work space.

STUDIO EQUIPMENT

Listed below is a group of basic tools and furnishings found in most ceramic work spaces.

- Work tables
- Potter's wheel (a necessity for some, optional for others; see below)
- Forming tools
- Shelves for work
- Shelves for materials
- Stool or chair
- Damp storage (optional)
- Sink (optional)
- Sprayer (optional)
- Spray booth (optional)
- Gram scales (.05–500 grams and 1–10,000 grams; described below)
- Electric kiln (at least .2 cubic meters) or fuel-burning kiln (at least 1 cubic meter capacity)
- Electric kiln for test firing (12,000 cubic centimeters) (optional)

"ECONOMY CLASS": AN INEXPENSIVE STUDIO

A small ceramic work space equipped with all the necessities for building and firing hand-built pieces can be designed that takes up little space and is inexpensive. Space restraints may limit you to a small electric kiln for firing small pieces. These kilns need no special wiring and use normal house current. Such work spaces require only a work table and some shelving to be complete. They are appropriate as a starting studio for the beginner or as a temporary studio for the experienced ceramist.

TOOLS

Tools for General Use

- Plastic bucket for water
- Needle tool for cutting and scoring
- Wooden knives for cutting and shaping
- Kitchen sponge
- Large natural (sheepswool) sponge

- Pair of scissors for cutting templates
- Thin zinc/aluminum sheet (a zinc lithography plate) for durable templates (available from printers, newspapers, and offset lithographers)

Useful Tools for Throwing

- Loop tool for trimming the clay
- Sponge mounted on a long dowel for cleaning the interior of the thrown piece
- Chamois for smoothing the lip of the piece
- Pair of calipers for measuring lids

Tools for Glaze Formulation and Application

- High-quality dust mask
- Gram scales (0.1–500 grams and 100–20,000 grams)
- Sieves for clays and glazes
    large 10-mesh stainless-steel kitchen sieve
    large 30-mesh, 60-mesh, and 100-mesh sieves (from ceramic supply houses)
    small 60-mesh sieve for preparing test lots of glaze (an "enameling sifter" is readily available from craft supply houses)
- Glaze pencil
- Three brushes
    $\frac{1}{2}$-inch-wide stiff artist's bristle brush
    $\frac{1}{2}$-inch-wide soft brush (a Japanese hake brush is excellent for this purpose)
    2-inch-wide sponge brush
- Sprayers
    atomizer sprayer
    external-mix compressor-driven sprayer
    external-mix airbrush
- 30-power magnifying scope for examining the surface of a glaze.

FIG. C–1   Eric James Mellon in his studio in Bognor Regis, West Sussex, England.

- Small, fine-grained natural sponge, either a cosmetic sponge or an "elephant ear" sponge)
- Rib, or ribs, for smoothing and shaping (wooden, plastic, or metal)
- Three or four thin sheets of plastic for wrapping wet clay

Useful Tools for the Hand-Builder

- Slab roller for rolling uniform sheets or slabs of clay (see below)
- Disposable-blade knife or scalpels for cutting the clay. Scalpels are available through craft supply catalogs or at pharmaceutical supply houses and university bookstores

THE POTTER'S WHEEL

The potter's wheel is one of our most important forming tools. While potters have been throwing on the wheel for millennia, the design of the wheel is still very much unsettled and a number of schemes are employed. For several reasons, no one design is perfect. The potter's wheel must be powerful, easily controlled, and capable of a wide range of speeds, varying from a few revolutions per minute to 200 revolutions per minute or more. These are demanding specifications.

We tend to distinguish between kickwheels

FIG. C–2 The Brent wheel, a variable-speed, belt-driven electric potter's wheel. Courtesy of American Art Clay Company.

and those whose sole source of power is a motor. Kickwheels derive their power (at least part of the time) from the kicking action of the potter's foot. To increase the wheel head speed the potter merely kicks faster; to slow it, the potter kicks more slowly or brakes the flywheel's speed. Many kickwheel designs also allow for motor drive, where the power is transmitted through a friction wheel to the flywheel. The power in motor-driven wheels may be transmitted by a friction drive or by belts or gears.

Kickwheels are reliable and durable and excellent for throwing small and medium-sized forms. Unfortunately, the motor drive is inefficient and thus is not suitable for throwing large pieces. They are also fairly expensive and tend to vibrate.

Motor-driven wheels, on the other hand, are excellent for throwing large forms. They can overpower small forms, however.

Furthermore, their controls are often poorly designed and badly built, and speed is especially difficult to control at the low end of the scale, just where control is needed most.

If you are interested in purchasing a kick-wheel, look for a one that is well built and does not vibrate excessively. If you would rather buy a motorized wheel, look for one that is quiet and compact and has responsive controls and good speed control, even at the lowest speeds. A good motorized wheel should not vibrate excessively.

SLAB ROLLERS

Slab rollers are a near-equivalent of the potter's wheel for hand builders and can speed up the hand builder's work considerably. Slab rollers are expensive, take up a good deal of room, and need to be adjusted and repaired periodically, but they do make strong, uniform slabs.

CERAMIC GRAM SCALES

An accurate gram scale is a necessity for measuring glaze ingredients and making ceramic recipes. Spring-loaded scales are the least expensive but also the most inaccurate. Most ceramists use triple-beam balance scales, in which parallel beams are used as tracks for three different sliding weights. As the weights are moved along their calibrated tracks, the beam is brought to a horizontal resting position where the weight of the material can be read.

The scale you use must compensate for the weight of the container. In most balances the container is placed on a small platform. Below the platform is a chamber that holds the weights used to compensate for the container's weight. Set all sliding weights at zero, unscrew the weighing platform from the chamber, and place the weights in the chamber as needed until the beam is level.

Electronic scales are quicker in their action than standard balance scales and do not require the addition, subtraction, or movement of weights. They compensate almost automatically for the weight of the weighing container and their digital readout allows quick, accurate readings. Accurate electronic scales are not inexpensive, but they are well suited for ceramic work.

At some point in your work you may want to invest in a large-capacity gram scale. A number of ceramic suppliers and scientific supply houses carry large-capacity gram scales (100–5000/20000 grams) that are well-made and reasonably priced. Large-capacity electronic gram scales that are accurate for ceramic work can be found in department and specialty gourmet stores.

APPENDIX D
Using Computers in Ceramics

Ceramists are not immune to a fascination with the latest technological innovations. Like scientists and engineers, we too deal with technology. In fact, the similarities between the world of the scientist and our own have often been remarked upon.

For ceramists, the computer is at once different from most things in our world and yet familiar— different in that the computer is concept oriented, whereas our material, clay, is tangible and palpable. On the other hand, the computer is a tool for manipulations, for moving and changing, and we are movers and changers par excellence. Furthermore, in a small irony, the heart of the computer, its memory chips, is made from silica.

Computers are useful to ceramists in a number of ways.

FOR GLAZE AND CLAY BODY ANALYSIS
What was once a time-consuming job is now effortless and quickly accomplished with computer-aided glaze and clay body analysis. These programs are so effective that no doubt in a few years almost all glaze analysis will be computer-aided. The emphasis will then shift to the process of helping ceramists understand what the figures in an analysis mean.

FOR DEVELOPING GLAZE RECIPES
One computer program, called an "expert system," can be used to develop glazes. In this program, a complex problem is broken down into a long series of questions and decisions based on the if/then principle. Typical statements are: "*If* you have 75% soda feldspar, 10% white clay, and 10% dolomite in a recipe and you want to fire to cone 6, *then* you will need to put the rest of the total into a strong melter from the following list." This will be an invaluable way to teach glaze formulation.

FOR HELP IN FIRING
Expert systems also can be used to help the ceramist fire fuel-burning kilns. The problems in-

volved in firing fuel-burning kilns, especially in reduction, are complex and subject to such variables as the weather, the nature of the kiln load, the type of fuel, and the atmosphere in the kiln. While the reduction fire does not lend itself to automation (and that is a source of strength, not weakness), many of the variables can be organized in a systematic way that makes sense.

FOR PROGRAMMING ELECTRIC-KILN FIRING

We are in a period of development of the programmed fire for the electric kiln. Most strategies use measurements of both time and temperature to control the firing. It will be interesting to see if systems can be devised that will combine these strategies with a mechanism that can sense the behavior of a firing cone or similar device.

DATABASES AND CAD

A database is simply a group of records that contains related information and can help the user access the desired information quickly. A recipe book is an example of a database. We can set up a database of ceramic recipes and locate every recipe that contains a designated material (for example, titanium). Some programs take this further by letting us put complex limits on the search, such as "look for recipes that contain both ma-

terial *x* and *y* and ignore all others (especially those which contain *only x* or only *y*)." These programs will also allow the searcher to locate all recipes that contain a material within certain percentages.

CAD stands for computer-aided design. Ceramists have begun to use computers to help in the creation and design of their surface ornament, especially imagery that is geometric and repetitive.

THE FUTURE

Ceramists are beginning to use computers with enthusiasm. We can speculate that in the future computers will help us form our material. For example, it is possible to imagine a new kind of ceramic-forming device: a variable throat extruder. The form could be developed as a complex mathematical description stored in the memory of the computer until needed, or in a strategy more natural to the studio potter. It could be derived from an input device worked by the ceramist. The input from this device, sensitive to movements in all three dimensions, would be interpreted as instruction for the creation of complex extruded forms. Such a device would require great virtuosity and an understanding of clay— the kind of challenge potters accept with élan. It would have a tremendous impact on our craft and provide us with further proof that our medium allows us to grow and change.

APPENDIX E
Celsius and Fahrenheit Temperature Chart

32° F	0° C	1400° F	760° C	2200° F	1204° C
70° F	21° C	1600° F	871° C	2300° F	1260° C
212° F	100° C	1800° F	982° C	2400° F	1315° C
500° F	260° C	2000° F	1093° C	2500° F	1371° C
1000° F	537° C	2100° F	1149° C		

APPENDIX F
Recipes for Clay Bodies, Glazes, and Vitreous Engobes

CONE 04 RECIPES

Clay Bodies

STANDARD TALC BODY

Ball clay	50
Talc	50

This is the standard 50/50 low-fire clay body. I was surprised to find from the computed analysis that a standard 50/50 low-fire talc body is low in alumina and high in flux.

ROBIN LEVENTHAL'S CLAY BODY #1

Ball clay	20
Dolomite	5
Soda frit	5
Red clay	50
Soda spar	20

This body is fairly workable and durable. After a few weeks it becomes highly thixotropic.

ENGOBE 04-1 R.Z./ROBIN LEVENTHAL

Ball clay	34
Soda frit	11
Gerstley borate	11
Soda spar	42
Titanium	2

This engobe is dry surfaced and durable.

Glazes

ROBIN LEVENTHAL'S OPAQUE GLAZE

Ball Clay	10
Boron frit	54
Gerstley borate	24
Zirconium opacifier	12

glass makers = normal
clay = normal
secondary fluxes = normal

The most significant secondary flux in this glaze is Gerstley borate. It readily accepts both stain and standard colorants. This glaze is durable and reliable and has little visual texture.

ROBIN LEVENTHAL'S CLEAR GLAZE

Ball clay	8
Flint	8
Soda frit	38
Gerstley borate	6
Zinc	2
3134	38

glass makers = high
clay = normal
secondary fluxes = low

The most significant materials in this glaze are the two frits, one a sodium frit and the other a boron frit. Its transparency is encouraged by its high glass makers and moderate clay content. Unfortunately, this glaze crazes. It is difficult to create a cone 04 clear glaze that contains no toxic materials and does not craze.

ROBIN LEVENTHAL'S 1B CLEAR GLAZE RECIPE

Ball clay	10
Boron frit	30
Soda frit	20
Gerstley borate	24
Spodumene	14
Zinc	2

glass makers = somewhat high
clay = normal (though a bit high for a transparent glaze)
secondary fluxes = normal

The most significant fluxes in this glaze are sodium, calcium, boron, and lithium derived, respectively, from a soda frit, a boron frit (both frits are also sources of calcium), Gerstley borate, and spodumene. This glaze crazes less than the previous one, but because of its clay content (which is high for a clear glaze) is slightly milky.

MOHAWK GREEN F

Gerstley borate	30
Kaolin	16
Lithium carbonate	2
Soda spar	38
Whiting	12
Zinc	2
Copper carbonate	3

glass makers = very low
clay = high
secondary fluxes = high

The most significant fluxes in this glaze are sodium, calcium, boron, and lithium, derived from soda spar, Gerstley borate, and lithium carbonate. Its color is a rich saturated green and has a fairly strong visual texture.

CONE 02 RECIPES

Clay Bodies

RED BODY

Ball clay	25
Red clay	50
Talc	25

Color: light brick red. Low absorption. Good workability.

IVORY-COLORED BODY

Ball clay	20
Goldart	40
Soda spar	10
Talc	30

Color: light buff, ivory. Good workability.

Glazes

CHEMUNG BASE

Ball clay	10
Soda frit	54
Gerstley borate	24
Zirconium opacifier	12
Copper carbonate	3

glass makers = normal
clay = normal
secondary fluxes = high

A shiny, translucent glaze that takes stain color well. Its most significant flux is sodium derived from soda frit and boron derived from Gerstley borate. Its turquoise color is derived from the reaction of copper to sodium.

SPENCER BASE

Ball clay	10
Boron frit	54
Wollastonite	24
Zirconium opacifier	12
Cobalt carbonate	1.5

glass makers = normal
clay = normal
secondary fluxes = normal

The most significant flux in this glaze is calcium. It has no visual texture and its surface is smooth and waxy. The color is a soft blue.

BALDWIN BASE

Ball clay	10
Boron frit	46
Red clay	12
Spodumene	20
Zirconium opacifier	12
Iron oxide	6

glass makers = normal
clay = high
secondary fluxes = very low

The most significant fluxes in this glaze are the boron frit and spodumene (a lithium-containing feldspar). Its color is a soft ocher cream with some visual texture.

WELLSBURG SHINY BROWN GLAZE

Barnard clay	30
Gerstley borate	48
Spodumene	20
Titanium	2

glass makers = low
clay = high
secondary fluxes = very high

The most significnat fluxes in this glaze are boron, iron, and lithium. Boron is derived from Gerstley borate, Barnard is a source of iron, and spodumene is a source of lithium. Its color is brown and its surface is quite shiny with some visual texture.

BARTON SPODUMENE BASE

Dolomite	10
Boron frit	34
Red clay	22
Spodumene	22
Zirconium opacifier	12
Iron oxide	6

glass makers = normal
clay = high
secondary fluxes = low

The most significant flux in this glaze is lithium derived from spodumene (a lithium-containing feldspar). Its surface is satin or satin shiny and the color a warm ivory.

TIOGA CLEAR GLAZE

Ball clay	4
Flint	24
Boron frit	48
Spodumene	22
Zinc	2

glass makers = extremely high
clay = very low
secondary fluxes = extremely high

This kind of recipe is desirable for transparent glazes. Its most significant fluxes are lithium (derived from spodumene) and zinc, both of which aid melting. Craze-free on both the buff and red bodies, it has a tendency to a slight opacity.

ROSSTOWN DRY-SURFACED GLAZE

Ball clay	3
Flint	50
Gerstley borate	26
Spodumene	16
Titanium	3
Zinc	2

glass makers = very high

clay = extremely low
secondary fluxes = normal

The most significant fluxes in this glaze are lithium derived from spodumene and boron derived from Gerstley borate. The surface is extremely dry and it is not appropriate for use on functional pieces. Although high in glass makers, it is not shiny because its secondary melters are too low to form a glassy melt.

MOHAWK GREEN
Originally written for cone 04, it also works (and works well) at cone 02

Gerstley borate	30
Kaolin	16
Lithium carbonate	2
Soda spar	38
Whiting	12
Zinc	2
Copper carbonate	3

glass makers = low
clay = high
secondary fluxes = very high

The most significant fluxes in this glaze are sodium, calcium, boron, and lithium, derived from soda spar, Gerstley borate, and lithium carbonate. The color is a rich saturated green with a fairly strong visual texture.

CONE 3 RECIPES

Clay Bodies

BUFF BODY

Ball clay	20
Goldart	55
Talc	25

A durable, workable body, light ochre yellow in color.

BUFF BODY

Ball clay	60
Goldart	15
Talc	25

This body is durable and quite workable. The color is a buff yellow, and it works well with glazes.

Ball clay	10
A.P. Green fire clay	10
Goldart	55
Red clay	25

This body is ochre orange in color. While it darkens many glazes, it is compatible with most of them.

Glazes

GRANBY BASE

Ball clay	12
Soda frit	28
Gerstley borate	10
Opax	10
Soda spar	38
Tin oxide	2

glass makers = normal
clay = normal
secondary fluxes = normal

The most significant flux in this glaze is sodium derived from both the soda feldspar and the soda frit. This is a smooth satin shiny glaze that is durable and opaque due to its zirconium and tin content. It is an excellent base glaze that works well with most colorants and stains.

FAIRDALE CREAM

Ball clay	12
Dolomite	10
Soda frit	24
Gerstley borate	10
Opax	12
Soda spar	10
Spodumene	20
Titanium	2

glass makers = normal
clay = normal
secondary fluxes = normal

The most significant fluxes in this glaze are lithium derived from spodumene and sodium derived from soda frit and soda feldspar. The color is a soft ivory cream and the surface is mat.

DEWITT DARK TAN

Ball clay	8
Barnard clay	8
Dolomite	16
Boron frit	24
Opax	12
Soda spar	10
Spodumene	20
Titanium	2

glass makers = normal
clay = high
secondary fluxes = normal

The most significant fluxes in this glaze are iron derived from Barnard clay and lithium derived from spodumene. The color is a dark earth-colored tan. The surface is strong and durable and marked with a tight pattern of visual texture.

FULTON GLAZE

Ball clay	10
Soda frit	30
Gerstley borate	18
Opax	10
Soda spar	30
Titanium	2
Cobalt carbonate	1.5

glass makers = normal
clay = normal
secondary fluxes = normal

The most significant flux in this glaze is sodium derived from soda frit and soda feldspar. It is bright blue in color and the surface is shiny and unmarked by visual texture.

CLASS BASE

Flint	14
Boron frit	32
Gerstley borate	12
Iron oxide	5
Red clay	22
Soda spar	14
Titanium	1

glass makers = normal
clay = high
secondary fluxes = low

The most significant fluxes in this glaze are iron derived from red clay and boron derived from boron frit and Gerstley borate. This is a durable, reliable dark base glaze that can be used with a number of colorants.

CLASS BLACK

Add 2% copper carbonate to the Class Base recipe to get a rich black.

CLASS BROWN

Add 8% black iron oxide to the Class Base recipe for a rich brown.

CONE 6 RECIPES

Clay Bodies

BUFF BODY

A.P. Green fire clay	10
Flint	14
Goldart	62
Potash spar	14

A light cream-colored clay body with good workability.

RED BODY

Ball clay	12
Flint	10
Kaolin	33
Red clay	45

A brick-red body with good workability.

TRANSPARENT AMBER VITREOUS ENGOBE

Flint	10
Boron frit	20
Red clay	40
Soda spar	30
Iron oxide	12

glass makers = high
clay = very high
secondary fluxes = none

The most significant fluxes in this vitreous engobe are iron derived from its red clay, boron derived from the frit, and sodium derived from soda feldspar. Its dark reddish-brown color is derived from its iron content and is influenced by a fairly high sodium content derived from soda spar and boron frit.

Glazes

EMERALD TRANSPARENT

Ball clay	8

Gerstley borate	22
Nepheline syenite	51
Titanium	2
Wollastonite	14
Zinc	3

Add 3% copper carbonate.

glass makers = high
clay = normal
secondary fluxes = normal

The most significant fluxes in this glaze are calcium derived from wollastonite and sodium derived from nepheline syenite. It is a fairly durable glaze. The surface is mat with a lot of visual texture. Its cool green color is derived from copper influenced by sodium (derived from its nepheline syenite content).

NEW SOFT WAXY TRANSPARENT GLAZE

Ball clay	8
Flint	15
Gerstley borate	20
Nepheline syenite	38
Titanium	2
Wollastonite	14
Zinc	3

glass makers = high
clay = normal
secondary fluxes = normal

The most significant secondary fluxes in this glaze are sodium derived from nepheline syenite and calcium derived from wollastonite. It is shiny and fairly durable. Because of its balanced recipe and its titanium and zinc content, it resists crazing.

CATLIN BASE

Ball clay	8
Gerstley borate	15
Soda spar	22
Spodumene	12
Titanium	3
Wollastonite	30
Zirconium opacifier	10

glass makers = high
clay = normal
secondary fluxes = normal

The most significant fluxes in this glaze are lithium derived from spodumene and calcium derived from wollastonite. The surface is satin shiny and has some visual texture. Its viscosity is fairly low and it fills interstices well. The color is a white softened by the presence of titanium.

Dolomite	*18*
Boron frit	*12*
Red clay	*12*
Soda spar	*32*
Spodumene	*15*
Titanium	*1*
Zirconium opacifier	*10*
Iron oxide	*12%*

glass makers = normal
clay = normal
secondary fluxes = normal

The most significant fluxes in this glaze are calcium/magnesium derived from dolomite and lithium derived from spodumene and titanium. The color is a dark tobacco brown, which becomes mustard color where thick. Its color is derived from iron (from the red clay and iron oxide) and influenced by lithium and titanium.

The version without colorant is a soft cream breaking to a light amber.

ZAKIN BASE II

Ball clay	*6*
Dolomite	*18*
Gerstley borate	*22*
Soda spar	*36*
Titanium	*8*
Zirconium opacifier	*10*

3% copper carbonate (can also be used with no colorant)

glass makers = very low
clay = low
secondary fluxes = extremely high

The most significant fluxes in this glaze are titanium and calcium/magnesium derived from dolomite. Because of its titanium content, this glaze is more durable than its low glass-maker content would indicate. Titanium also encourages its strong visual texture and satin mat surface. The green color is derived from copper softened by calcium/magnesium (from dolomite) and titanium.

ZAKIN BASE III

Ball clay	*6*
Dolomite	*18*

Gerstley borate	*22*
Spodumene	*36*
Titanium	*8*
Zirconium opacifier	*10*

Used by itself and with 3% copper carbonate.

glass makers = very low
clay = low
secondary fluxes = extremely high

This glaze is much like Zakin Base II above. The most significant fluxes are lithium derived from spodumene and titanium. The color is a muted light amber, and the mat glaze has only a hint of shine. Its visual texture is very rich. Durability is enhanced by the titanium, and color and visual texture are influenced by the spodumene and titanium.

With 3% copper a soft green.

ZAKIN IV   (ZAKIN IIIA)

Dolomite	*18*
Gerstley borate	*22*
Red clay	*10*
Spodumene	*32*
Titanium	*8*
Zirconium opacifier	*10*

Used with 12% iron oxide.

glass makers = extremely low
clay = low
secondary fluxes = extremely high

The most significant fluxes in this glaze are lithium derived from spodumene and iron derived from red clay and titanium. This glaze has no visual texture. Its smooth velvety surface is reminiscent of a barium mat glaze. The color is iron red derived from a red clay and red iron oxide.

CONE 6 LOW-CLAY BODY RECIPES

Note: Don't add ceramic colorants such as cobalt, chrome, or manganese to the clay body. Instead, use ceramic stains. Because clay bodies are constantly handled during the forming process, colorants can be dangerous.

LOW-CLAY TRANSLUCENT BODY

Kaolin	*36*
Flint	*25*
Soda spar	*26*
Talc	*08*

| Frit 3124 | 03 |
| Bone ash | 02 |

This white translucent body lends itself to use in translucent tiles and ceramic collages but in general is not very workable. Because it slumps in the firing, it is useful as a tile body (a slumping tile placed on a flat support guarantees a flat tile).

Since this body is quite vitreous, it will stick to the kiln shelf. Use it with a special kiln wash of 50 ground soft brick/50 dolomite.

LOW-CLAY BODY #1

Frit 3124	06
Kaolin	52
Talc	42

This body is of moderate melting power and has a slight sheen. Adding 8% black stain (a highly melting stain) produces a rich black. Many other stains work well, though not chrome-tin pinks, which are bleached by the talc. The body is only moderately white, is not particularly translucent, and is limited in workability. It can, however, be used to create three-dimensional forms because it does not tend to slump.

LOW-CLAY BODY #2

Frit 3124	06
Kaolin	50
Talc	34
Soda spar	10

This highly-melting body works well uncolored or with colorants that are fairly refractory.

LOW-CLAY BODY #3

Kaolin	34
Soda spar	26
Flint	24
Frit 3124	10
Wollastonite	06

This body is quite opaque compared to the others in this series. It is dry surfaced as well and is a nice white in color.

CONE 9 RECIPES

Clay Bodies

BUFF BODY

| Dolomite | 8 |

A.P. Green fire clay	12
Goldart	58
Kaolin	22

A buff-colored body with excellent workability.

BUFF TALC CLAY BODY

A.P. Green fire clay	12
Goldart	60
Kaolin	22
Talc	6

A buff-colored body with excellent workability.

PORCELAIN BODY (CLASSIC)

Flint	25
Kaolin	50
Potash spar	25

This is the classic porcelain recipe that ceramists in the Western world have used since its development in Germany. It is a pure white body with a highly limited workability.

WOODBOURNE II VITREOUS ENGOBE

Ball clay	8
Dolomite	28
Potash spar	24
Red clay	20
Talc	20

glass makers = low
clay = very high
secondary fluxes = normal

The most significant fluxes are iron from the red clay and calcium/magnesium derived from dolomite and talc. With no colorant, it is a rich burnt orange to cream. The mat surface is soft and waxy.

WOODBOURNE III VITREOUS ENGOBE

Ball clay	8
Potash spar	24
Red clay	24
Talc	14
Whiting	30

glass makers = low
clay = very high
secondary fluxes = normal

The most significant fluxes are calcium/magnesium derived from talc and whiting. The color is a mottled iron green and the surface is a soft, waxy mat.

WOODBOURNE III VITREOUS ENGOBE WITH IRON

Ball clay	8
Potash spar	24
Red clay	24
Talc	14
Whiting	30
Iron oxide	12

glass makers = low
clay = very high
secondary fluxes = normal

The most significant fluxes in this vitreous engobe are calcium/magnesium derived from talc and whiting, and iron derived from red clay and iron oxide. The surface is a highly mottled, runny, waxy mat and the color is rich caramel brown.

Glazes

NORTHFIELD II TRANSPARENT GLAZE

Ball clay	10
Flint	18
Gerstley borate	12
Potash spar	42
Titanium	2
Wollastonite	14
Zinc	2

glass makers = extremely high
clay = normal
secondary fluxes = very low

The most significant fluxes are potassium derived from potash feldspar and calcium derived from wollastonite. The transparency is encouraged by its high glass-maker content. Add 3% copper for an Emerald Transparent.

NORTHFIELD TRANSPARENT III

Ball clay	8
Dolomite	16
Flint	18
Potash spar	40
Titanium	2
Wollastonite	14
Zinc	2
Copper carbonate	3

glass makers = extremely high
clay = low normal
secondary fluxes = low normal

The most significant fluxes in this glaze are potassium derived from potash feldspar and calcium derived from wollastonite. Transparency is encouraged by the high glass-maker content.

ALLEN CREEK IV

Ball clay	10
Dolomite	32
Potash spar	24
Talc	24
Zirconium opacifier	10

glass makers = low normal
clay = normal
secondary fluxes = high

The most significant fluxes in this glaze are calcium/magnesium derived from talc and dolomite. It is buff white to burnt orange in color with a soft-looking surface. Add 3% copper carbonate for a green.

WEBSTER II

Ball clay	12
Potash spar	28
Spodumene	10
Talc	35
Whiting	15

Add 3% copper carbonate.

glass makers = very high
clay = normal
secondary fluxes = very low

The most significant fluxes in this glaze are calcium/magnesium derived from talc whiting. The color moves from burnt orange to gray-green.

WEBSTER III

Ball clay	12
Potash spar	20
Spodumene	10
Talc	35
Titanium	8
Whiting	15

glass makers = high normal
clay = normal
secondary fluxes = normal

The most significant fluxes in this glaze are calcium/magnesium derived from talc and whiting, titanium, and lithium derived from spodumene. The glaze flow is rich and the color is orange tan to white to dark green-gray.

Ball clay	15
Spodumene	12
Talc	46
Titanium	12
Whiting	15

glass makers = normal
clay = high
secondary fluxes = normal

The most significant fluxes in this glaze are calcium/magnesium derived from talc and whiting and lithium derived from spodumene and titanium. For a soft green, add 3% copper carbonate.

ANNOTATED BIBLIOGRAPHY

BOOKS

Berensohn, Paulus *Finding One's Way with Clay.* Simon & Schuster, New York, 1972. This book is mostly about feelings and ideas by an artist who has thought deeply about the creative process in clay.

Conrad, John W. *Ceramic Formulas: The Complete Compendium.* Macmillan, New York, 1973. Many of the formulae here are nicely done and very useful.

Cooper, Emmanuel *Electric Kiln Pottery.* Batsford, London, 1982. This book is by an English potter who earns much of his living from work fired in the electric kiln.

Darling, Sharon (with a contribution by Richard Zakin). *Teco: Art Pottery of the Prarie School.* Erie Art Museum, Erie, Pa., 1989. A thorough discussion of this important American Art Pottery studio.

Evans, Paul. *Art Pottery of the United States: An Encyclopedia of Producers and Their Marks.* Feingold Lewis, New York, 1987. A complete guide to the American Art Pottery movement.

Frith, Donald E. *Mold Making for Ceramics.* Chilton, Radnor, Pa., 1985. A useful guide for the ceramist who wants to work with molds.

Hamer, Frank. *The Potter's Dictionary of Materials and Techniques.* A & C Black, London, 1975. This is a useful guide to ceramic materials, techniques, ideas, and technical history in dictionary form.

Hopper, Robin. *The Ceramic Spectrum.* Chilton, Radnor, Pa., 1984. Robin Hopper deals with color and glaze character in a thorough and personal way.

———. *Functional Pottery.* Chilton, Radnor, Pa., 1986. Hopper writes with conviction about a subject he believes in passionately.

Lawrence, W.G., and West, R.R. *Ceramic Science for the Potter,* Chilton, Radnor, Pa., 1982. A technically oriented text, it is authoritative and useful. It is aimed at the needs of the studio ceramist.

Leach, Bernard. *A Potter's Book,* Trans-Atlantic Arts, Hollywood-by-the-Sea, Fla., 1962. This book is a kind of epistle in praise of clay from a man who took the potter's mission most seriously.

Nelson, Glen C. *Ceramics.* Holt Rinehart & Winston, New York, 1978. This handbook is well and simply written and made to be useful.

Norton, F.H. *Ceramics for the Artist Potter.* Addison Wesley, Reading, Mass., 1956. The author explains technical material to ceramic artists very effectively. His diagrams are especially clear and useful.

Parmelee, Cullen W., and Harman, C.G. *Ceramic Glazes.* Cahners Books, Boston, Mass., 1973. This book is technical, thorough, and useful.

Rhodes, Daniel. *Clay and Glazes for the Potter.* Chilton, Philadelphia; A & C Black, London, 1958. This handbook is an intelligent and sensible overview of the field.

Weiss, Peg, ed. *Adelaide Alsop Robineau: Glory in Porcelain.* Syracuse University Press, Syracuse, N.Y., 1981. This highly specialized book will tell you a great deal about the history of ceramics in our country and about an important figure in that history.

Wood, Nigel. *Oriental Glazes.* Watson-Guptill, New York, 1978. This book is an excellent guide to the way in which the Chinese potters created their glazes.

Zakin, Richard. *Electric Kiln Ceramics.* Chilton, Radnor, Pa.; A & C Black, London, 1981. A guide for the ceramist who wants to use the electric kiln.

JOURNALS

American Craft, 401 Park Ave. South, New York, N.Y. 10016. This well-designed magazine covers all aspects of the crafts, including ceramics.

Ceramic Review, Carnaby St., London W12 1PH. Well-illustrated journal covering every subject of interest to potters.

Ceramics Monthly, Box 12448, Columbus, Ohio 43212. This well-illustrated magazine covers every aspect of the ceramic world, with special emphasis on the ceramics of North America.

Studio Pottery, Box 70, Goffstown, N.H. 03045. Written by and for people who spend their lives in the clay field. Each issue focuses on a theme.

INDEX OF ARTISTS

SUBJECT INDEX

elements in, 3
guidelines for, 129
high-fire, 94–97
with high-impurity clays, 75
lead, 73
low-fire, 81–92
materials for, 8, 51–53
mid-fire, 92–94
opacified, 75
for porcelain bodies, 97
recipes for, 53–54, 260–268
and safety, 254
salt, 60–61
Shino, 66
slips under, 106
smooth-surface, 57
spodumene, 77–78
testing, 101
textured, 55–56
transparent, 96
volatile, 60–61
wood-fired, 61
glazing, 85
Greece, 246–247
grog, 14, 15–16, 159
colored, 36
grolleg clay, 66, 113
ground silica, 6, 14, 18, 52
Grueby studio, 250

Han Dynasty (China), 51, 61, 243
hand-built forms, asymmetrical, 188
hand-built sculpture, 154
Haniwa period (Japan), 154, 245
hay, 68
high-clay glazes, 75
high-fire glazes, 94–97
high-impurity clays
for coloring, 36
in glazes, 52
Holland, 54
humor, in clay, 24–25

imagery
applying, 102
carved or engraved, 43
molded, 44
pressed, 43–44
sgraffito, 104, 114
ingredients, glazes classed by, 74–79
inlays
of colored clay, 30
cracks between, 34
reverse, 206

intaglio glazing, 99–100
intuitive glaze analysis, use of, 131
Iran, 246
iron, 75
in glazes, 52
iron oxide, 252
color from, 117
molecular formula and weight of, 122
Islamic/Spanish pottery, 54
Islamic tradition, 247
Italy, 54, 247

Japan, 58, 71, 244–245
Haniwa period, 154, 245
pottery in, 145
sculpture in, 146
joining pieces, with slip, 183
Jomon potters, 43, 244–245

Kamakura potters, 245
kaolin, 14, 125
in glazes, 51
molecular formula and weight of, 122
for porcelain, 21
kickwheels, 257
kiln sitters, 229–231
kiln wadding, 228
kilns, 221–227
anagama, 66
atmosphere in, 221–222
in China, 243
cooling, 235
loading, 228–229
for raku, 73
safety using, 254
types of, 223–227
Korea, 245–246
Kyo-Yoki, 245

Leach, Bernard, *A Potter's Book*, 71–72
lead, 252
in majolica, 54
substitution strategies for, 81
lead frits, 52, 252
lead glazes, 51, 73, 78, 243
lead melters, 81
limit guides (Schmitz), for molecular analysis, 126–127
Limoges porcelain, 66
lithium, 36
lithium carbonate, 53, 252
molecular formula and weight of, 122
lithium feldspars, 77, 252
loading kilns, 66, 228–229

pinholes, 53, 74, 80
   from vitreous slips and engobes, 108
plaster of paris, 210
Plastic Vitrox, 29
   molecular formula and weight of, 122
plasticity, 11
platelets, 11
platinum, 55
polychrome techniques, 31
Pop Pottery, 251
porcelain, 66, 95
   absorption percentage for, 41
   recipe for, 22
porcelain bisque, 29
porcelain bodies, 23, 25, 29
   glazes for, 97
porcelaneous bodies, 21, 23
potash feldspar, 14, 15, 52, 74, 96
potassium glazes, 74
potter's wheel, 188, 194, 195–197, 256–257
pour technique, to apply glaze, 100
praseodymium, 117
pre-Columbian America, 248–250
pre-Columbian Mexico, 154
pre-Columbian potters, 109
prepared clay bodies, 38
press molds, 35, 43–44, 205–207
pressed imagery, 43–44
propane, 225
Pueblo potters, 46
pug mills, 39
pumice, molecular formula and weight of, 122
pyrophyllite, molecular formula and weight of,
   122

quartz, 17, 240
quartz inversion, 18

raku, 68, 71–74
   dangers of, 73
   kiln for, 73
   post-firing treatment of, 73–74
   recipes for, 70–71
   slip for, 69
recipes, 9–10
   analysis of, 120–132
   for bisque slip, 87
   for clay bodies, 18, 87, 220, 260–268
   computer development of, 258
   for crackle clear glaze, 69
   for earthenware, 151
   for glazes, 53–54, 132, 260–268
   interpreting, 131–132
   for majolica, 87

   materials-based evaluation of, 128–132
   for porcelain, 22
   for raku, 70–71
   for raku slip, 69
   for transparent glaze, 96
   for vitreous engobes, 108
red clay, molecular formula and weight of, 122
reducing agent, 55
reduction firing, 95, 221
   and color, 32
   and cone 9, 223
   cone 9 in gas kiln, 237–238
   for porcelain, 97
Renaissance, 247
respirator, 253
reverse inlay process, 206
Rochester Institute of Technology, School of
   American Craftsmen, 127, 151
Rookwood studio (Cincinnati), 250
rutile, 74, 117

safety, 252–254
saggers, 228
salt glazes, 60–61
salt kilns, 225
sand, as filler, 16
sandblasting, 44
Sassanian period (Iran), 246
sawdust
   as filler, 16
   firing with, 46–48, 68
scales, 257–258
sculpture, 21, 145, 147, 154, 159, 169
   absorption percentage for, 41
   hand-built, 154
   in Japan, 146
   mixed media in, 154, 159
   technical problems with, 159, 169
seasoning process, 180
secondary fluxes, glaze recipes with, 54
secondary melters, 52–53
self-glazing clay bodies, 34–35
sgraffito imagery, 104, 114
Shang dynasty, 243
Shino, 245
Shino glazes, 66
Shoji Hamada, 245
shrinkage, 40, 42
silica, 4, 16–18, 60
   glaze recipes with, 53
   ground, 6, 14, 18, 52
   hazards from, 252
   materials containing, 252–253
   molecular formula and weight of, 122